THE NEW SOCIAL CONTRACT

Beyond Liberal Democracy

Gary Gerrard

University Press of America,® Inc.
Lanham · New York · Oxford

Copyright © 2002 by
University Press of America,® Inc.
4720 Boston Way
Lanham, Maryland 20706
UPA Acquisitions Department (301) 459-3366

12 Hid's Copse Rd.
Cumnor Hill, Oxford OX2 9JJ

All rights reserved
Printed in the United States of America
British Library Cataloging in Publication Information Available

Library of Congress Cataloging-in-Publication Data

Gerrard, Gary.
The new social contract : beyond liberal
democracy / Gary Gerrard.
p. cm
Includes bibliographical references and index.
1. Liberalism. 2. Democracy. I. Title.
JC574 .G47 2001   320.1'1—dc21   2001054035 CIP

ISBN 0-7618-2169-4 (cloth: alk. paper)
ISBN 0-7618-2170-8 (pbk. : alk. paper)

∞™ The paper used in this publication meets the minimum
requirements of American National Standard for Information
Sciences—Permanence of Paper for Printed Library Materials,
ANSI Z39.48—1984

To Barbara with all my love

"Where shall we find a form of association which will defend and protect with the whole common force the person and the property of each associate, and by which every person, while uniting himself with all, shall obey only himself and remain as free as before."

Jean-Jacques Rousseau, *The Social Contract*

CONTENTS

Preface		ix
Introduction		xi
PART I	The Physical and Evolutionary Origins of Life, Society, Morality and Individualism	
Chapter I	The Complexity of Life	3
Chapter II	Biological Society	23
Chapter III	The Emergence of Morality	29
Chapter IV	The Morality of Equality	53
Chapter V	Reflections on Human Nature	85
Part II	Translating the Morality of Equality into the Political Theory and Political Practice of an Individualistic Society	
Chapter VI	The Origin and Purpose of Rights	95
Chapter VII	The Social Contract in Theory	113
Chapter VIII	The American Experiment	125
Chapter IX	Creating an Individualistic Society	153
Chapter X	Interpreting the New Social Contract	173

Chapter XI	Life in an Individualistic Society	227
Chapter XII	Revolution or Evolution	239
Notes		243
Index		263

Preface

This book began following my first exposure to the great political philosophers. They all seemed to be just making up their own rules, and lacking the proper respect endemic to youth, I thought I could make up my own as good as theirs; so, like an impetuous, defiant child told he cannot do something and intent on doing it, I started writing. I finished undergraduate and law school and became a trial and appellate lawyer, but the thought of constructing a better political philosophy remained, and this book is the result of my unguided, haphazard study and thoughts.

I have made many choices to finish this book, and probably they have all been wrong. First, I began with the belief that I was writing philosophy, and that philosophy, particularly political philosophy, is valuable only if the average person can understand and use it. Therefore, I chose to write for as general an audience as possible. When I started looking for a publisher, I realized I had surely failed in that effort.

Second, when the manuscript was accepted by a publisher that targets an academic audience, I panicked. I was sure that my lack of academic background and training would be so obvious that the book would be laughed at. In spite of nearly thirty years of thinking and reading about the subjects I draw upon in the text, I was, and am, certain I have missed important, even decisive works of others. Because I had no editor to work with, I hired a recent Ph.D. hoping to buy an insurance policy against appearing a fool. Having lost my youthful hubris and gained respect, I many times seriously considered trashing the manuscript. Choosing not to was also probably a mistake.

Third, I considered adding better references to try to support and bolster my credibility. I accepted other's advice not to do that. My choice; my mistake.

Fourth, I employed some rhetorical devices that may have failed. In the *Rhetoric*, which I have preached for years is every trial lawyer's most valuable resource, Aristotle advises presenting an argument in such a way as to allow one's audience to reach the desired conclusion before or without telling them what it is. That way they will believe it to be their own and will not give it up easily. I have often marshaled the facts more than analyze them, hoping my readers would reach my conclusions on their own.

Finally, I chose to follow my arguments to their logical conclusion even if they are controversial. Quite likely I will please no one and offend everyone, but for different reasons.

I have, however, found consolation as I bring this long trek to a close. Henry Kissinger writes in *The White House Years* that the historian's problem has changed from there not being enough source material about what happened to there being so much no one can sift through it all. And, Edward O. Wilson in *Consilience* observes that, "In 1797 when Jefferson took the president's chair at the American Philosophical Society, . . . [m]ost [American scientists] could discourse reasonably well on the entire world of learning, which was still small enough to be seen as a whole." Scientific knowledge has grown exponentially since the 1700s, and in the process, expertise has fragmented and higher education has turned into "congeries of experts" whose success depend on staking a claim to an atomic slice of human knowledge by establishing one's expertise in and making discoveries about that slice. Gone are the days of Renaissance men or women who could master all the branches of human knowledge. Wilson argues for a unification of all the sciences and the humanities in a process he describes as consilience.[1]

I take comfort in the thought that even in another thirty years, I could not sift all the facts or become an expert in all the fields relevant to this project. I have searched for the facts and tried to understand the science necessary to arrive at, and hopefully add slightly to, a consilience sufficient to the purpose. Alas, there is no field of human knowledge I would not like to know as an expert, but there are too many books and too little time. I can only accept the well-deserved criticism for my many errors.

This book surely proves that I do not have the profound mind of a philosopher, but merely the plodding, practical mind of a lawyer. Indeed, I have approached the problem as a lawyer. First, what are the facts? Any good lawyer, and all people with an opinion, search for, sift and present the facts to support their opinions with confirmation bias. Second, for the client to win, there must be a theory to make the facts coherent and understandable and to produce the conclusion that the client is right. That theory is the rule of law, and the lawyer must find in a paper ocean of irrelevant and contradictory rules of law the rule that both fits the facts and results in the client winning. And, if the lawyer can find no existing rule, he must make up a new one and try to persuade the court to adopt it. Why? So his client will win.

As is most often the case, expert testimony is required to explain the facts so that jurors and judges can understand and make sense of them within the theory provided by the law and in order to make a decision that is consistent with and gives practical effect to the rule of law applied to the real people in the case. Quite literally, the law is a process of consilience, all the way from jurors deciding a slip and fall case with expert testimony about the coefficient of friction between the plaintiff's shoe and the wax on the floor, all the way up to the United States Supreme Court deciding whether Microsoft has monopolized the personal computer operating system market.

My client in this book is, however, not a person but my conviction that happiness, however individually conceived, is the goal of life; that no one person's happiness is more valuable than another's; that no person, ought to be able to achieve his happiness by taking whatever happiness another has already achieved; and, that the most desirable condition to live in would allow each and every person the greatest possible opportunity to achieve his happiness.

I have gathered and presented facts to support and explain my case. I have looked for a rule of law to win this case, and found them all wanting. So I have made up my own rules. This case, however, must be decided by the court of public opinion.

I have given the reasons for adopting the new rule. I have presented the facts as ably as I can. I have compared the proposed rule with others similar in motive and result to show that I am not trying to remake the world or the law in my own image. And, I have argued that the object of current law is universal equality, and it will be better achieved with the rule I propose.

The most important contributor to this work is my wife, Barbara, who patiently listened to me talk about this book for over twenty years, surely thinking that I would never really finish it, and praying that I would so she would not have to hear about it anymore.

I wish to thank Scott D. Schmalhorst, of San Antonio, Texas. When the idea first occurred to me, he encouraged me in this project rather than dismissing it. I want to thank Clark Wolf, Ph.D., of the University of Georgia Philosophy Department for reading the first draft of the manuscript and giving me suggestions on how to improve it. Clark offered encouragement, responded to my many e-mails and patiently pointed out my errors and omissions. I also want to thank my former professor who introduced me to Lenore Ealy, Ph.D., who offered many valuable suggestions on reorganizing and improving the manuscript, all of which I greatly appreciate. Lenore's suggestions resulted in substantial improvement in the presentation of the ideas that follow.

Finally, I want to thank Phyllis Stewart, whom I have met only over the internet. She encouraged me to finish the book and provided helpful criticism of both the substance and the style.

Introduction

Francis Fukuyama created a minor stir in 1989 when he suggested in an article, "The End of History," that the collapse of the Soviet Block signaled the end of man's ideological history and that liberal democracy is the "final form of government." Liberal democracy may be the best form of political society yet devised, but it is not the end of political history. Political liberalism, that is, participatory political institutions, individual rights and limited government, leaves unresolved some basic social conflicts. These conflicts have always been present in political society, while advances in the social sciences have made others more acute.

Political liberalism is a product of the emergence of individualism, that is, a belief that every human life is valuable in itself and not merely as the biological means to perpetuate the human species. Probably the most famous, though certainly not the first,[2] political expression of individualism was in the American Declaration of Independence when Thomas Jefferson wrote:

> We hold these truths to be self-evident, that all men are created equal; that they are endowed by their Creator with certain unalienable rights; that among these are Life, Liberty, and the pursuit of Happiness. That, to secure these rights, governments are instituted among men, deriving their just powers from the consent of the governed.

This passage tersely summarized John Locke's political philosophy in his *Second Treatise on Civil Government.*[3] After the American Revolution, an amalgam of Locke's political philosophy, English liberties and British constitutionalism became the foundation for the United States Constitution and Bill of Rights.[4] While Locke and the founding fathers made significant advances in political philosophy and political practice, they only partially resolved the most basic issues of political society.

As a practicing trial and appellate lawyer for more than 20 years, I know that every case requires applying abstract legal principles to real events involving real people. The judgment of a court is when principle becomes reality. Moral and political philosophy, and constitutional law, all too often fail to transcend adequately the boundary between theory and practice. Declaring the universal equality of man is a noble ideal and may be enough to start a revolution, but putting that ideal into everyday practice after the revolution is won is far more difficult. After the American Revolution, the men of noble ideals and intentions were unable to reconcile slavery with their ubiquitous declarations of the equality of man as the reason for the Revolution.[5] The Constitution commands due process and equal protection of the law, again noble ideals, but it leaves to judges in courtrooms across the country the job of translating these ideals into the law of the land by deciding individual cases.

Our ideals about how people ought to live together is our political philosophy, and the law embodies it. If there is no court to appeal to or if the court will not recognize the ideal of universal equality as a rule of law and enforce it, when the universal equality of *a* man or *a* woman is denied, as it was for Negro slaves, universal equality can only be a noble sentiment or the law a hypocrite. There are only two ways to decide whether someone has violated society's political philosophy: in a court of law or the violence of the streets, as the French Revolution proved. This is not only the way it is, it is the only way it *can* be.

Trial lawyers are the foot soldiers of political philosophy. What do soldiers do when their orders are unclear? They can argue about what they have been ordered to do, as lawyers are prone to do, and then attack the closest hill. Or, if circumstances permit, they can ask for more specific orders. After many years in the trenches, I have come to believe that the founding fathers as our generals of political philosophy faced us in the right direction, but their orders about exactly where to go and how to get there are unclear. I will make a case not for discarding universal equality as the foundation of our political philosophy, but rather for a more specific statement of what universal equality means and how to translate it into law so that the basic political and social problems that now keep society in a constant low boil may be finally and satisfactorily resolved.

The fundamental problem unresolved by our political philosophy or the Constitution is when may coercive force be used, not just by government but by private individuals as well. The failure to answer this question is like diabetes, which produces many seemingly unrelated secondary diseases such as vascular disease, heart disease, blindness, polyneuropathy, and even coma, all of which can be cured only by treating the primary disease, not its specific symptoms. Inadequately restrained coercive force produces many secondary social problems. Locke forcefully advocated government limited by the purposes of political society. The founding fathers significantly limited government's powers in the Constitution, and the Bill of Rights imposed additional limits on the federal government, though not on the state governments. Neither the original Constitution nor the Bill of Rights has a single provision that addresses the relations among private individuals even though the vast majority of social life involves relationships with private persons, not government officers or employees.

American history has revealed two basic weaknesses in these limits on government. First, according to Locke's theory, the purpose for which political society is formed is to protect the life, liberty and property of each citizen. The power of government is limited by the "law of nature," which is essentially reason applied to accomplish the purpose of political society. As such, the law of nature was, and is, no law and no real limitation on the power of a political majority to impose its will by force on a minority. Second, in moving from theory to practice, the founding fathers did not rely on the law of nature to limit the federal government's powers. Instead, they created a written constitution with checks and balances that set ambition against ambition. They separated the powers of the three branches of the federal government, created a federal system by delegating specific powers to the federal government and leaving the remaining powers and functions of government to the states.

Despite their significant advance in turning political philosophy into political practice, the founding fathers system of competing powers still did not answer the fundamental question: when may coercive force be used? Blessed with the greatest freedom, opportunity and toleration of any nation on earth, the United States attracted people from all corners of the world and created a cacophony of diverse cultures, religions and philosophies that constantly compete for the coercive force of government to impose their views on the rest of society. Until this most basic problem of coercive force is solved, society will remain tied in a Gordian's knot of diverse factions competing for the "legitimate" coercive force of government.

In the 2000 presidential election, the Democratic candidate, in my view, unabashedly appealed to majority might makes right. His campaign pitted the old against the young on Social Security and Medicare, the rich against the poor in a shameless appeal to tax the "richest one percent" and redistribute it to others, and blacks against whites on issues such as affirmative action. Republicans made similar appeals to the Christian Coalition, right to life and business groups to build their electoral majority, but that is precisely the point. Electoral politics is about assembling a majority to acquire the coercive force of government, and the constitutional limits on the use of that power are simply inadequate.

The Constitution, of course, has some specific institutional checks on majority rule, but the fundamental question remains. May 99% of the electorate foist the lion's share of the tax burden of maintaining society on the "richest one percent?" And lest this be dismissed as too extreme an example, can 51% of the electorate foist 90% of the tax burden on the 49% with the highest annual incomes? This is not a hypothetical question. Numerous sources have reported that 10% or less of Americans pay over 60% of personal income taxes. And, government at all levels is constantly called on to support private activities with public dollars.

In a television interview shortly after the presidential election, a California Democratic Congresswoman was asked about the maximum personal tax rate she would support. After mentioning the richest one percent several times and how they should not be the primary beneficiaries of a tax cut, she refused to say that there should be any maximum tax rate on personal incomes. While few people are likely to worry that Bill Gates will be taxed into poverty, the absence of any limit on the power of the majority to take with due process of law the property of some citizens, insures that there will always be economic class warfare in liberal democracy.

As Chief Justice Marshall observed early in our history, "[T]he power to tax involves the power to destroy."[6] The Sixteenth Amendment to the Constitution authorizes an unapportioned personal income tax. But constitutional authorization heightens, rather than diminishes, the question of the limits on majority rule. Wealth redistribution through taxes authorized by the super-majority necessary to amend the Constitution, does not remove the basic problem of when and for what reasons a single individual may stand against the overwhelming will and collective power a constitutional majority?

The power to destroy with taxes, which is the current method of attacking cigarette smoking, leads to a second facet of the problem of coercive force: when may a majority use force to prevent an adult from smoking, or drinking alcohol or using "recreational" drugs? Prohibition failed so miserably with alcohol that it was repealed, and there are growing calls to legalize many drugs. And again, to prohibit such products or practices by constitutional amendment does not resolve the problem. Prohibition was imposed, and repealed by constitutional amendment. Could the Thirteenth Amendment banning slavery be repealed?

Besides taxes or cigarettes, alcohol or drugs of choice, may the government prefer one person or group over another in providing employment, services or education? May a majority declare war, draft a minority of dissenters into armed service and compel them upon threat of prison or death to fight a war they oppose? May a majority decide that some personal contact between consenting adults is unhealthy, unnatural, sinful, or immoral, and outlaw it, and punish anyone who violates the law?

In short, the Sixteenth and Eighteenth Amendments and the most recent presidential campaign show that the limits on majority rule are still unclear. Without clearly defined limits on when and for what reasons a majority may use force to compel obedience by any person who disagrees with the majority, the deliberately ambiguous political rhetoric, "do the right thing," will continue to be the justification for abuses of majority rule in liberal democracy.

Any society dedicated to the equality of *all* its members in the pursuit of happiness, what I shall call an individualistic society, must confront the diversity of conflicting views about what happiness is and how to achieve it. Absent an infallible answer to both questions, any individualistic society must accommodate these diverse ideas. But, must it accommodate all such ideas? Must society, in the name of free speech or the pursuit of happiness, tolerate the views of the likes of NAMBLA, the North American Man/Boy Love Association that advocates pedophilia or Neo-Nazi or White Supremacist organizations that advocate the murder of blacks, Jews, gays or other unpopular minorities? If not, where shall the line be drawn between the tolerable and the intolerable?

The diversity of even permissible views often results in divisive debates and confrontations that have the potential for destroying, or at a minimum obscuring, the shared beliefs that our political society was founded on and gives it cohesion. Thus, by tolerating diversity without adequate limits on coercive force, political liberalism risks fostering its own destruction. Social liberals view the coercive power of government as the greatest tool to promote their view of the general welfare of society, and social conservatives and religious fundamentalists view social ills as the result of a decline in moral and religious values and the coercive force of government as the instrument to restore the moral character of the nation. These conflicts surface in political disputes over abortion "rights," drug abuse, sexual preferences and lifestyles, sexually transmitted diseases, and unwanted pregnancies, among others.

Another secondary facet of the coercive force problem appears in the debate over issues of so-called social justice such as affirmative action, race relations, universal health care, welfare and gross disparities in wealth and its redistribution. Every interest group claims "rights" by appealing to a supposedly higher authority, either religious or moral, when no legal right exists. If a political majority can be assembled, those "rights" can become legal rights enforceable with the coercive force of government. "Human rights" are often discussed, claimed and violated without any clear understanding or agreement about what exactly a "right" or a "human right" is. Without a firm understanding of what "rights" are, the political battles for majority power to create or eliminate legal rights will continue to fuel the antagonisms that keep society simmering.

Yet another facet of the failure of the Constitution to resolve the problem of coercive force is revealed by the political struggle over appointments to the Supreme Court. How should judges decide constitutional questions? Should they read the Constitution literally and strictly and enforce only the specific text, the so-called strict constructionist view, or should they view the Constitution as an outline of a particular political philosophy that the Constitution charges them with the responsibility to fill in the details. Even the strict constructionist must go outside the text to decide exactly what due process and equal protection mean. And, the text of the Constitution does not authorize the Supreme Court to declare an act of Congress or a state legislature unconstitutional and void. The Supreme Court claimed that necessary power on its own.

To put the issue more concretely, the words "abortion" and "privacy" nowhere appear in the Constitution or Bill of Rights, nor, for that matter, does the phrase "liberty to contract," but the Court has used each of these phrases to strike down state and federal legislation. Following Franklin Roosevelt's Court Packing scheme of the 1930's, one justice, Justice Roberts, changed his mind about the proper role of the Supreme Court and singlehandedly reversed the role of the Court in reviewing social welfare legislation and the federal government's limited authority.

Abortion and affirmative action are merely the current issues that challenge the Court's role as the protector of the individual from the coercive power of a majority in both the state and federal governments without specific authorization or clear direction from the Constitution. The first issues laying down this challenge arose as early as 1798 and have continued unresolved and unresolvable to this day for the simple reason that the Constitution does not provide an answer.

Locke's political theory and the tradition of English liberties failed to adequately limit government's authority and power over the individual because reason alone, even in the service of the most intelligent and best intentioned judges and politicians, leaves too much room for abuse of political power. History demonstrates that political power unchecked by an adequate immune system metastasizes throughout any political body, and the tumor is growing.

Because the Constitution has no clear, specific and comprehensive standard, judges of the Supreme Court more than any others must make up constitutional law as they go. The Supreme Court is a *de facto*, perpetual constitutional convention. Without a specific legal standard, and faced with conflicting constitutional principles, the Supreme Court has already committed two grievous errors, one almost fatal. In *Dred Scott v. Sandford*,[7] the Supreme Court approved a slave owner's use of coercive force over the life and body of another person, and added to it the coercive force of the government, and gave momentum to Civil War. After the Civil War extended universal equality by abolishing the private and governmental coercive force necessary for slavery, the Court approved majority imposed inequality with its separate but equal doctrine in *Plessy v. Ferguson*.[8] The wounds inflicted by both decisions have yet to heal.

A separate, but still related problem is the modern version of the eternal conflict between determinism and free will. Are people responsible for their actions? On the one hand, all adults are presumed to have the mental and moral capacity to obey the law, but modern science keeps nibbling away at this cornerstone of the law. On the other hand, every criminal defense lawyer is obligated to argue that his client is not responsible for his actions because of something in his past.

The Menendez brothers claimed they were not responsible for executing their parents because their father had sexually, physically and mentally abused them as children, thus rendering the murders an act of "self-defense." Ronny Zamora claimed he was not responsible for murdering his neighbor because "involuntary subliminal television intoxication" rendered him insane.[9] More recently, a thirteen year-old boy accused of killing a six-year-old playmate with a professional wrestling style body slam, claimed he was not responsible because he was imitating what he had seen in a television commercial. John Hinckley was found not guilty of attempting to assassinate President Reagan because he was insane. Others claim "diminished capacity" because they were voluntarily under the influence of drugs or alcohol. Courts and juries often reject these defenses, but the point is that they are made, and with more frequency and success.

Minors who commit violent crimes present a special challenge to define and enforce personal responsibility. Some juvenile crimes are so heinous that it seems even a child, especially a teenager, must have understood that what he was doing was wrong. Because minors can be tried as adults, either age alone does not reliably determine the ability to understand and comply with the law, or the desire to punish children outweighs our understanding of their ability to understand and control their behavior.

Modern theories of psychiatry, psychology and sociology that espouse cultural or environmental determinism undermines the common belief and legal principle that adults know the difference between right and wrong and more importantly can refrain from doing wrong acts. The error, however, is not in social science. The error is in believing that modern science, the very activity that has brought man to the brink of understanding the essence of the universe, has rendered man a hopelessly impotent, automaton incapable of choosing at least some of his own actions. A better understanding of the nature of moral capacity is necessary to remove doubts about the adult and juvenile criminal justice systems, and create a comprehensive theory of personal responsibility. If moral capacity can be adequately identified, then society would be well served to distinguish clearly between those persons with and those without moral capacity and treat each according to their capacity.

The answer to the riddle of the legitimate use of coercive force by both private individuals and government requires reexamining the nature of morality which underpins our political philosophy. Part I of this book proposes a new conceptual framework for a theory of moral capacity and a morality of equality as the clearer statement of the foundation of the political philosophy of universal equality. But the score of the greatest symphony is not music without a conductor and trained musicians, and the noble sentiments of political philosophy are mere words without the orchestra of the law to play them. An orchestra of many individual musicians with different instruments all playing a different melody and competing to be heard above all the rest can produce a terrible cacophony. With the score of Beethoven's Ninth Symphony before them, that same diversity of instruments and voices can produce an *Ode to Joy*. Political ideal and political reality can become one when the cacophony of diversity is transposed into the polyphony of an individualistic society. Part II of this book proposes a New Social Contract, a written, legally enforceable contract, that unites the ideal of universal equality as expressed in the morality of equality with the coercive force of the law.

All theories or explanations have foundational assumptions from which they proceed. Thomas Hobbes, John Locke and Jean-Jacques Rousseau began their social contract theories with a postulate of a state of nature in which all men were born equal. As the foundation for political society, the state of nature has a number of problems. Among these are uncertainties about the state of nature: was it a historical or an actual condition or a hypothetical condition from which to postulate how reasonable people might agree to join together to promote their mutual self-interest? Whether hypothetical or historical, any description of the state of nature undermines the theory by opening it to criticisms of relativism and bias.

To avoid these problems, I begin with a proposition I believe no one can disagree with: that the universe behaves essentially in predictable ways. While the science of complexity is still in its infancy, certain principles have been confirmed that seem to unify apparently unrelated phenomena. One principle is that all complex systems are integrations of less complex systems. From the integration of simpler systems more complex systems with new properties emerge. The new properties exist only if, and only as long as, the simpler systems function.

Beginning with the premise of predictability of inanimate physical systems, I propose a conceptual framework of life and animal society as systems of increasing complexity, with the human brain and human society assumed to be the most complex physical systems. This framework leads to a theory of moral capacity as an emergent property of cognitive complexity which produces a conscious belief that each and every human's satisfaction of his desires is equally valuable. This theory explains why some people act morally, some immorally and some amorally, and also why some have a sense of morality toward other animals as reflected in animal cruelty laws and organizations such as the SPCA (Society for the Prevention of Cruelty to Animals) and PETA (People for the Ethical Treatment of Animals). Morality is not about the rational pursuit of self-interest, but about choosing the means to satisfy one's desires without lessening any other person's possessions. Moral choices are not calculations of rational self-interest made out of fear of undesirable consequences. They are choices made from a conscious conviction that every person's life, liberty and desire for property is as valuable as one's own. I propose a specific first principle of the morality of equality that distinguishes between what I call constructive power and destructive power.

All animal societies require certain systems of lesser complexity. This level of complexity I call biological society. Because morality is a property of human social interaction, biological society is a system of lesser complexity necessary for individual moral choices. An individualistic society is the extension of the morality of equality to all members of society, that is, the equal value of all persons in the pursuit of their happiness. An individualistic society emerges from biological society by conscious design from the less complex systems of human biological society and individual moral capacity.

If all people had moral capacity and human biological society satisfied the biological requirements of every human in it, an individualistic society could emerge without any need for government. But every human does not have moral capacity, and biological society does not benefit everyone. Therefore, Society (throughout this book, when capitalized, "Society" refers to the individualistic society I propose) through its government, must use coercive force when necessary to maintain the complexity of biological society for all persons incapable of doing so on their own. These conditions of biological society are the physical necessities, and this is the first half of the answer to the riddle of the legitimate use of coercive force.

Not all humans have moral capacity, and those who do will not always choose to act morally. Thus, Society must clearly distinguish between those people with moral capacity and those without it and use coercive force when necessary to prevent nonmoral and immoral people from using destructive power against members of Society. This is the other half of the answer to the legitimate use of coercive force in Society.

The necessity to maintain biological society for all members of Society and the desire for a world in which all persons act according to the morality of equality is the *ought* of the political philosophy of an individualistic society. The New Social Contract is the legal document that unites political philosophy with the coercive force of law. It is the fundamental charter of Society which clearly specifies how coercive force may be used, by both private individuals and government. It is Society's symphonic score that transposes cacophony into polyphony.

I argue that the morality of equality already is the leitmotif of American law, but it has not yet come into sharp focus, like science before Newton showed that the forces that control the orbits of the planets and stars also control falling apples and touchdown passes. The morality of equality is the secular calculus of equality harmonizing political philosophy, law, government, and conscious individual social relations. In our postmodern, deconstructed age of relativism, the very word morality evokes cynicism, but the morality of equality is not a competitor in the contest between diverse religious and secular views of the world. As the fundamental law of Society, it protects equally the religious zealot, the adamant atheist, the secular humanist, and everyone in between from interference by anyone with a contrary view about the appropriate ends of human life.

PART I

The Physical and Evolutionary Origins of Life, Society, Morality and Individualism

Chapter I

The Complexity of Life

For any political theory to be acceptable in a diverse society, it must begin from a point of common belief. A civilized society cannot long exist with widely divergent views about life and how it ought to be lived without a morality acceptable to all or the constant repression of discordant views. What is that common belief shared by the religious fundamentalist, the atheist, the theologian and the scientist?

Every religion has a creation story to explain how the world came to exist, and in general, how it works. Whether God created the universe or it exploded with a big bang, all agree it exists. And, whether the universe operates according to the will of God or laws of nature, everyone accepts, based on experience, that matter and energy interact in very predictable ways.

The belief that the universe is directed in subatomic detail by the active, omnipotent will of God, is entirely compatible with the belief that the laws of nature determine everything. Science is either discovering laws of nature or predicting the will of God. The most ardent theist accepts the predictability of nature every time he looks both ways before crossing the street; yet the most skeptical scientist cannot say why the laws of nature are as they are.

The belief in laws of nature that produce predictability creates two problems: first, all events are not predictable, and second, total predictability compels a clockwork view of the universe that makes human life as predestined as the path of a stone skipped across the surface of a pond. Of course, the inability to predict accurately that a newborn infant will grow up to be a doctor, lawyer, Indian chief, drug addict, or serial killer does not disprove predestination or mechanical determinism from the moment of birth or conception or the big bang. Maybe these laws of nature have not been discovered yet. Because experience supports predictability according to fixed laws of nature, and because laws of nature are not inconsistent with any religion I know of, this common belief is a good place to begin. If proceeding from this point can produce a satisfactory theory of morality and political society consistent will all diverse views, then we will have the best of all possible worlds.

Francois Jacob, Nobel prize winner in Physiology or Medicine in 1965 for discoveries about the genetic control of enzyme and virus synthesis, has described how science has been divided into four basic fields: physics, chemistry, biology and psycho-sociology.[1] Each differs not only in the nature of its subjects, but also in the language and concepts each uses to describe and explain its subjects. These basic sciences can be arranged in a hierarchical order according to the complexity of their subjects from physics to chemistry to biology to psycho-sociology. In order for science to provide a "unified world view," the basic problem is to explain the more complex phenomena with the terms and concepts of the simpler science–a process known as reductionism. The question is, can it be done.

Jacob notes that science in the last few centuries has made revolutionary advances toward a unified world view. Many fields of inquiry were once seen as isolated and explainable only with separate terms and concepts. Modern science unified several divergent fields so that they now appear to be different facets of the same phenomenon. Newton's laws unified terrestrial and celestial mechanics. Thermodynamics and mechanics were unified by statistical mechanics; optics and electromagnetism by Maxwell's theory of magnetic fields; and, chemistry and atomic physics by quantum mechanics. Biochemists also demonstrated that both inanimate and living matter are composed of atoms that obey the same physical laws. But, if total reductionism is the goal, then sexuality, pain, justice and democracy must eventually be explained with quantum mechanics–an apparent absurdity.

Jacob claims that the nature of complexity requires different concepts and language to adequately explain increasingly complex objects. For instance, molecules are made of atoms and must obey the laws governing the behavior of atoms, but molecules also have new properties such as forming isomers, polymers, acids or bases. And, the molecules actually found in nature and produced in laboratories are only a small fraction of all the possible interactions of atoms. Thus, chemistry studies a "special case" of physics. Likewise, biology studies a "special case" of chemistry. The biological organisms that actually exist, including humans, represent only a very limited range of all possible chemical combinations. And, while there are several million biological species, that number is small compared to those that could exist.

While more complex systems have new or emergent properties, Jacob explains that each is made up of an integration of simpler systems. All of the constraints of each simpler system also constrain the more complex ones. The emergent properties of each greater order of complexity are, however, the more important. As Jacob says, "The law of perfect gases is no less true for the objects of biology or sociology than for those of physics. It is simply irrelevant in the context of the problems with which biologists, and even more so sociologists, are concerned."

Jacob also observes that, "complex objects are produced by evolutionary processes in which two factors are paramount: the constraints which at every level control the systems involved; and the historical circumstances of the actual interactions between the systems." Constraints govern simpler systems more than history. As systems become more complex, the balance shifts toward history. And, as complexity increases, new constraints appear. For instance living systems must reproduce or they cease to be living systems; animals that live socially, must have systems of cooperation that increase the probability of survival and reproduction of the social group, though not necessarily every individual; and, modern human society has many economic systems all of which are necessary for the production and distribution of food and other products and for security against external threats. These constraints on social systems of lesser complexity will be important when considering the necessities that are prerequisite to moral choices and without which an individualistic society cannot exist.

Complexity as a scientific discipline has received increasing attention in the last twenty to thirty years. The basic ideas of emergent properties and the evolution of systems have been applied to such diverse disciplines as computer science, artificial life, psychology, particle physics, economics, market behavior, political science, evolutionary biology, genetics, consciousness, and language, to name a few. Emergence also seems to be related to chaos and the self-organization of systems, and thermodynamics. Another Nobel laureate, Ilya Prigogine, provided fundamental insights into the relationships between far from equilibrium thermodynamics, chaos, and self-organization as properties of systems from which life emerged. More recently, Prigogine has applied these principles to argue against determinism.[2] There are now scientific journals devoted to complexity and college courses that apply principles of complexity to a broad spectrum of subjects. The scientists at the prestigious Santa Fe Institute study complexity in many diverse fields. Perhaps a new Newton or Einstein will devise a calculus of complexity and unify all the diverse phenomena that have or will emerge in the universe, and give us a complete psychology of God.

The basic properties of complexity, integration with cumulative constraints, emergence of new properties, and evolution, provide the building blocks for a conceptual framework for understanding ourselves as individuals and in society, and our moral and political philosophy. Each is a complex system with emergent properties that have evolved from less complex systems and that is constrained by its component systems of lesser complexity. While this framework is not scientific, nor is it intended to be, Jacob also observed that the analysis of complex objects at different levels is also valuable, as shown by the success of understanding heredity through simultaneous analysis at the molecular level of biochemistry and the "black box" level of Gregor Mendel's genetics.

The discussion that follows proposes a hierarchy of concepts about life as emergent properties, leading up to human life. Although not scientific, these concepts are intended to be refutable empirically. For instance, the proposition that moral capacity is an emergent property of cognitive complexity which requires the integration of certain less complex cognitive capacities can be disproved empirically by identifying instances of moral behavior by an individual who lacks one or more of the systems of lesser complexity. There are many examples of nonhuman animal behavior that demonstrate the evolutionary origins of human moral capacity.[3] Such examples do not, however, disprove moral capacity as proposed herein, any more than showing that elephants or dogs reason and use sounds to communicate would disprove the proposition that humans are the only animals capable of abstract reasoning with language.

It has been said that the human brain is the most complex object in the known universe. If that is true, and the principles of complexity are fundamental to all physical systems, then logically the human brain and human society are emergent properties that require concepts different from those necessary to explain adequately the less complex component systems. If humans are the most complex, and if complex systems are always constrained by their simpler components, then humans are but a special case of animal physiology and behavior,[4] and conscious, rational morality or ethics is an emergent property of those systems. Most, if not all, the complex properties of humans, including morality, should be evident to some degree in other animals.

With these principles of complexity in mind, I offer a conceptual framework for analyzing humans both as individual organisms and in society, that may improve moral and political philosophy.

The Three Elements of Life

All life has three basic properties: will, power, and right. Every biological organism, from the prokaryotic bacteria to humans has these three properties in common.

Let us begin with a few definitions:

Effect: an existing state of matter.
Objective: a particular future state of all possible future states.
Cause: to direct, control or influence the movement of matter to become.
Purpose: to select an objective.

Will

Will is the purpose to cause an effect.

[To select {a particular future state of all possible future states}] [to direct, control or influence the movement of matter to become] [an existing state of matter].

All matter moves, and every movement leads to some new existing state. The difference between inanimate matter and living matter is that inanimate matter moves only according to the laws of physics and chemistry, while every living organism moves at least sometimes purposefully. When Professor Sven Gard of the Nobel Committee presented the Nobel Prize to Francois Jacob, Andrew Lwoff, and Jacques Monod, he described how their accomplishments had "laid the foundations for the science of molecular biology." He noted, "Action, coordination, adaptation, variation–these are the most striking manifestations of living matter." These all manifest purposeful movement: movement other than solely by the laws of physics and chemistry; movement guided by a will.

Ilya Prigogine has also proposed a mechanism by which physical systems as they are forced far away from thermodynamic equilibrium, reach a point of chaos that requires the system to "choose" between a particular order called a *dissipative structure*. Prigogine's work shows that the self-organization of the system in response to being pushed away from equilibrium is the process that leads to life. This is quite similar to the concept I propose. In essence, life is a self-organized structure, but it is capable of surviving, that is,of maintaining itself far from equilibrium, and to replicate its self-organized structure. This is the objective of the simplest living matter.

A living organism acts when its movement has the purpose to cause an effect, which is the objective of the movement. Will gives the movement of matter its purpose. The will selects the objective to be caused or achieved by the movement. Living matter does obey the physical laws of nature, as it must; but, some of the movement of living matter according to the physical laws of nature has an objective. Will is the emergent property of matter, the special case of physics and chemistry, that is a higher order of complexity that differentiates chemistry from biology.

This concept of will might be criticized as merely a label without explaining the cause of the phenomena to which it is applied, and that is true, but Newton used the word gravity similarly when at the conclusion of his *Principia Mathematica,* he conceded that he had "not assigned the cause of this power," and that "it is enough that gravity does really exist and act according to the laws which we have explained, and abundantly serves to account for all the motions of the celestial bodies, and of our sea." For present purposes, it is enough that there are complex systems that exhibit purposeful movement.

When the balls are spread out on a pool table, they cannot move other than by the physical laws of nature. When a player strikes the cue ball intending to cause it to collide with the eightball and knock the eightball into the corner pocket, the player's will selects the particular future state of the eightball resting in the corner pocket from all possible future positions of the balls. He then directs or controls the flow of energy to cause that objective to become an effect, an existing state. The cue ball and eightball's movement is not life; the player's movement that sets the balls in motion is life. If a violent wind were to blow the cue ball into the eightball resulting in the identical final position as caused by the player striking the cue ball, the movement of the cue ball and eightball would still be random, not purposeful.

To say that the wind's movement is random, or more accurately, orderly but not purposeful, presumes a certain state of human understanding. If some will set the wind in motion to cause the eightball to come to rest in the corner pocket, then the wind would be the equivalent of the cue stick striking the cue ball. Some may say that the wind is God's cue stick, but to accept that explanation without evidence of the existence of the will of God as reliable as that of the will of the human player, is simply to equate the laws of nature with God. To attribute events whose objective or cause is incomprehensible to the will of God hardly improves our understanding of either the laws of nature or God. Even if the will of God set the wind in motion, that alone tells us nothing about the nature of God or her denomination, only her skill at pool.

This is not an idle or dead end point. Without an infallible explanation for the cause of the emergent property of will that distinguishes inanimate matter from life, it is as much a matter of faith to believe life is due solely to the laws of nature as it is to believe that God blew the breath of life into a lump of clay. Whatever one believes, a high degree of predictability continues to unite all views.

Outside a living cell, a virus is essentially inanimate. When introduced into the right living cell, the virus acts to duplicate itself. To *act* means to move with the purpose of achieving an objective. The virus moves with the purpose to cause its structure to be duplicated. The exact same constituent atoms in a less complex arrangement would not reproduce their structure when introduced into a cell. Thus, at some point, the arrangement of atoms becomes sufficiently complex to move toward a specific future state of all possible future states.

When a paramecium in a drop of water moves, some of its movement, unlike the movement of the water molecules around it, has an objective. Although many interrelated processes have been identified, we cannot say precisely what causes the paramecium to do *everything* it does, but in general it moves with the purpose to find enough food and maintain the conditions necessary for it to survive and reproduce.

The will of the simplest living matter I shall call *autonomic will* since it is solely the result of the internal structure and biochemical processes within the organism and its responses to external stimuli. Some living organisms operate solely upon the autonomic will, e.g., plants, single-celled animals, animals without a nervous system, and a human in a coma. More complex than viruses and single-celled animals are the plants and animals with cells with differentiated functions, but the purposeful movement of the simplest multi-celled organisms is still governed by the autonomic will.

A higher order of complexity emerges with the evolution of a central nervous system and a brain that receives and processes information about the world inside and outside of the organism through various senses, such as sight, smell, taste, hearing and touch, and for some animals, heat, polarized light or electrical potential. Henceforth I will ignore plants because they do not seem to have a central nervous system. Some animals have a sufficiently complex nervous system that they can perceive the world through their senses and thereby become aware or conscious. Only in the past few decades has the full power of the scientific method been turned on the physical processes that we take for granted as consciousness.[5]

I am not proposing a definitive definition of consciousness, only that consciousness exists as an emergent property of life and in very simple creatures. If Stuart Hameroff and others are correct about the simplest conscious events occurring in microtubules of single-celled organisms, perhaps consciousness is itself one of the emergent properties necessary for life. Distinguishing between the most elemental conscious events and more complex ones is, as is usually the case, not a precise matter. Nevertheless, by consciousness I mean the level of complexity necessary for the processing of information about events both internal and external to the organism and, more important, the control of the animal's purposeful movement in response to those events. This eliminates reflex actions of the nervous system and the other autonomic systems necessary to sustain life in organisms without a central nervous system or at the cellular level of complexity.

Consciousness exists through much of the animal kingdom. All animal body coloring that serves to camouflage the animal or make it appear larger or more dangerous or ferocious prove animal consciousness, not of the camouflaged animal, but of the animal the camouflage affects. Body coloring proves that many, if not most, animals perceive the world around them and act sometimes based on those perceptions.

Acts controlled through consciousness, result from what I shall call *conscious will*. In other words, when the objective of the animal's movement becomes a part of the animal's consciousness and the movements to achieve the objective are selected and controlled through the consciousness, that part of the animal's will is a conscious will. A hungry crocodile has the conscious will to eat. It looks for a potential meal, and then chases, catches, kills, and eats it. The crocodile's conscious objective is to identify, capture and eat its prey. The animal's consciousness controls its movements to achieve these objectives.

Only part of the will is conscious. Other purposeful processes controlled by the autonomic will operate concomitantly with the conscious will, as evidenced by numerous autonomic processes within the human body necessary to maintain life, such as the heart beat and rate, the maintenance of body temperature, metabolism, growth and maturation, the peristalsis of the intestines, breathing during sleep, the constant beating of the cilia of the lungs, the autoimmune systems' defense against foreign bodies and the endocrine systems responses to environmental stressors. All of the most essential life functions are controlled by the autonomic will. Thus, animals with conscious will are a special case of all animals. They have conscious will superimposed on or emergent from their autonomic will.

Although an act may be controlled through the consciousness, its ultimate objective is still determined by the autonomic will. For instance, hunger results from biochemical changes due to the depletion of nutrients and the increase of waste products. Increased heart rate results from biochemical changes in the blood caused by the byproducts of exercise or by hormones such as adrenalin. The increased heart rate in response to exercise is not controlled through the animal's consciousness, although the exercise may be. The intermediate objective, that is, the means used to locate, catch, kill and eat its prey to extinguish the conscious feeling of hunger and to readjust the level of various biochemicals, are consciously controlled. The ultimate objectives, i.e., the ends, of readjusted level of blood components, are not created in the consciousness. The autonomic will determines the ends and the conscious will controls some of the means used to achieve it. Consciousness is a biological adaptation, an emergent property, to improve the animal's ability to achieve its autonomic will, like scales, lungs, teeth or legs.

The crocodile is no doubt conscious of its intermediate objective when it looks for, attacks and kills its prey. Another way of saying this is that the crocodile desires to catch, kill and eat its prey to satisfy its hunger. *Desire* is a consciously selected objective. Thus, conscious will can be restated as the desire to cause an effect.[6]

A male sparrow may consciously perceive a female, and consciously control its acts to try to mate with her, but the male sparrow does not choose to desire a mate any more than the crocodile chooses to be hungry. Rather the final objective is selected by the sparrow's autonomic will. The sparrow has no more choice about whether to seek a female to mate with than it does to have wings and fly. And, the crocodile has no more choice about whether to kill its prey for food than it does to have scales and a tail. The conscious control of the animal's acts, at least at this order of complexity, is merely a tool to improve the means to achieve the autonomic will.

The more complex the central nervous system the more complex or varied the animal's responses to external conditions, such as the capacity for *learned behavior,* that is, the ability to adapt behavior to repetitive external stimuli. Most animals have some degree of learned behaviors.

Indeed, there is some evidence that even the paramecium can adapt to repetitive stimuli.[7]

At first learned behavior is an autonomic response such as that produced by the paramecium or Pavlov's dog. This learning is *autonomic learning*. Like the autonomic will, autonomic learning is found in animals with higher levels of learning ability. Although Pavlov's dog had consciousness, it did not consciously control whether to salivate when a bell rang. Not surprisingly, humans can be conditioned to produce conditioned responses like Pavlov's dog, and a conditioned human cannot with conscious effort prevent her body from giving a conditioned response. Clearly, consciousness does not control this kind of learned or adaptive behavior.

In addition to autonomic learning, many species appear to consciously learn from one generation to another. Animals raised in captivity from infancy often can be returned to the wild only with difficulty if at all. Most mammal predators are very vulnerable if returned to the wild after being raised in captivity, like Elsa in *Born Free*. Each must learn how to hunt, either individually or as a group, and to kill to feed itself. *Conscious learning* is an emergent property of behavior adapted and controlled through the consciousness.

A capacity for conscious learning increases an animal's possible responses to external conditions, whereas the autonomic will reacts in a fixed or conditioned pattern. The beaver may only survive in the wild by building its dams and lodges, whereas humans may survive naked in the equatorial jungles, wrapped in furs in the frozen arctic, in tents or huts or castles or in a space station. The theory of evolution states that if a capacity is conducive to survival, the animal with it is more likely to survive and reproduce and thus pass on that capacity to its offspring. If the beaver's forests and streams disappear, likely so will the beaver. If the jungle turns to desert, humans can consciously adapt. If adaptability to diverse environmental conditions is the measure of the advancement of evolution of living organisms, humans would likely be close to the top. Bacteria probably still have the advantage over humans.

At some point in animal evolution, again precisely where is not critical, an individual animal consciously changes its behavior based on an understanding of external conditions. These conscious changes of behavior are the first instances of reasoning.

Ginger, my miniature poodle, learned that my wife feeds her and our two cats on the back porch each evening at the same time. The cats often do not eat all their food. Ginger can look out the closed French doors in the kitchen and see the food in the cats' bowl, but she cannot get to it. At first Ginger whined and scratched at the door until we let her out. Then we realized Ginger just wanted to go out to eat the cats' food, so we stopped responding to her whining and scratching. At the opposite end of the house is another set of French doors that leads to the back yard. Most often, when Ginger needs to go out to relieve herself, she whines and does a little dance by this door until we let her out. In short order, Ginger figured out that if we would not let her out the kitchen door, we would let her out the other door, and she could simply run around the house to the back porch and get the cats' leftovers.

Ginger's behaviors were quite complex. She successfully manipulated her "smarter" masters to serve her purpose. She turned my wife and me into her tools to open the door. Her behavior was clearly consciously controlled and reasoned. It required many conscious and complex mental steps requiring not only a perception of the external world, but an understanding of how the external world works. Without this understanding, she could not arrive at the correct sequence of acts to reach the food. Ginger must have understood (1) the spatial relationships of the house and grounds, (2) how to get from one point to another by going in the opposite direction from the goal that could be seen just a few feet away; (3) how her own behavior could influence the behavior of an animal of another species to produce a desired result, and (4) when to repeat that behavior to cause the other animal to open a door that blocked her way.

This is a feat worthy of many humans. Ginger consciously adapted her behavior to get the food to satisfy her desire, which is only possible with a consciousness of numerous relationship among all the objects and acts involved and how to manipulate them to achieve her objective. This consciousness of relationships is *understanding*.

Reasoned behavior[8] occurs when an animal adapts its behavior in a way unique to its experience and understanding of its world. The animal mentally manipulates relationships of which it is conscious to arrive at a plan or sequence of action to achieve its objective. It is highly unlikely that the set of conditions found at our house ever occurred for any other dog in our dog's family tree. Thus, it is even more unlikely that her ability to adapt her behavior to get the cats' food was influenced by any autonomic or conscious learning of previous generations. Understanding and reasoned behavior both emerge from greater mental complexity.

Reasoned behavior can, however, become merely consciously learned behavior. Individual tool-using animals such as chimpanzees and humans can have behaviors that required reasoning about the world without each individual animal that displays the behavior having the same degree of reasoned understanding. The first chimpanzee to use a blade of grass to extract termites from a mound, must have had an understanding of its world sufficient to originate the behavior. Others only needed to copy it through conscious learning.

A Japanese Macaque monkey on Koshima Island also demonstrated even more sophisticated reasoning. A troop of monkeys were fed wheat kernels. One day the keepers mixed sand with the wheat, which would make it difficult to separate the wheat from the sand, or so the keepers thought. Almost immediately, one of the female monkeys picked up a handful of the sand and wheat, went to the edge of a nearby stream and dropped it in a still area. The sand sank. The wheat floated. The monkey picked the wheat off the water surface and ate it. Other monkeys then mimicked the behavior.[9] Archimedes would have been impressed.[10]

This example illustrates another important point. Animals can reason without language and without formal, abstract concepts of cause and effect. The macaque did not need to know Archimedes' law of specific gravity or to measure the relative densities of wheat, sand and water in order to consciously manipulate those relationships to reason that by putting a handful of sand and wheat into water the sand would sink and the wheat would float. Palestinian youths who throw stones at Israeli troops do not need to know Newton's laws of motion or to calculate the mass of the rock, the force of their arms or the angle of departure of the rock from their hand in order to hit their target. Most spatial reasoning does not seem to require language. In fact, try as one might, language is of little benefit in working a Rubic's Cube.

Language does seem to vastly improve the ability to reason, as well as increase communication and social organization and cooperation. By compartmentalizing and refining the consciousness of relationships, language facilitates the combination and manipulation of relationships to arrive at new relationships. Any sentence will serve as an example. Each word represents one or more objects, acts or relationships, and by combining and recombining words, the relationships are linked and interrelated. That language serves this purpose is supported by the ape language studies that demonstrate the ape's ability to form rudimentary sentences. There is even an African Grey parrot named Alex that has shown an ability to speak short, comprehensible English sentences.

What does it mean to choose? An animal that functions entirely upon an autonomic will does select its objective, but this selection is not conscious. A choice requires the conscious selection of an objective, but it also requires a consciousness of alternatives from which to choose, for without two or more possible courses of available action, there is nothing to choose. In other words, the animal must be conscious of two or more possible future states. It cannot consciously select one objective over another if it is not conscious of each alternative future state. The animal must also be conscious of some relationship involved in the alternative actions, for without some understanding of each alternative, it cannot be conscious of the difference between the available alternative future states. Let us examine some examples.

While the paramecium may move away from excessive heat or other life threatening condition, it does not choose to do so. Such movement is controlled by the internal systems of the paramecium as are all of its other purposeful movements. If the north pole of a magnet is moved close to the north pole of another magnet, the second magnet will move away from the first. The paramecium moves away from various conditions by other physical processes. Pavlov's dog did not choose to salivate when a bell rang. No one chooses for his heart to beat. Thus, all autonomically controlled and autonomically learned behaviors do not result from choice.

The weaver bird builds its nests of only one material. Even after four generations of birds have been raised in captivity without the materials to build its nests, when returned to the wild, they build the same nests of the same materials as generations before. The reed bunting and the tree pipit sing their own song even if they have been raised without ever hearing it before. The chaffinch, deprived of ever hearing its own song, will learn to sing another bird's song such as the linnet, but having learned the linnet's song, when it hears its own song it will sing its own and never imitate the linnet's again. And, if the linnet is raised with birds other than its species, it will learn to sing any song but its own.[11] If all nesting behaviors of birds throughout the world are available alternative courses of action, they are nevertheless not alternatives for the weaver bird. If the songs of all birds are available alternatives, they are not alternatives for the reed bunting or tree pipit, but perhaps they are for the linnet.

Even a rat may be capable of choices. A rat taught to traverse a maze to reach its food, may become conscious of the spatial relationships of the maze and choose to follow the most direct route.[12] The instances of rats taught a maze who escape onto the top of the maze and take a direct route to the food, suggests that some rats understand the spatial rela-tionships not only within the maze, but from a perspective outside of it.

Humans appear to have the greatest capacity to consciously recognize and understand their alternatives, although that capacity is not absolute. Like all emergent behavioral capacities, the ability to choose varies from species to species that possesses it, and from individual too individual of each species. Such variance is to be expected if evolution occurs gradually and in discernable steps of increased complexity.

All choices have inherent constraints. First is the conscious recognition of the alternative actions available. If a person decides to go to town and walks there and back because she did not know there is a car in the garage, or that the bus stops in front of the house, she cannot choose those alternatives because she is not conscious they exist. Humans are often like a rat in a maze with invisible walls, never conscious of all of their alternatives.

The second constraint is the understanding of the relationships that affect the alternatives, that is, the consciousness of the consequences of each available alternative action. Without an understanding of the consequences, there is no opportunity or basis for choosing one alternative over another. This would be like the person knowing about the car and the bus, but not knowing whether it is faster to walk, drive or take the bus.

Human understanding of the world is necessarily imperfect. We cannot foresee all the consequences of an act, much less all of the consequences of one act compared to all other possible acts when choosing among them. As a species if not as individuals, humans constantly try to understand the world by discovering the relationships to better foresee the consequences of our acts and the events of nature, but foresight is limited. Certainly our understanding and foresight are better than a dog or chimpanzee's, but it is still limited. And, as between individual humans, the capacity for consciousness of alternatives and the relationships between them also varies significantly.

Does the dog, chimpanzee, human or any other animal have free will? A stone does not have free will because it does not have will. There are simply some qualities a stone does not have such as gender, society, justice, or consciousness, and will is one of them. Of course, it is equally pointless to attribute qualities such as consciousness or justice to prokaryotic organisms, because they do not have the level of complexity necessary to exhibit these qualities. The autonomic will selects a future state of all possible future states. Conscious will is a special case of will that selects the future state and controls the organism's acts to cause it to become an existing state. Choice is a special case of conscious will, when the conscious process selects the objective from an understanding of conscious alternatives and their consequences and then causes it to exist. "Free" will is a qualification or special case of will, like "conscious" will is a qualification of will. So what quality of will is meant by the modifying adjective "free?" Free will is the conscious selection of an objective from consciously available alternatives and consciously controlling the acts to cause the objective to become an existing state based on an understanding of the expected consequences. It is a choice.

We have troubled ourselves greatly over the question of whether determinism and free will are mutually exclusive. In the system of wills resulting from ever greater orders of complexity proposed here, free will is really a question of whether consciously controlled actions can determine events, or whether all events are determined on an unconscious atomic or even subatomic scale by laws of nature which control all conscious processes rather than vice versa.

Molecular biologists have explained in great detail many of the processes of a living cell as ordinary chemical reactions. No one has yet offered a predictive model for the movement of a single cell, much less a multi-celled organism, both internally and in response to its environment. Such a model would have to provide the precision and predictive power for living matter that quantum theory provides for atoms and molecules. If such a model is developed, it will also have to explain the human brain, and why I like squash, but I retch at the thought of boiled okra. I doubt I will live to see such a theory, and I will leave to those who do, unraveling its implications for free will. Thus, it seems that predictability and complexity are inversely proportional.

What can be said with some confidence is that physical systems that select a particular future state from all possible future states and cause that future state to become an existing state do exist. Every biological organism is such a system. Further, some biological systems have the additional capacity to choose some of their objectives. The behavior of these systems cannot be reliably predicted by any known law of nature. The very existence of will and choice are variables in the equation of how matter moves that renders the current laws of physics and chemistry inadequate to explain, much less predict, the acts of living organisms.

I cannot identify the precise physical mechanism that accounts for the difference between the movement of matter with and without will, but whatever that mechanism is, it is an emergent property of complexity. Quite plainly, will is as physical a phenomenon as is light. We see both every day, which proves that consciousness exists, even though a precise mathematical formula for it may be as elusive as the arrow of time or dark matter.[13] Objects in the heavens and on earth danced to the same tune before Newton discovered the score. Time ran slower at the top of Mt. Everest than at the Dead Sea before Einstein told us it did. To add the adjective "free" to will, is merely another way of describing the will's choice of an objective.

Free will as a choice is always constrained, never absolute. None of the acts controlled by the autonomic will can result from free will. The desire for food, for sex, to fight or flee, to mark and defend a territory, to build a dam or a nest, are all ends, i.e., objectives, selected by the autonomic will for the consciousness to try to satisfy. In this sense, Ginger may have chosen how to get to the cat's food she desired; thus she may have had free will about how to get the food, but she had no choice to desire food in the first place. An animal's capacity for choice, that is, to perceive the world, to recognize alternatives and the consequences of each, is limited, and so is its choice, and therefore its free will.

The evidence for choices by other species may be equivocal, but no one can doubt that humans make choices every day. It is essential to keep in mind that choices are never completely free. When one goes to a restaurant, looks at the menu, and chooses what to order for dinner, each item on the menu is an alternative from which to choose. One understands at least some of the consequences of each choice, i.e., the expected taste, appearance and satisfaction of each item on the menu. Within the framework of the known alternatives and an understanding of the consequences of each, one is free to choose. If one orders without knowing the specials not on the menu, one is not free to select what one is not conscious is an alternative. Likewise, if one does not know that the cook has put poison in one of the items on the menu, choosing that item is still an act of free will, although the consequences are not fully understood. Thus, free will exist only within the scope of known alternatives and the understanding of the consequences of those alternatives. Because neither consciousness of the available alternatives nor the consequences of each is perfect, free will is never perfect; yet, we have as much free will as our understanding of our alternatives allows.

The importance of this description of free will and choice will become clearer when considering what it means to act morally and when a person may be appropriately condemned or punished for a particular act. Moral choices and the rule for making those choices will be the foundation of the New Social Contract.

Free will is not, however, volitional will. Humans seem to be the one animal capable of *volitional will*–of the ability to perceive and understand their alternatives sufficiently to be conscious of and to control, at least partly, their autonomic will and thereby to choose some of their ends not just the means to achieve them. By understanding the autonomic will and how it influences human behavior, humans can choose whether and how to satisfy certain desires, and can choose to create other desires when the basic desires of the autonomic will are essentially satisfied as when they are sufficiently fed and protected. The ends created by the autonomic will cannot be eliminated. They are as much a constraint on our complex systems as our physical shape, but they can be essentially satisfied. As the ancient Greeks observed, human civilization began when the basic "animal" needs were met and time was left for other pursuits. The autonomic will influences the other pursuits, but some are subject to the volitional will.

Humans may act either from the desires provided by the autonomic will, like a hungry crocodile, or the self-created desires of a volitional will. Humans act only from non-volitional will until they choose to create their own desires and the means of achieving them. The capacity to choose one's will, to choose both the ends and not just the means to those ends, truly distinguishes humans from other animals.

Evidence of the human capacity for volitional will is frequently found in behaviors that appear self-destructive. When someone goes on a hunger strike to gain attention for her cause, she must recognize the autonomic will for food to survive, yet the volitional will chooses to deny that autonomic will as the means to achieve a perceived greater goal. Catholic priests, knowing that there is a very strong autonomic will for sex and procreation, take a vow of celibacy for the perceived greater goal of service to their God. Buddhist monks in Viet Nam set themselves on fire to protest the war in their country, and thus became martyrs as many others have done for a cause they believed in.

As we learn more and more about the biological mechanisms of human behavior, how certain groups of brain cells recognize and respond to specific stimuli, how certain chemicals influence behavior, e.g., testosterone increases sexual desire and aggression, oxytocin produces love or pair bonding, the constant temptation will be to reduce the world and human behavior to mechanistic and deterministic processes that deny free will. This reaction, however, misses the very essence of human free and volitional will.

By understanding that a group of cells ordinarily produces a particular response and that it may not be the desired act in a particular situation, a person may recognize the response for what it is and choose whether to act on it or in a different way. Most people are afraid to speak in front of an audience. It produces a fight or flight response that can lead to disabling panic attacks. By understanding the neurophysiological and endocrine autonomic responses of the body, a person can choose to control those responses and give a speech. Understanding and bringing the autonomic will under conscious control is how the volitional will is created, not destroyed. Thus, every newly understood biological mechanism creates greater opportunity for freedom of will, not less, and we must resolutely resist the temptation to allow such discoveries to defeat responsibility for our choices.

Will, of any kind, is, however, nothing unless it is coupled with power.

Power

Power is the ability to cause an objective to become an effect.

The ability [to direct, control or influence the movement of matter {for} ...][a particular future state of all possible future states][... to become] [an existing state of matter].

Stated another way, power is the ability to direct the flow of energy to achieve the objective of the will. Will without power is nothing. Power without will is matter moving according to the laws of physics and chemistry. Will with power is life. If the crocodile cannot move to its food or away from danger, it will die. Its will cannot be achieved. When hungry, if it is blind, it lacks the power to see its prey, chase and kill it. If it can see, but has a broken leg or cannot run or swim fast enough or is too weak to make the kill, then it lacks the power to satisfy its desire to eat. A girl in an iron lung may have the will to dance, but not the power.

Power has different forms. The most obvious form is *physical power,* the ability to change the location or form of matter. Every organism has the power to change the form, combination, and organization of its constituents necessary to survive, and usually to reproduce. With most animals, power also includes the ability to run, to fly, to swim, to do all those acts that achieve the will. Every living organism has physical power in some degree or it would not be alive.

A few animals augment their physical power by using *tools.* Every tool exists because it enhances the ability to achieve its user's will. Tools may be as simple as the chimpanzee's blade of grass to catch termites or the sea otter's rock to break open a shell or as complex as a nuclear weapon or a Space Shuttle. Obviously, the ability to make and use tools varies greatly between humans and other tool-using animals and among individual humans. The more an animal can fashion and use tools, the greater its physical power to satisfy its desires.

The second form of power is the *power of alliance.* This power comes from the combined acts of two or more living organisms. Some animals of the same species live together in groups or societies. In each society it will be found that the combined acts of the group improve the species' ability to defend itself, to gather food or to procreate, or all of these. In social relationships, animals cooperate and combine their individual power and increase the power and benefit to each individual. This increased power can be a simple addition of individual power or a geometric increase. Wolves and other predators that hunt in packs greatly improve their chances of killing their prey over a lone hunter. Human society produces tremendous increases of power from the cooperation of individuals.

The power of alliance can exist only if the individuals share a common will. Of course, the individual wolf, wild dog, lion, bee or ant, do not choose to cooperate with others of their kind. They share a common autonomic will to cooperate and live and hunt socially. Humans are almost certainly autonomically social animals, but they also can choose to create a power of alliance to try to achieve a shared common conscious objective such as by forming a partnership, a corporation, a church or a political society.

The power of alliance is enhanced for humans by the *power of persuasion*. Persuasion occurs when an animal satisfies its own desire by inducing another animal to choose to act in a desired way. Through this power many individuals can come to share consciously the same will and act together to achieve it.

Although persuasion is not unique to humans, its nonhuman precursors are of little importance to how human society operates. Persuasion in the animal world is interesting mainly to demonstrate how capacities for conscious action can be found in many animals other than humans, even though humans seem to have developed it to a far greater degree. Human persuasion is discussed in more detail in Chapter III on morality.

Economic power exists exclusively in human society because only humans exchange tools. Economic power is the combination of all the other powers: physical, including tool making and using, alliance, and persuasion. When we use and exchange our tools, excluding weapons when used against ourselves, we use economic power. Making tools or performing services requires physical power. This physical power is aided by the power of alliance, as when several people work together to build a house. The power of persuasion is used to form the alliances necessary to make the tools or perform the services and to get other people to exchange something for them.

Right

A right is that which cannot be denied its possessor.

"Right" has many connotations and definitions. Like will and power, this definition applies to all life, not just human life. Power and will exists the moment life begins. They did not originate when humans first appeared or became conscious of them. Power and will are a part of life and nature, not human inventions. If only humans have rights, they cannot be inherent in life like power and will are. Rather, such rights must be human inventions that exist only in the moment of human existence. Human created "rights" are discussed in Chapter VI. Since the birth of philosophy, humans have sought to find a source of rights greater than themselves and their agreements and customs. Implied in the search for a nonhuman authority is the fear that if rights are merely human inventions, then each person may invent his own rights.

There is only one natural right; one right that inheres in nature, in life itself, and cannot be denied any living creature, one that exists totally independent of humans. That is the right *to try* to achieve any objective the will selects. This right is as extreme as can be stated. It includes the right *to try* to steal, murder, rape, commit mayhem, and every other atrocity committed by man. All the greatest horrors committed by humans are man's natural right.

In animals other than humans, so far as we know, only power limits the animal's satisfying its desire. If an animal has the will and the power, the act will be done.[14] For humans, the consciousness of the future and the understanding that acts have remote consequences may result in a choice not to do an act that a person has the power to do to avoid those consequences. Or, a person may choose to achieve the same objective by using alternative means that avoid the undesirable consequences.

The realities of life and the physical world, including the animals and humans that inhabit it and how they behave, are all part of the constraints that determine whether an animal has the power to achieve its will. When the antelope outruns the lion, both use their power to achieve their will: the lion to kill the antelope, and the antelope to escape the lion. Neither's right to try can be taken by the other. The antelope that escapes has the power to achieve its will to survive, while the lion does not. Nature and life do not guarantee success, but the right to try to succeed, to try to achieve the will, can never be taken away. Even death does not deny the natural right to try. When the lion kills and eats the antelope, neither's right to try is taken. Both tried; one succeeded; one failed.

Chapter II

Biological Society

As life evolved from the single-celled organisms that first appeared more than three billion years ago, some species adapted to their environment by living in close proximity to each other and developing cooperative or coordinated behaviors. Fish swim in schools; bees and ants live in Colonies; hyenas, wolves and lions all live and hunt in groups, and by doing so they became social animals. Animal societies thus became systems of greater complexity than the individual animals that are its members. Elephants, chimpanzees, gorillas and humans all developed social behaviors.

If evolutionary biology is correct, animal societies evolved because cooperative behavior, like physical adaptations, increased the species' or genetically isolated group's ability to survive and reproduce. Other animals evolved survival strategies without the cooperation of others of their species. The tiger, jaguar, and polar bear, to name only a few, live essentially solitary lives. Living socially may provide three possible advantages: (1) improved access to food, (2) improved protection from predators or competitors and (3) improved rate of reproduction of offspring that also survive to reproduce. For example, lions are probably the most social cats, but their society improves the care of young to reach maturity more than the other goals of social cooperation.[1] E. O. Wilson, the father of socio-biology, has said in explaining the evolutionary origins of altruism:

> The mathematical models of population genetics suggest the following rule in the evolutionary origin of such altruism: If the reduction in survival and reproduction of individuals owing to genes for altruism is more than offset by the increased probability of survival of the group owing to the altruism, then altruism genes will rise in frequency throughout the entire population of competing groups. To put it as concisely as possible: the individual pays, his genes and tribe gain, altruism spreads.[2]

The mathematics of population genetics applies whatever the trait or behavior. Evolution works through the statistics of population dynamics and the individual organism is merely a datum in the formula.

When a species that lives socially faces environmental conditions that eliminate the advantages provided by their social organization and behaviors, it must either evolve new social behaviors to meet the new conditions or cease living socially and become like the tiger or polar bear, or it will become extinct. The social organization and behaviors of a species that improve its survival and reproduction are systems of lesser complexity necessary for a species to live socially. This order of complexity necessary for a species to live socially is what I mean by *biological society,* society whose individual and collective behaviors are determined by the mathematics of population genetics.

Modern human society has been enormously successful as a biological society, but its essential biological function and constraints have not and cannot be eliminated. We have developed agriculture and domesticated and selectively bred animals for food. We have elaborately complex systems of economic production and distribution of food and other goods and services that extend around the world and are often referred to as "globalization." We have organized and armed some individuals as police for internal protection and as soldiers for external protection. The industrialized nations have sophisticated systems of medical care to treat injury and disease and medical technology to produce children for infertile couples, even though there is no risk of the human species becoming extinct if they do not have children, and even though there are plenty of orphaned children who need substitute parents.

Human society is so successful that only rarely does anyone think of it as a biological society. The more common focus is on society's failures to deliver all of the advantages of social cooperation to the poor or homeless or elderly who must die or resort to crime because they do not have sufficient food, shelter, clothing or medical care. For these people, human biological society is a failure, even though it is an overwhelming success for the rest. In other words, the human species thrives, while some humans die. Biological society can be extremely effective from a biological, evolutionary standpoint, while at the same time the life or death of any one individual is irrelevant except as a datum in the statistics of population genetics. This is the unmistakable message of Wilson's description of the mathematical models of the evolution of altruism. The individuals who benefit the most in biological society are the strongest, the most powerful.

As social animals, we tend to think of ourselves as unique in the animal kingdom, but we are not. If human society ever ceases to perform its biological functions, humans will respond the same as any other species by either evolving new social behaviors, living individually or becoming extinct. Human history is littered with societies that have thrived and then disappeared. The ancient Assyrian, Roman, Egyptian, and Mayan civilizations are but a few examples. Each flourished, some for centuries, and then disappeared. The exact reasons are unclear, but when each social system deteriorated and failed to adapt to or defend against internal and external threats or improve the availability of food, it became extinct.

All animal societies have a social structure. These structures vary significantly, but in most mammals, and especially primates, the social structure centers around a single dominant individual or an alliance of several individuals. There appears to be a strong correlation between the complexity of a species' social structure and behaviors and the intelligence of individual animals, which seems to facilitate individual and social adaptability and social cooperation.

Humans are the only animals to have consciously designed at least part of their social structure. As early as the Assyrians and Egyptians, some human societies have been organized by the choices of the dominant individuals. In one sense, this is only a progression of the social organization of other primates that have dominant individuals who rule their social group according to their desires and personality. Dominant does not mean exclusively physical strength. For humans and other great apes, intelligence and the ability to understand, predict and manipulate the mental states of other individuals is as important as physical strength. The integration of these complex systems of individual intelligence, understanding of the mental states of other individuals, and the conscious ordering of social relationships and behaviors within a biological society will become clearer in the next chapter about morality as an emergent property of individual cognitive complexity in society.

Many human societies have been consciously organized. The Spartans organized their society around the military life, not just in response to hostile neighboring societies, but also as a choice of the goal of life. At seven years of age, all Spartan males were taken from their homes, raised in a communal camp, and trained in military discipline and skills. Infants perceived to be weak or inferior, or the wrong gender, were put to death immediately. Infanticide was a common practice in ancient times, not just in Sparta. Evolutionary biologists explain infanticide as a version of population genetics at work.

Around the same period, the Athenians were in their Golden Age with its emphasis on individual freedom and democracy. The Romans replaced the Tarquin kings with the Republic, and then later Augustus Caesar, while maintaining the appearances of the Roman Republic, became the first emperor of the Roman Empire. The Christian kingdoms of Medieval Europe were organized on the divine right of kings and feudalism. The reformation of the sixteenth century and the enlightenment of the eighteenth century revived the belief in the importance of the individual. These two movements culminated in the political arena in the doctrine of individualism and limited government as most eloquently expressed in the American Declaration of Independence.

Viewing human society as a complex system composed of an integration of simpler systems, allows us to look for those systems that are necessary for the continuation of human biological society. If there are systems without which humans cannot continue to survive as a separate, social species, like wolves, elephants or chimpanzees, these systems are essential to human biological society. A multitude of cultural practices or behaviors may exist only in human society and vary greatly from one human society to another, but unless human society could not survive as a biological society without them, then they are not essential to human biological society. Some of the cultural practices or specific behaviors may be essential for other properties to emerge, but not for human biological society.

Biological society is not, however, the yardstick for measuring human society or what it is capable of becoming, but rather a minimal constraint. Human society is clearly capable of much more complexity than that necessary for the mere survival of the human species as a social animal. Human biological society is so successful that it has the unique potential for emergent properties that allow the individual human animal to become more than a datum in a mathematical model of human population dynamics. The human animal in society has the capacity to become an individual, valuable and important because he or she is alive here and now, not because of some possible genetic contribution to future generations. Individualism can emerge only when the systems of lesser complexity from which it emerges continue to function. Thus, biological society as a system of lesser complexity constrains the emergence and continuance of individualism.

All animal societies operate on will, power, and right, the systems of lesser complexity necessary for the existence of life. The dominant members of a society, animal or human, with the power to achieve their will, do so, as is their natural right. Describing human society with words such as right, duty, and justice cannot change the evolutionary origins, the physical constraints of these systems of lesser complexity, or the biological function and operation of human society. No matter what we do, life is physical and individual. Evolution may operate according to the formulas of population genetics,[3] but individual animals, and humans, live and die. At least as a description of how the world works, the Greek sophists were right when they argued that might makes right. Whether that is how it *ought* to be, is another matter which will be discussed in detail in Chapter VI on rights.

As I have defined a right–a natural right–it is independent of human thought, action or existence. It is an inseparable property of all life. It is the combination of the will and power that is a living organism. If this is an accurate conception of life, might is power, and right is power plus will trying to achieve the will's objective. Nothing can separate will from power any more than energy can be separated from mass. To separate might from right is to end life.

The amoeba is not merely a collection of carbon, hydrogen, oxygen, nitrogen and other atoms. And, neither are humans merely protoplasmic vessels transferring the human genome from one generation to the next, like ants passing a chemical signal one to the other as they march back and forth along a line. I may be a substitute for a variable in the mathematical formulas for gene expression, but I am more. Evolution may be how I got here, but is that what I am now?

If the biological world is where we came from, and from which we cannot escape, how can we be anything other than the captives of population genetics models? The answer is we are capable of emergent properties that allow us to choose to be individuals. Let us now turn to how this choice is made.

Chapter III

The Emergence of Morality

Chapter I proposes that individual animals are complex systems with inherent constraints and emergent properties. Chapter II proposes that biological society is a yet more complex system composed of individual animals with all the constraints on the individual animals and with new constraints and emergent properties necessary for society to exist. The questions addressed in this chapter are what exactly is moral behavior, how and why the property of morality emerges from the individual in biological society, and what additional complex systems are necessary for morality to emerge.

Animals have many behaviors that seem cruel or deceitful. Lions may eat their own cubs during a long drought or kill a lion from another pride that wanders into their territory. When wolves hunt in packs, they invariably target the most defenseless as their prey. The newborn wildebeest is also a favorite of the lion and hyena. Hyenas will drive off weaker predators such as the cheetah from its kill before it can eat. The crocodile lies submerged in the murky shallows of a watering hole with only its fixed eyes above the water, waiting patiently for a sudden explosive attack on any unaware animal that comes to drink.

The Bronze Cuckoo lays her eggs in the flycatcher bird's nest. The flycatcher incubates and raises the cuckoo's chicks to maturity, even teaching them to fly. Before laying its egg in the body of a live caterpillar, the female Ichneumonidae or digger wasp guides its sting into each ganglion of the caterpillar to paralyze but not to kill it so the wasp larva can eat the live caterpillar from the inside out.

We often empathize with the animal killed, whose food is taken or who is deceived, but we do not condemn as immoral the lion for eating her cubs or killing a rival. We do condemn as morally unfit the human mother who abandons her baby or tries to kill the mother of the girl competing with her daughter for a spot on the high school cheerleading squad. We do not condemn the wolf for killing a newborn lamb or the hyena for taking the cheetah's kill, so why do we condemn the murderer and the thief. We do not condemn the crocodile for killing with stealth or the Cuckoo for tricking the flycatcher, but we do condemn the liar, the adulterer, the forger, and the hypocrite. Why do we not condemn the digger wasp for turning the caterpillar into a living feed bag, yet we reserve our greatest condemnation for the likes of Hitler, Dr. Joseph Mengele, Ted Bundy and Jeffery Dhalmer, who enjoyed inflicting great suffering on their innocent and helpless victims?

We could not lay moral blame on someone because his heart beats, or his body temperature remains normal because the autonomic will controls these actions. These acts are no more morally blameworthy than is a rock dropped over a cliff for falling into the sea. Moral blame is meaningless unless the human or animal chooses its acts. We ignore the morality of all animal cruelties because for all we know animals cannot choose how they act to survive and reproduce. Choice requires a consciousness of alternative courses of action and the expected consequences of each alternative. Is the lion conscious of an alternative to eating its cubs during a drought? Is the digger wasp conscious of an alternative to laying its eggs in the caterpillar's body? If an animal cannot choose to act differently, it cannot be morally condemned for doing what it must to survive and reproduce.

This view has not always been true. In *The Common Law*,[1] Oliver Wendell Holmes, Jr., began his treatise on the English and American common law with a discussion of the history of liability. Holmes argued that the source of all legal theories of civil and criminal liability derived from a common desire for revenge based on a moral sense of blame. Holmes cited the rules of law of the ancient Greeks, Romans, Jews and Teutonic tribes for the liability of animals and inanimate objects. In Exodus, it is said: "If an ox gore a man or a woman, that they die; then the ox shall be surely stoned, and his flesh shall not be eaten; but the owner of the ox shall be quit." According to Plutarch, in the time of Solon, "If a dog bites a man, the dog is to be delivered up bound to a log of four cubits long." And, quoting AEschines, "We banish beyond our borders stocks and stones and steel, voiceless and mindless things, if they chance to kill a man." In primitive cultures, if a tree fell on a man, or he fell from the tree, and he died, the tree was delivered to the relatives or chopped to pieces. In England during the time of Edward I, the tree was forfeited to the crown as a deodand. As late as the sixteenth century of Henry VIII, if a man's sword was used by another to kill a man, it was forfeited to the crown as a deodand, regardless of the owner's innocence in the crime.

Holmes noted that others have explained this desire for revenge on animals and inanimate objects with the personification of inanimate objects common in primitive or savage people and children. This explanation suggests that children and primitive people believe that inanimate objects and other animals have a consciousness and capacity for choice.

While moral judgment applies only to choices, all choices are not subject to moral judgment. Choices require a consciousness of alternatives and an understanding of the consequences of each. An animal may act to further its self-interest without being conscious of itself or what furthers its self-interests. It may even choose acts that further its self-interest without being conscious of itself. With some notable exceptions, the vast majority of animal behavior does appear to serve the self-interest of the animal. Self-interest mediated by natural selection is the very foundation of Darwinian evolution. But, before an animal can *choose* to act for its own self-interest the animal must be conscious of its own self.

Self-consciousness is an emergent property of consciousness. It is the consciousness of one's own consciousness and the relationship of oneself as separate and distinct from other objects and animals. Without a consciousness of the self, an animal cannot select an alternative based on the expected consequences to itself.

Wolves may choose to attack a newborn calf instead of a mature bull based on a consciousness that it is easier and less risky to kill a calf. Surely killing the calf is in the self-interest of the wolves so they can eat and survive. The wolves may choose their prey, but unless they are self-conscious, they cannot choose to achieve their self-interest because they are not conscious of their self.

If a man fathers a child but is not conscious that he has, he may choose to act in a way that benefits the child, but if he is not conscious the child exists, he cannot choose his acts based on the expected consequences *to the child*. He may benefit the child by sending the mother money because he loves her or she is blackmailing him. By choosing to send the money, the man does not choose to benefit a child he is not conscious exists, like the wolf cannot choose to benefit a self unless it is conscious it exists. If the man is conscious of the child, he may choose to send the money to benefit the child. The physical acts and their consequences may be identical, but in one instance the act is chosen to achieve the desire to help his child, and the other is not.

If instead, the man chooses not to send the mother money because he is not conscious of the child, he cannot be morally blamed for not supporting his child. If he knows about the child and chooses not to send the money, then surely he is morally blameworthy.

A number of experiments have been done to test whether animals have self-consciousness. These experiments, while crude, use the same techniques used to test when human infants acquire self-recognition.[2] They analyze the animal's reactions to its image in a mirror, on videotape or in a picture for signs that the animal recognizes that the image is of itself rather than another animal of its own species, or not at all. To date, only chimpanzees, orangutans and humans have passed this test of self-consciousness.

At a minimum, the ability to recognize one's own image in a mirror seems to be a starting point of self-consciousness. This is not to say that an animal without self-consciousness cannot consciously discriminate between itself and other objects in its environment, or even between other members of its own species and other species and inanimate objects. Surely dogs that mark their territory with scent glands and body waste do that. Rather, self-consciousness begins with consciousness of one's own consciousness. If an animal cannot recognize its own image, likely it cannot recognize itself as conscious. Without that consciousness, it cannot choose its acts based on a consciousness of the consequences of each upon itself. That is, it cannot make choices based on conscious self-interest.

While the scientific demonstration of self-consciousness in other species is difficult, we unreservedly accept that humans are self-conscious. Further experiments with animals may eventually demonstrate self-consciousness in other species and in so doing confirm the belief of many people about the mental abilities of their dogs and other animals. For now, the evidence supports two conclusions: one, self-consciousness is an emergent property of mental complexity, and two, humans, by a certain stage of mental development, are self-conscious and can choose to act in their own self-interest.

Being self-conscious, however, does not mean that an animal is conscious that others of its species are also self-conscious.[3] Deceptive behavior and empathy provide the first evidence for the emergence of the consciousness of others' consciousness, or other-consciousness.

What appears to be deceptive behavior has been observed in many animal species. Body coloring camouflages the animal or makes it appear larger or more dangerous to its enemies. When the body coloring distorts other animals' perceptions, they are often deceived.

Behaviors also alter other animals' perception. The American avocet and the black-necked stilt perform a broken wing display to potential predators to draw them away from their nest and young.[4] The females of some firefly species mimic the flash patterns of males of other species to lure them to mate, only to eat them.[5] It seems most unlikely that the avocet, the black-necked stilt or the firefly chooses to deceive its predators or prey. Their behaviors are almost certainly hardwired or conditioned, yet some animals do appear to choose to deceive other animals. Such deception requires the conscious manipulation of the mental states of the other animal, which, of course, requires a consciousness of the other animal's mental state.

Figan, one of the chimps Jane Goodall[6] observed for years in the wild, saw a banana Goodall had placed in a tree, but he ignored it until Goliath, a dominant male who was sitting under the tree, moved off. Then Figan retrieved the banana. Explanations other than Figan's consciousness of Goliath's mental state are possible; however, this is strong anecdotal evidence.[7] Menzel claims one leader of his captive chimpanzee group, when shown a source of food, drew others away only to return later to eat the food herself. When the others became aware of this behavior, they watched her carefully for deceptive cues.

A number of experimenters have had some success in teaching chimpanzees, and orangutans, representational systems approximating language. The methods used and conclusions drawn from these studies have proved controversial, but the source of the controversy seems to be the different assumptions made by critics about the apes' innate mental abilities. Each group of experimenters seems to have demonstrated that their apes can communicate rudimentary meanings using a limited set of symbols.

These studies have provided further examples of behavior interpretable as consciously deceptive. Lana, a chimp taught computer lexigrams, misrepresented what was in her food dispenser when dignitaries were visiting the laboratory.[8] Lucy, a chimp taught gestures based on American Sign Language, was taught the possessive, "Lucy's book," and her handler, "Roger's book." During a later training session, Lucy ran away with someone else's book. When asked whose book it was, Lucy signed,

"Lucy's book." Lucy was also required to clean up when she made a mess. When confronted with a mess she made, she was asked whose it was. She pointed an accusing finger at those about her until she finally cleaned up her mess.

The same researcher observed an incident with two other chimps when they were competing over a favorite water hose. One suddenly rushed to the cage door, looked out and gave a natural alarm call for danger outside. The other chimp immediately dropped the hose and rushed to the door while the first one went quietly back to regain the hose. "Gotcha!"

Another chimp, Nim, would use the signs "dirty," which represented a desire to defecate or urinate, and "sleep," which represented wanting to take a nap or go to bed, to avoid undesirable situations or events, such as ending an apparently boring task required by his teacher, or to delay transfer to another teacher. Nim often exhibited almost human signs of lying when using the signs inappropriately, such as avoiding eye contact and having a slight grin on his face.

H. Lyn Miles[9] has proposed a developmental approach to deception in apes which identifies the types of activities labeled deceptive, and characterizes them according to psychological complexity and sophistication attending each type. Miles notes that much depends on how deception is defined. Is it body coloring that confuses a predator or the conscious manipulation and distortion of the conscious perception or understanding of another animal? Miles' approach is developmental because it assumes each level requires more sophisticated, or complex, mental processes than the preceding one.

Level 1: Simple Error

Only an appearance of deception is present, such as the erroneous use of a sign. Koko, a language trained gorilla, when asked what is funny, signed "that red" for a green frog. Koko may have consciously used the sign wrong as an effort at humor, but she may just as easily have used an erroneous sign.

Level 2: Over extension

This level also represents only an appearance of deception from the animal having a larger domain for the sign than the experimenter. The animal does not make an error or mistake, but uses the sign in a more general meaning than the adult human who has greater discrimination in using the sign. An example is Chantek, a language trained orangutan, using the sign "dirty" to represent bathroom, where he likes to play, as well as where he goes to defecate and urinate.

Level 3: Instrumental Association

At this level, the animal has an association between a sign or signs and a desired outcome, but it has no intention to deceive and no awareness that others interpret the sign differently. An example is Nim's use of "dirty" to avoid training sessions. The use of the sign is associated with an intention to achieve a certain end, and includes the behavior of the human in that intention, but does not necessarily involve inducing a false belief in the human. Our dog getting us to open the door for her seemed to us a trick, but probably was the dog only doing what got her what she wanted.

Level 4: Intentional Deception

This is the common meaning of deception. The animal is aware of an alternative reality or goal achievable by the misuse of a sign. Misuse is thus intentional and premeditated. Actions and signs indicate one intention, but when the intention is fulfilled, another is apparent. This requires suppression of some cues that might reveal the deception. Menzel's chimp's false alarm call to regain the hose was an intentional deception.

Level 5: Deception with False Cues

This requires substitution of cues that are contrary to the deceptive message as well as suppressing cues that might reveal the deception. Chantek hid an eraser from his trainer, but signed and behaved as if he had eaten it by opening his mouth for the trainer to see inside and signing "food-eat." At this level, Chantek actively tried to thwart the trainer's recognition of a falsehood by providing false messages to support the falsehood. At level 4, the animal provides true messages to support the falsehood.

Not surprisingly, child developmental psychology shows many parallels to the development of mental capacity of apes. Self-consciousness is developed through experience and mental maturation. Extensive experiments with human children from birth through age twenty-four months have shown that as late as eight months of age, the human infant shows no evidence of self-perception or differentiation between self and others. By age twenty-four months, the child is aware of itself as separate from other objects and people, of the cause-effect relationship between its own body movements and a moving visual image. It can recognize its own features, and it has an internal image of its own face that it can compare to external visual images both in a mirror and on videotape. And, it can verbally label unique fetural attributes of itself as the self.[10]

At about two years old, children are apparently self-conscious, but totally unconscious of other people's consciousness. This is evidenced by their inability to use intentional deception or deception with false cues. When the child learns to deceive others, "telling the truth" becomes a habit, or in the terminology of Harvard psychologist, Jerome Kagan,[11] a standard, that most adults try to instill in their children, some with more success than others. Also during this stage of mental development, the first evidence of other-consciousness appears.

Another indicator of children's development of consciousness of others' mental states is the emergence of empathy. Like self-consciousness, empathy has nascent precursors in infancy.[12] Before one year-old, infants exhibit *global empathy*, which is a distress response paralleling another's distress, such as when one infant in a nursery cries and others follow. When the child acquires *person permanence,* which is an awareness of other people as separate physical entities, though not at first as separate mental entities, the infant exhibits alternating distress. With a firmer hold on person permanence, the older child more reliably recognizes the other's separate distress. These developments in person permanence parallel the development of self-consciousness described above.

Between two and three years of age, the child begins to develop an ability for role-taking or perspective-taking which is essentially imagining the world as another person experiences it. This basic capacity has three facets: *perceptual role-taking,* which is literally imagining the visual perspective of another person; *cognitive role-taking,* which is imagining the thoughts and emotions of another; and, *affective role-taking,* which is inferring another's emotional state from their behavioral cues, such as wincing when seeing another fall down or get hit by a hard object. These abilities begin between two and three years old, but they continue to mature and improve throughout childhood, allowing increasingly accurate interpretation of a greater variety of other's expressive and situational cues in various social settings.

The development of these abilities is evidenced by the appropriateness of the child's offers of assistance. When the child is in the first stages of acquiring person permanence, it recognizes another's distress and has a sympathetic or affective reaction to it, but the child's offers of assistance are often inappropriate, such as trying to give a candy cane to a parent crying after a fight with a spouse. With increased sophistication in role-taking, the child gains accuracy in understanding the other's mental state and its cause, and its offers of assistance are more appropriate. Instead of a candy cane, the child may offer a hug and "I love you."

Language skills also reinforce the maturing role-taking abilities and allow the use of complex symbolic cues. A verbal description of an unseen person's situation may evoke an empathetic reaction and understanding as keen and real as actually experiencing the person's situation. As children acquire *person identity*, which is the ability to view others as having stable identities, attitudes, experiences and internal states, the child can construct concepts of general life experiences and generalize to classes or chronic aspects of life in general with less reliance on cues from specific situations. A young child visiting another child in the hospital who is terminally ill, but happy and friendly during the visit, may feel happy in response, while an older child or adult can see the tragedy and sadness of the ill child's situation rather than its momentary emotional state. Adults can abstract certain life conditions for people in general and empathize with the homeless, refugees, famine victims etc. as a class.

We do not lay moral blame on very young children because, like animals, they do not have the mental complexity necessary to choose their actions. For a very long time, different legal systems have recognized that children below a certain age are incapable of criminal or negligent acts. Although children, even very young ones, seem to have innate capacities suggesting a moral sense of right and wrong, several mental developments are necessary for a child to acquire full moral capacity. Jerome Kagan notes in *The Nature of the Child* that children as young as two years-old have some understanding of when an object is not as it is expected to be, and they often exhibit anxiety as a result. A young child presented with a doll missing its head, will often show it to an adult with clear distress and perhaps a question "who broke it." It is not only the question but the distress that Kagan claims shows signs of moral development. The reaction has both a cognitive and an emotional component.

The three-year-old perceives certain acts or events as "bad" and others as neutral. When asked whether hitting another is bad or wrong, the child responds "yes" it is wrong. When asked if closing a door is bad or wrong the child produces a confused lack of response like, "that does not compute." I suggest this difference is because the child has a nascent consciousness that hitting another is bad, not just because a parent may disapprove, but because of the child's emerging consciousness of and identification with the mental state of the other child, while the door has no consciousness to be affected by slamming it. On the other hand, when a child, or even an adult, runs into a door and experiences pain, he will often blame the door, and parents will often sympathize by reinforcing the child's complaint, "Bad door." Maybe Holmes' was right.

Later the child develops the ability and desire to conform to rules or standards of performance provided by its care-givers, and it again shows distress when it fails to conform to those standards. The adolescent child develops an apparent need for logical consistency between its beliefs and between its beliefs and actions. At this stage, children begin to question all rules of behavior, standards, and even basic beliefs about the world and the people in it, and they begin searching for an acceptable source of authority for social and moral rules.

There are several complex systems that must all be present for what I call other-consciousness to emerge. One is the cognitive capacity for self-consciousness. Another is the cognitive and emotional capacity for empathy in being able to imagine the mental and emotional state of others. Another is the child's ability to apply reason to understand the relationships between his self-consciousness, and others' consciousness. The human infant lacks each of these mental complexities, but the process of physiological and cognitive maturation of the brain necessary for other-consciousness to emerge continues from birth through adulthood. Experience, teaching and conditioning by adults all aid the emergence of other-consciousness.

Other-consciousness is not just the intellectual maturity necessary for rational thought. It includes the psychological and emotional development to imagine the emotional state of others, not just their thoughts. It is not simply the ability to follow and accept the logic of an argument about why one person's desires are no more valuable than one's own. The complexity necessary to be conscious of other people as equal to oneself, to see and feel and think about the world as other people do, emerges in stages until the fully mature, other-conscious person is so thoroughly convinced of the equality of the self and some other people if not all people that the equality seems self-evident. Other-consciousness is not just a cognitive ability to imagine the world as another person sees it. It is not just an emotional, sympathetic reaction to the suffering of others. Except for abstract reasoning with language, which apparently is unique to humans, all of the complex systems necessary for other-consciousness to emerge can be found to some extent in some other animals, which is consistent with other-consciousness being an evolved, emergent property. Some, if not all, human emotional states have biochemical correlates such as the effect of oxytocin in producing emotions of love or affection for children or mates. All these complex systems must exist for other-consciousness to emerge as a conscious conviction that others are equal to the self. Other-consciousness is as close as we can get to a God's eye view of others and ourselves.[13]

Locke argues that children are born without knowledge or understanding. (Locke's and my use of "understanding" are not synonymous.) They must acquire "reason" before they are capable of becoming a member of society.[14] To Locke, "reason" includes all developments in childhood necessary for a child to understand he is an equal to everyone else. The child does not attain reason until he knows the "law of reason" and is thus subject to that law and capable of pursuing his own will within the "permission of that law."

Locke presumes the child acquires reason at age twenty-one, unless he is a lunatic or idiot. Until the child acquires reason, it is subject to the "jurisdiction" of the parents, or if orphaned, a guardian. In other words, the parent is authorized and obligated to provide for the necessities of his or her child and to educate it to acquire reason in order to become a member of society.[15]

Locke is surely right in two respects: first, children are not born with moral capacity; they must acquire it. Second, an extended period of development, experience and education is necessary to produce the mental complexity sufficient for a person to come to see other persons as his equal, if ever. Locke describes this mental development as follows:

> This equality of men by nature the judicious Hooker looks upon as so evident in itself and beyond all question that he makes it the foundation of that obligation to mutual love amongst men on which he builds the duties we owe one another, and from whence he derives the great maxims of justice and charity. His words are:
> > The like natural inducement hath brought men to know that it is no less their duty to love others than themselves; for seeing those things which are equal must meet needs all have one measure; if I cannot but wish to receive good, even as much at every man's hands as any man can wish unto his own soul, how should I look to have any part of my desire herein satisfied unless myself be careful to satisfy the like desire, which is undoubtedly in other men, being of one and the same nature?

> To have anything offered them repugnant to this desire must needs in all respects grieve them as much as me; so that, if I do harm, I must look to suffer, there being no reason that others should show greater measure of love to me than they have by me showed unto them; my desire therefore to be loved of my equals in nature, as much as possibly may be imposeth upon me a natural duty of bearing to them-ward fully the like affection; from which relation of equality between ourselves and them that are as ourselves, what several rules and cannons natural reason hath drawn, for direction of life, no man is ignorant.[16]

Locke and Hooker's arguments for the equality of man reflect a mature other-consciousness. Their views of equality, though presented from a Christian perspective, are not uniquely Christian. Most of the religions of the world have similar concepts of equality. Pagan Greece and Rome and ancient Judea had advocates for the equality of all men. The pervasiveness of expressions of equality in religious teachings and moral, social and political philosophy is strong evidence that other-consciousness exists and is an emergent property of human consciousness. Self-consciousness and other-consciousness are necessary for moral capacity, but they are not sufficient.

Before children become fully morally capable, they are subject to a separate criminal justice system designed to accommodate their limited ability to understand their choices, and conform their actions to legal standards. Although the idea is currently under serious attack, the juvenile justice system exists because children cannot conform their behavior to legal standards before they reach the maturity necessary for other-consciousness. The juvenile justice system is intended to help children develop the necessary abilities to understand and conform to the adult criminal law, not to punish them for not having developed them.

The adult criminal law punishes choices, not just acts or their consequences. For most crimes, the prosecution must prove the defendant intended to commit the crime.[17] Suppose a person goes to a doctor's office with an umbrella on a rainy day. On the way out, he picks up the wrong umbrella, one much more valuable than, but similar looking to, the one he came with, and walks out the door. To prove theft, the prosecution must prove that the person left the office with the umbrella knowing it was not his and intending to take it. If the person takes an umbrella not knowing that he has taken the wrong one, no crime has occurred because he did not intend to take another's umbrella.

To translate this common legal analogy into the terms of choice as I have formulated it in Chapter I, the person does not choose to take another's umbrella because he is not conscious of or understand the consequences of the alternatives, i.e., to take another's umbrella or put it back. Without being conscious that the umbrella is not his own, he cannot choose to take another's umbrella. Without choosing to take another's property, one is not criminally or morally blameworthy, just mistaken. The consequence is the same, one person is without his umbrella, but the consequence is not condemned or punished. The act of taking another's property is not punished; the choice to take it is. Remember, the choice to take another's property is an act of free will. To take an umbrella without understanding the consequence and selecting that alternative from another alternative is merely an act, not a choice.

The insanity defense reveals the last element of the kind of choice necessary for criminal responsibility or moral blame. The insanity defense has existed since antiquity. Roman law did not punish the child or the insane for murder. "'The one,' say they, 'is protected by its innocence, the other by his misfortune.'"[18] The Emperor Marcus Aurelius wrote to the judge in the case of Aelius Priscus, who had killed his mother. "He is sufficiently punished by his misfortune."[19] In 1582, an English Court held that "a man or a natural fool, or a lunatic in the time of his lunacy, or a child who apparently has no knowledge of good or evil," could not be guilty of a crime.[20] And in 1794, the rule was stated that if a person who "'doth not know what he is doing, no more than * * * a wild beast' he might escape punishment."[21]

The statement of the rule with widest application today[22] is found in *M'Naghten Case*. Daniel M'Naghten, an Englishman with a persecution complex, attempted to assassinate Robert Peel, the Prime Minister of England. By mistake, M'Naghten killed Peel's secretary. In 1843, M'Naghten was tried and found not guilty by reason of insanity. Lord Chief Justice Tindal instructed the jury as follows:

> Under the law a person is sane and responsible for his crime if he has sufficient mental capacity to understand what he is doing and to understand that his act is wrong. If at the time of an alleged crime a defendant was, by reason of mental infirmity, unable to understand the nature of his act or its consequences, or was incapable of distinguishing that which is right from that which is wrong, he was legally insane and should not be convicted.[23]

A more modern, but less accepted definition, is the one adopted by the American Law Institute, a group of law professors, judges and lawyers who try to shape the law into what they believe it should be. It states:

> (1) A person is not responsible for criminal conduct if at the time of such conduct as a result of mental disease or defect he lacks substantial capacity

either to appreciate the criminality (or wrongfulness) of his conduct or to conform his conduct to the requirements of law.

(2) The terms 'mental disease or defect' do not include an abnormality manifested only by repeated criminal or otherwise anti-social conduct.'[24]

Criminal or moral blame is withheld from the insane not because the person was not conscious of his alternatives or because he could not foresee the consequences of his acts, but because he was not conscious of how to choose between the alternatives, i.e., right ones and wrong ones. John Hinckley may have intended the exact consequences that resulted when he shot President Reagan, but in choosing to do it, a jury found he was not conscious of the rules for choosing between his alternatives, simply stated as right and wrong, or he could not conform his conduct to the rules.

The insanity defense provides the last element of moral capacity. There is no dispute that John Hinckley was a rational person. He had an objective to get Jodie Foster's attention. He understood, i.e., he was conscious of, alternative courses of action that were available to achieve his desired objective. He wrote letters to Foster, without the desired effect. He planned and embarked on a course of action requiring many levels of preparation and sequences of action to get close enough to President Reagan and shoot him. And, he carried out his plan well enough. Hinckley lacked, however, a consciousness of what the law calls right and wrong to guide him in selecting the morally acceptable–the right or legal–alternative course of action to achieve his will or the ability to conform to those rules. With all the mental capacities to select his objective and to plan and execute his attempt to kill the president, without the additional consciousness of how to choose between his alternatives, he was sick, or more precisely mentally deficient, not morally or criminally blameworthy. The specific rules for making such choices will be discussed in the next Chapter.

Whether John Hinckley or any other specific criminal defendant actually was insane when he did the act for which he is prosecuted is not important here. The important point is that the criminal law, as an expression of morality, withholds moral blame and punishment from any person who chooses to do an act that would otherwise be a crime if he did not know the difference between right and wrong, i.e., if he was not conscious that there is a rule for choosing right versus wrong alternative courses of action. It is as if the person who picks up another's umbrella in the doctor's office is not conscious that taking an umbrella he did not bring with him is a consequence to be avoided, or like charging someone with theft for picking up a toothpick or mint at the cash register when leaving a restaurant. Without this consciousness of the relationship between right and wrong alternatives to choose from, Hinckley, or any other insane or mentally deficient person, is no more morally blameworthy than the lioness that eats her cubs.

The insanity defense shows the final emergent property of the individual animal necessary for morality to emerge. Without self-consciousness, one may act in an autonomically self-interested way, but one cannot choose to achieve one's self-interest. A person with self-consciousness can choose an alternative that best achieves her self-interest, but without other-consciousness, she cannot make choices based on the consequences on others' consciousness. Nor can she consciously equate her own consciousness and self-interest with the consciousness and self-interest of others. If she has other-consciousness, and recognizes a conflict between accomplishing her self-interest and the effects of her acts on someone else, she must also be conscious that there are rules for resolving that conflict that she must follow. Without a consciousness that certain alternatives produce right consequences and others produce wrong consequences, she cannot choose the right versus the wrong alternative. Let us now examine what makes one alternative right and another wrong.

We live in a world with physical limits. Living organisms must compete within those physical limits to achieve their will. All life is essentially a competition to survive and reproduce. Humans are not exempt from this competition. Competition produces conflicts between predator and prey, between rivals for territory, for mates, for social dominance, and for all the resources necessary to achieve the will. But, these physical conflicts can also produce internal conflicts. These internal conflicts produce the distress, anxiety, emotional turmoil, or the discomfort of logical inconsistency between conscious objectives of opposing internal systems.

Choices about how to achieve one's conscious self-interest often produce a conflict between the conviction of equality that is other-consciousness and conscious self-interest. In other words, the other-conscious human can foresee that she has several alternatives to achieve her self-interested objectives, and some of these alternatives will have consequences upon those for whom she has other-consciousness. When these consequences conflict with the conviction of equality between the self and others, they produce the internal conflict manifested as a conscious state usually described as anxiety, distress, angst, shame, guilt, a guilty conscience, or even depression. In simplest terms, a right alternative is one that satisfies the conviction of equality of other-consciousness and thus relieves or avoids this internal conflict, and wrong ones do not or even exacerbate that conflict.

If self-interest alone were the criterion for making choices, then the most effective alternative with the least risk to achieve the will would always be "right." The rational calculation would be, "Do I have sufficient power to take what I want, and are the risks of doing so worth the possible benefit?" Rational self-interest cannot determine right and wrong, however, because it does not give equal weight to the consequences of each alternative on others.[25] Thus, it cannot resolve the internal conflict between conscious self-interest and other-consciousness.

Let us now turn to a classic of literature, Daniel DeFoe's *Robinson Crusoe*, first published in 1719, for a practical, though fictional,[26] illustration of how the internal conflict between conscious self-interest and other-consciousness produces the internal conflict that moral rules are needed to resolve.

In this classic adventure tale, Robinson Crusoe is shipwrecked on a deserted island off South America. During this time, he retrieves supplies from the shipwreck, selects the best site for his castle and builds and fortifies it against possible attack. He plants a garden with seed salvaged from the ship. He secures guns, powder and shot from the ship and uses them, without any hesitation, to kill goats and birds for food. The first half of the book describes in great detail Crusoe's conscious, rational pursuit of his survival and comfort while alone on the island.

Crusoe had animals with him, a dog, a parrot he taught to speak, and numerous cats. The dog died of old age after sixteen years. The cats were so prolific that Crusoe had to drive the young away, except for ". . . two or three favorites, which I kept tame; and whose young when they had any, I always drown'd; and these were part of my family." But, he treats his family of animals as no more than objects to satisfy his desires for food, companionship and entertainment. He never hesitates to use them for his self-interest, and he never considers whether his actions are right or wrong.

Natives from other islands visit the island, and Crusoe observes their cannibalistic feasts. After observing one such feast and finding the gruesome leftovers, he resolves to intervene in the next one. As he contemplates killing these cannibals, Crusoe begins to consider

> . . . that if I kill'd one party, suppose ten, or a dozen, I was still the next day, or week, or month, to kill another, and so another, even *ad infinitum,* till I should be at length no less a murtherer than they were in being man-eaters, and perhaps much more so.

For the next fifteen months, Crusoe is in a state of anxiety over the danger to himself and the dilemma of killing other men. His only fear on the island is

> ... falling into the hands of cannibals and savages, who would have seiz'd on me with the same view as I did of a goat or a turtle; and have thought it no more a crime to kill and devour me, than I did of a pidgeon or a curlier.

Although the cannibals would not hesitate to kill and eat him, Crusoe has some degree of other-consciousness for them and the consequences on them of his proposed actions which provokes a dilemma of how he should act to achieve his desire to escape the island. This dilemma exists only because of the effects his actions will have on those for whom he has other-consciousness. This is a true moral dilemma. If his escape plan required him to chop down every tree on the island, and kill all his cats, dog, parrot and goats, he would have no hesitation because he has no other-consciousness for any of them. Neither considering nor doing these actions produces the mental and emotional anxiety or distress that necessitates a moral choice.

Crusoe was raised a Christian, and he believes in the Christian God and the Golden Rule, but he concludes that capturing one of the savages is his only way to escape:

> ... my only way to go about an attempt for an escape was, if possible, to get a savage into my possession; and if possible, it should be one of their prisoners, who they had condemn'd to be eaten, and should bring thither to kill. But these thoughts still were attended with this difficulty: that it was impossible to effect this without attacking a whole caravan of them and killing them all; and this was not only a very desperate attempt and might miscarry, but on the other hand, I had greatly scrupl'd the lawfulness of it to me; and my heart trembl'd at the thoughts of shedding so much blood, tho' it was for my deliverance. I need not repeat the arguments which occurr'd to me against this, they being the same mentioned before; but tho' I had other reasons to offer now, viz., that those men were enemies to my life and would devour me if they could; that it was self-preservation in the highest degree to deliver myself from this death of a life and was acting in my own defence, as much as if they were actually assaulting me, and the like. I say, tho' these things argu'd for it, yet the thoughts of shedding human blood for my deliverance were very terrible to me and such as I could by no means reconcile myself to for a great while.

However, at last, after many secret disputes with myself and after great perplexities about it, for all these arguments one way and another struggl'd in my head a long time, the eager prevailing desire of deliverance at length master'd all the rest, and I resolv'd, if possible, to get one of those savages into my hands, cost what it would. . . .

Crusoe faces a true moral choice of how to resolve the conflict between his self-interest in escaping the island and his other-consciousness for the savages and the consequences of his choice of how to escape. His self-debate contains elements of the "natural" rights political philosophy of Hobbes and Locke that is summarized in Chapter VII. Both made self-preservation the first "natural" right. Quite possibly DeFoe, as a well-read Englishman of the early 1700s, was familiar with and incorporated elements of natural rights philosophy into *Robinson Crusoe*.

After adopting his escape plan, another two years passes before Crusoe rescues Friday from being eaten by one of the landing parties of savages. And, while Crusoe cares for Friday as he does his other animals, he also teaches Friday to call him "master," and to be handy and to speak and understand enough English to be useful. Friday is more than just another animal that Crusoe uses to serve his self-interest. Friday is a "faithful, loving, sincere servant . . . perfectly oblig'd and engag'd; his very affections were ty'd to me, like those of a child to a father; and I dare say, he would have sacrific'd his life for the saving of mine upon any occasion whatsoever." Crusoe describes his other-consciousness for Friday and the other savages:

. . . that He [God] has bestow'd upon them [the savages, for Friday was a savage and a cannibal] the same powers, the same reason, the same affections, the same sentiments of kindness and obligation, the same passions and resentments of wrongs; the same sense of gratitude, sincerity, fidelity, and all the capacities of doing good, and receiving good, that he has given to us; and that when He pleases to offer to them occasions of exerting these, they are as ready, nay, more ready to apply them to the right uses for which they were bestow'd than we are.

Crusoe's other-consciousness was independent of the savages having other-consciousness for him. He knew they killed and ate other humans, and would eat him. The internal conflict shows how some, but not all, humans may face moral choices about how to treat animals, i.e., SPCA (Society for the Prevention of Cruelty to Animals) and PETA (People for the Ethical Treatment of Animals) although the animals do not themselves have other-consciousness. The internal conflict between self-consciousness and other-consciousness produces the need for moral rules to resolve these conflicts. The more an individual's other-consciousness equates others with their self-consciousness, the more acute is the internal conflict and the greater the need for moral rules to resolve it. Had Crusoe had other-consciousness for his cats' kittens, or the goats or birds on his island, his choice about how to act toward his family of animals would have produced a similar moral conflict to the one he had when choosing his acts toward the savages.

The savages may well be other-conscious individuals, but their other-consciousness only extended to their own family group or tribe, not to their meals any more than Crusoe's extended to "a pidgeon or a curlier." Part of the problem of morality is toward whom does one act morally. Is it wrong to slam a door, or eat a chicken or kill a baby?

Next, Crusoe and Friday rescue a Spaniard from another landing party of savages intent on eating Spanish stew. In the process they kill seventeen savages and rescue Friday's father, who had also been destined to be dinner. With these companions, Crusoe now saw himself as a beneficent autocrat:

> My island was now peopl'd, and I thought myself very rich in subjects; and it was a merry reflection which I frequently made, how like a king I look'd. First of all, the whole country was my own meer property, so that I had an undoubted right of dominion. Secondly, my people were perfectly subjected; I was absolute lord and lawgiver; they all ow'd their lives to me and were ready to lay down their lives, if there had been occasion of it, for me. It was remarkable too, I had but three subjects, and they were of three different religions; my man Friday was a Protestant, his father was a pagan and a cannibal, and the Spaniard was a Papist; however, I allow'd liberty of conscience through my dominions. . . .

Other-consciousness is an emergent property of individual humans, not necessarily of all humans. But, is it just one among many ideas about morality? Are all human wills equal, or is the satisfaction of some more valuable, more important, than others? Was Crusoe's life and escape from the island more valuable than the life of the cannibals he killed?

Let us briefly revisit will, power and right. All biological organisms have will and power, i.e., movement toward a particular future state of matter. Organisms differ in the specific objectives of their will or, stated another way, the particular future state to which they purposively move, and in whether each organism has the power to achieve its objectives.

Nature knows no values. It places importance on nothing. No one star or planet, no one water molecule in the sea or grain of sand on a beach, no one bacterium, fish, bird or ape has any importance. Each is a part of the universal, unending movement of matter. The second law of thermodynamics states that over time all matter tends toward a state of highest entropy. In *The End of Certainty,* Ilya Prigogine gives an illustration from the nineteenth century physicist Ludwig Boltzmann. If a vessel is divided into two equal compartments and initially one side is a vacuum and the other contains a gas, when the divider between the two compartments is removed, over time the distribution of gas molecules will equalize between the two compartments, as will the temperature and pressure of the gas throughout the containment vessel. The system has then reached equilibrium. Once equilibrium is reached, the molecules will move between the two compartments so that on average each contains an equal number of molecules and produce a stable temperature and pressure within the vessel.

Is it possible for the system to spontaneously return to its initial condition of a vacuum on one side and all the gas molecules on the other? The answer depends on whether entropy is an irreversible process, which Prigogine attempts to answer in *The End of Certainty.* I confess to not fully understanding Prigogine's explanation, which is certainly not Prigogine's fault. If I understand him correctly, however, the answer has to do with equilibrium thermodynamics being a special case of thermodynamics which does not consider non-equilibrium or far from equilibrium systems which produce dissipative structures, self-organization, and emergent properties of greater order. In other words, complexity is produced by far from equilibrium systems.

Once the gas in the vessel has reached equilibrium, can it move to the initial state of half vacuum, half gas filled? Of course it can, and the probability of that occurring is not small at all, but the system considered must be expanded beyond the containment vessel and gas to include a first year physics student with a vacuum pump. When the complexity necessary for life is introduced into the system, the probability of various future states of the gas in equilibrium becomes fundamentally altered. Why? Because of all possible future states of the system, there is a complex structure within the system which selects from all possible future states of the system a particular state and then controls the flow of energy to cause that particular future state to become an existing state. The will of the physics student selects the future state of half vacuum, half gas in the containment vessel, and then controls the flow of energy to bring that state into existence. Of all the possible future states of the vessel, the student values the half vacuum, half gas-filled state, and then causes it to become an existing state.

Value comes only from the will selecting a particular future state of all possible future states. For animals with conscious will, another way of saying this is that to desire a thing is to value it. The physics student values the half vacuum half gas state, perhaps to demonstrate his knowledge of physics to his professor to get a passing grade. The male satin bower bird will go to great lengths to build a bower and furnish it with blue objects to attract a mate. The male bower bird values blue objects, not red ones, even if he is not conscious of what is valuable or why.

Since nature in the broadest sense has no will and therefore desires nothing, there is no value or importance to anything superior to the will of individual organisms. Some may argue for such a will and call it God. Perhaps Prigogine's work lends support to the teleological argument for God. Is the self-organization of far from equilibrium systems the creator's will creating life and humans? Perhaps, but I shall continue to refrain from that debate until an adequate explanation of the self-organization of far from equilibrium thermodynamics requires the existence of God any more than gravity, relativity, or quantum mechanics does. To find a universal will requires identifying an Aristotelian final cause toward which the world and all its constituents, animate and inanimate, are inevitably moving and the will that selected this particular future state of all possible future states of the universe. If we find this universal will, we will surely find God.

The ruthless competition of individual organisms to survive and reproduce, shows that the autonomic will values the self over every other individual organism. Altruistic behavior notwithstanding, the basic values of life appear to be survival, reproduction and the intermediate means to achieve both. Individual wills always conflict. The lion's will conflicts with the gazelle's, the wolf's with the lamb's, the wasp's with the caterpillar's. All biological organisms have a will that selects its objectives. They are all equal in having a will that values its objectives.

People often desire the same house, the same car, the same job or the same mate. All people who desire the same thing cannot achieve their desire. When one person desires a car, if he satisfies that desire by killing the first person he finds with a car and taking it, presumably the other person desires to live and keep his car. Thus, the person satisfies his desire by depriving another of his desire. Anyone who satisfies his desire in this way necessarily claims the satisfaction of his own desire to be more important or valuable than the other person's satisfaction of his will. This is, of course, the way all the biological world works. The most powerful achieve their will; the fittest survive and reproduce. Life evolves by the process described by the mathematics of population genetics.

In the nonhuman biological world, and for our evolutionary ancestors and those today without other-consciousness, the sole determiner of which will is the most valuable is power. When men began to reason about the world, they adopted the priority of power as the determiner of what is most valuable and made it into the conscious "principle" of might makes right. Socrates and the Sophists, and philosophers throughout the ages, have debated whether might makes right. Closer to our own time, the Social Darwinists used natural selection as a scientific prop for the sophists' side of the argument.

As Hobbes observed, even the single strongest man can always be overcome by a group of weaker men allied against him or a single person with cunning and deceit. To adopt power alone as the sole conscious principle of right and wrong for making choices necessarily contradicts one's self-interest, because no one and no group can be assured of permanent supreme power. Might makes right is the justification of one's own murder by anyone with sufficient power to do it. Thus, even pure, rational self-interest logically compels a belief in the equality of individual wills.

Reason is only one of the subsystems of complexity necessary for other-consciousness. When reason alone is the source of the belief of equality, whenever reason concludes that ignoring equality produces the greatest advantage, the consequences to others of one's acts become secondary to self-interest. The person who has only rational self-interest can and will, without any qualm, commit murder, rape or genocide, while still repeating the logic of equality.

It seems that evolution has not made individual power the most efficacious means for an organism or a species to survive and reproduce; otherwise, there would be no social animals, no sustained cooperation among individual animals. Social animals, and especially humans, have, as E. O. Wilson describes it, epigenetic traits or behaviors for social cooperation selected through the evolutionary processes of population genetics. Wilson describes these traits in humans as "hereditary biases in mental development, usually conditioned by emotion, that influence concepts and decisions made from them."[27]

Some of the behaviors of other animals are quite similar to rules of moral choice that approximate the equality of will of each member of the social group. Most mammals exhibit inhibited behaviors when competing for mates or territory. Male elephants engage in ritual combat, but it is rare for one of the combatants to be mortally wounded. Even the more primitive Komodo dragon engages in such combat, but not to the death. Dominance hierarchies in social groups are most often established by physical confrontations that end short of mortal injury. These hierarchies help avoid more lethal conflicts among individuals and promote cooperation that improves the probability of survival and reproduction for the group, if not for all individuals.

These pre-moral behaviors are produced by a long evolutionary history of unconscious processes. It seems logical that when the unconscious processes governing these behaviors were first raised into consciousness and verbally expressed, the conscious rules initially expressed the priority of the biological world: the power of the individual to satisfy his will. Might makes right is thus a conscious expression of how dominance hierarchies were, and maybe still are, established and maintained. Egoism and "rational self-interest" are the moral face of Darwinian natural selection of inhibited behaviors. Utility is the conscious expression of the rule of cooperation necessary for biological society to maximize the probability of the group's survival and reproduction.

This does not explain, however, universal equality as the standard of right and wrong. While universal equality has evolutionary and philosophical precursors, it can come about only when other-consciousness emerges. It requires the level of complexity necessary for the individual to consciously equate the value of achieving his desires with the value of all other individuals achieving their desires. There are many other systems of lesser complexity necessary for individual humans to reach this level of individual conscious complexity, but even that is not enough for universal equality to become the rule of human social interaction. Universal equality is the emergent property of a human society in which a sufficient number of individuals are other-conscious and powerful enough to make universal equality the rule governing the social interaction of members of the social group. This human society cannot exist if the systems of lesser complexity necessary for biological society to succeed for each and every individual do not also exist.

There are many stories of human cannibalism among otherwise highly civilized people when the benefits of biological society cease. No person can be expected to choose death over violating a rule of right and wrong, although some do. When an individual's choice is between life and the means necessary to sustain it or death, life is always the "right" choice. More accurately, there is no right or wrong choice. When people must choose between life and death, moral standards of universal equality simply do not apply any more than they do to the lion who eats its cubs.

When other-conscious individuals do not have to choose between life and death, the equal value of self-consciousness and other-consciousness establishes the rule of right and wrong when making choices about how, or whether, to satisfy one's desires. Other-consciousness produces a conviction that the satisfaction of one's own desires are no more valuable than any other person's satisfaction of his desires. This belief in the universal equality of all individuals makes it wrong for one individual to satisfy his will in a way that will deprive another individual of an existing state created by the other's will and power. This conscious belief in the equal value of individuals is the essence of individualism.

We have now arrived at what has been obvious to all other-conscious readers from the beginning: Locke, Hooker, Jefferson, Jesus and all the rest who have declared the universal equality of man were right. There are, however, reasons for having arrived at the same place by a different route. First, no resort to God or religious principles has been necessary. Science and theology do not conflict; they agree. The theological entanglements of Locke and other political philosophers who made God the source and authority for universal equality are avoided. Religion can reinforce or give emotional zeal to the emergence of other-consciousness and the belief in universal equality, but it is not necessary.

Second, if morality is an emergent property of the integration of complex systems, and if those systems have been correctly identified, no social or political system can eliminate any one of those systems without destroying the complexity necessary for individuals to make moral choices. In other words, we cannot have a society that requires people to choose between life and death and expect them to choose death.

Third, the equality of wills is more than a political ideal; it is a physical fact of the biological world. The universal equality of wills does not, however, determine the course of events. Power does. This too is a physical fact of the world if life is the order of complexity which unites will and power. If a social and political state in which all humans are other-conscious and choose to act according to a moral principle of equality is to become an existing state of matter, the power necessary to achieve that objective must be brought to bear.

Fourth, by identifying other-consciousness as the mental complexity necessary to make moral choices, and by understanding the rule of right and wrong for making them, we can determine whether children have moral capacity when they reach the age of maturity. If they have moral capacity, they can choose whether to become a citizen of Society and thereby accept the personal responsibilities it entails. Rather than simply assuming eighteen-year-olds have full moral capacity and waiting until they commit a crime to prove otherwise, Society will be forewarned of their limitations and may protect itself from their moral limitations. It offers a different approach to criminal justice, which will be discussed in more detail later.

Finally, if universal equality is an emergent property of a complex system that integrates both the complexities necessary for individual moral capacity and for biological society, we now have the essentials of human existence, the "state of nature," from which to consciously create the individualistic society we desire. Rational self-interest is never enough. Rational other-consciousness may be.

Chapter IV

The Morality of Equality

Moral philosophy is the conscious search for the rules to resolve the internal conflicts between conscious self-interest and other-consciousness. The human capacity for language and rational, even rigorously logical, discourse emerges before or even without mature other-consciousness. For those people who never acquire a mature other-consciousness, their self-interest is always more valuable than anyone else's. The belief in universal equality produced by other-consciousness, need not emerge. If it does, it first emerges as the internal conflict between conscious self-interest and other-consciousness. That internal conflict is resolved by choosing an alternative course of action that gives equal value to the desires of self-interest and other-consciousness. This chapter will propose a rule for making individual choices that gives equal value to all human desires and thereby resolves the internal conflict.

A brief review of other moral philosophies will illustrate how morality has progressed from the conscious expression of the unconscious motives of self-interest and social cooperation toward the recognition of universal equality and a morality of equality.

Four Moral Theories

Throughout western history there have been four basic approaches to morality. The first is might makes right. Perhaps the most famous presentation of this view is that of the Sophist, Callicles, in Plato's dialogue, Gorgias. Callicles argues that might makes right because the strong make and enforce the rules of right and wrong in society. In one sense, might makes right is not a moral principle, but rather a description of how society works. It is a shorthand description of the dominance hierarchy of biological society. The powerful may be a single person or a group using the power of alliance. This description of biological society is quite accurate because power–might–does determine whether any person's will is achieved. When wills conflict, the most powerful prevail. Whether this is "right," depends on whether the most powerful humans have progressed beyond the unconscious mathematics of population genetics to become other-conscious individuals.

As a principle for guiding other-conscious individuals in making choices to avoid the internal conflict between conscious self-interest and other-consciousness, might makes right has nothing to offer because it simply denies the other-consciousness necessary for moral capacity and the need for moral rules. This version of might makes right merely states that power determines whether any individual's desires are satisfied; those with adequate power use it to satisfy their desires; those with insufficient power cannot satisfy their desires; and that is not only how it is, in fact, but how it *ought* be. Other-conscious individuals, however, reject power as the sole determiner of whether an individual's desires are satisfied, especially when other people are used as the means to satisfy those desires.

If a man wants a house, and he tries to build it by himself, whether he achieves his desire depends on whether he has the power to find and assemble the necessary materials. If instead he enslaves five men and forces them to build the house, power still determines whether the house is built, but the man satisfies his desire for a house by taking the other five men's liberty and labor. Alternatively, the man could hire five men willing to build his house. Each alternative will result in the same house being built. Each has consequences for the man who desires the house, and for those who build it. Morality provides the rule for choosing between alternatives. For other-conscious individuals, the satisfaction of one man's desire for a house is of equal value to the satisfaction of the desires of those who will build it.

The first alternative of building the house without involving anyone else creates no conflict between other-consciousness and conscious self-interest. Enslaving five men to build a house will achieve the same desire. It might even be the most efficient, quickest and most cost-effective means, but it will also cause the five men to lose their freedom, time and labor. The master will get his house by using his superior power over the others. What the master gains, his slaves lose.

The slaves' labor is not free to the master, however. He must provide them with sufficient food, shelter and clothing to keep them alive long enough to build the house. Maybe what the master provides is equal to a fair wage. What if it is equal to the wage the five workers would accept to build the house, if they chose to do so? As long as the master forces the slaves to work against their will, he claims the satisfaction of his desire for a house to be more valuable than the slaves' choice how to pursue the satisfaction of their own desires by means of their own choice. He takes the slaves' freedom to satisfy his desires, whether or not he gives them everything they would have received if they chose to build his house for an agreed price.

For other-conscious individuals, these alternatives produce an internal conflict of moral dilemma. That other-consciousness is the source of the internal conflict and the need for a rule to resolve it is shown by the man who would never enslave other men to build a house, but who would never give a thought to owning mules and plowing his field with them. Morality is unnecessary without the conflict produced by other-consciousness for the objects affected by one's choice. That conflict can be adequately resolved only by choosing an alternative that allows each person to choose their own means to try to achieve their desires. If the five men choose to build a house for a price everyone agrees upon, this alternative resolves the internal conflict. No one's desires are changed, only the means of achieving them.

Another approach to morality is egoism, which makes self-interest the sole criterion for making choices. Egoism states that whenever a person is faced with a choice, she ought to choose the alternative that is the most desirable or beneficial to her regardless of the consequences to others. At its most extreme, egoism merely restates might makes right with self-interest the conscious criterion of choice. This is merely another conscious statement of natural selection.

This most extreme version of egoism is qualified by introducing the idea that in determining one's self-interest, not only must the short-term consequences of one's choice be considered, but also the long-term ones. The consequences of one's actions on others are not a direct part of the calculation of which alternative to choose, but if today the slaves build a house, and tomorrow they kill their master, it may not be in the master's long-term self-interest to enslave others to build a house. Note that the egoist considers only the consequence to himself when choosing between alternatives. Whether the egoist's house is built by beating, starving and imprisoning slaves or hiring well-fed, healthy, and content workers, is of no concern to the egoist unless there is an undesirable consequence to him, not the workers.

Psychological egoism softens egoism further by allowing consideration of the consequences of one's acts on others if it is in the egoist's self-interest because by doing so she feels better. Psychological egoism is more a description of the behavior of people who profess to act out of self-interest when they help others or refrain from harming others than it is a principle to guide choices. It allows the egoist to explain his acts without abandoning egoism.

As a principle to guide choices, however, psychological egoism is of little help. It reduces to, "If it feels good, do it," and it comes dangerously close to the epicurean and hedonistic principle that one should always seek pleasure and avoid pain, which may not be in anyone's self-interest. Pleasure does not equate to self-interest or we should all be drug addicts on a permanent high. Psychological egoism allows choices that ignore the consequences to other individuals if the person does not feel better or worse because of those consequences. Crusoe's cannibals could be perfect psychological egoists as they feast on an enemy.

Psychological egoism is a step toward the emergence of individualism. The psychological egoist may be other-conscious. If he must choose between hiring five men to build his house or enslaving them, he may feel better by choosing to hire them because that alternative resolves the internal conflict between self-interest and other-consciousness. Selecting that alternative gives equal value to the desires of all people affected. The psychological egoist need not know exactly why his choice makes him feel better. He just knows that it does.

The emotional and psychological components of other-consciousness are commonly referred to as conscience. When the internal conflict between self-interested desires and other-consciousness is adequately resolved, the anxiety or distress that conflict produces almost certainly will be removed and the person will *feel* better.[1] The conscience often creates great anxiety and distress in people who commit a crime even though they know they will never be caught? Another fictional story, Doestoyevsky's *Crime and Punishment,* illustrates not only the internal conflict created by the choice of means to satisfy one's desires, but also how the emotional and psychological distress that results from the wrong choice lingers in the conscience and the consciousness. For the other-conscious criminal, the only resolution of the internal conflict is confession, apprehension and atonement. Even then, the conflict is almost never completely erased.

Moral philosophy is complicated by the fact that not all adults have mature other-consciousness, and those who do may not understand the internal conflict it creates or how to resolve it when making choices. Egoism ignores the equal value of individuals. In the end, egoism is no different from might makes right because the egoist cannot satisfy any desire without the necessary power, and in a society of pure egoists, the mighty will satisfy their desires at the expense of the weaker, including those who are other-conscious. Thus, pure egoism makes conscious self-interest the rule for making choices, and psychological egoism permits other-conscious individuals to maintain their psychological, intellectual and emotional balance, but does not tell them how. Psychological egoism neither identifies nor resolves the basic problem of morality.

The Golden Rule, and its secular counterpart, Kant's categorical imperative, introduce other-consciousness to making moral choices. Do unto others as you would have them do unto you. Act only as you would want everyone to act. This rule may be viewed in three ways.

First, the Golden Rule may be the beneficent religious commandment that we should all help others and treat them with charity, kindness and mercy. In one sense, the Golden Rule substitutes the interests of others for the self-interest of egoism as the rule for making choices. In other words, we must choose only acts that will not harm others and will not allow others to suffer any misfortune without coming to their aid even at our expense because that is what we want others to do for us. A second alternative is that the Golden Rule allows each person to decide for himself how everyone should be treated, as long as he is willing to accept such treatment for himself, or more accurately, as long as he is willing to *say* he will accept it when, in fact, he never believes he will ever be on the short end. Finally, the Golden Rule may be merely a specific formulation of egoism. One's self-interest will be best served over the long run by acting as one would want all others to act toward him. As we shall see in Chapter VII, this is Hobbes view of the Golden Rule. None of these interpretations is, however, an adequate rule of morality.

Aristotle and other ancient philosophers held that slavery was justified as the natural consequence of the superiority of some individuals over others: man over woman, ruler over subject, and master over slave. Jesus apparently accepted slavery as an institution. He made no criticism of it in his teachings, and said, "Blessed is the slave whom his master, returning, finds performing his charge."[2] The Catholic church, presumably the ultimate authority on the Christian interpretation of the Golden Rule before the Reformation, itself owned many slaves during the Middle Ages. Pope Gregory I used ". . . hundreds of slaves on the papal estates and approved laws forbidding slaves to become clerics or marry free Christians."[3] In his will of 1149, the Archbishop of Narbonne left his Saracen slaves to the Bishop of Beziers, and no less than St. Thomas Aquinas defended slavery as a consequence of Adam's sin and a necessary in a world in which some must toil so others can be free to defend them.

The Catholic Church defends its history as a slaveholder by arguing that its treatment of its slaves improved their lives and was better than their alternatives.[4] Southern Negro slaves were surely unpersuaded by the same arguments. The Golden Rule is not sufficiently clear and specific to prevent the rationalization of self-interest over universal equality. Some of the greatest of the founding fathers fell victim to the same inconsistency between their declarations of universal equality and their practice as a slaveholder.

The reformed Christian church has fared no better. Martin Luther "quoted the Old Testament as justifying slavery. 'Sheep, cattle, men-servants, and maid-servants were all possessions to be sold as it pleased their masters. It were a good thing were it still so. For else no man may compel nor tame the servile folk.' Every man should stay patiently in the task and walk of life to which God has assigned him."[5] Slavery declined in Medieval Europe not because of moral or religious teaching, but because economic change made slavery uneconomical.

The most enlightened Christian politicians of the American South defended slavery before the Civil War in the finest tradition of Aristotle, Aquinas, and Martin Luther. On July 2, 1859, in a speech given in Augusta, Georgia upon retiring from Congress, Alexander Stephens, future Vice President of the Confederacy, spoke of slavery as the natural condition of the relation between the inferior, black, and superior, white, races. He defended slavery not only by invoking the ancient philosophers, Pythagoras, Plato and Aristotle, but also the Divine Law. He proclaimed that, "The wickedest of all follies, and the most absurd of all crusades, are those which attempt to make things equal which God, in his wisdom, has made unequal."[6] Stephens' other-consciousness apparently extended to his white southern brethren, but not to his Negro slaves.

Some may argue that the Golden Rule is adequate to guide other-conscious individuals in making choices, and the errors of the last two thousand years are due to man's weakness in understanding or following it. If man is that weak, if the Golden Rule allows good Christians to believe their self-serving rationalizations are true to the rule rather than due to the hypocrisy of men whose actions flout the words, then the Golden Rule is a failure as a rule for making moral choices.

In the end, each interpretation of the Golden Rule fails as a guide for making moral choices. The first fails because it is as strong a justification for of slavery as is might makes right. The weak or poor may demand that the powerful or wealthy do their bidding or turn over their wealth simply because they want or need it. Need and want used to enforce servitude or theft violates universal equality as surely as avarice and self-aggrandizement. And if this view allows the powerful or wealthy to act for the needy only when the powerful or wealthy feel like it, i.e., when they would want to be treated the same, then we have reverted to psychological egoism.

The second interpretation fails for the same reason that utilitarianism does, as we shall see. As nice as it sounds, it is incapable of specific, consistent application, and it allows everyone to indulge their own rationalization of right. It is just a nice sentiment in need of specific application, of no more value than a moral rule that says, "Do only good, and be happy."

Finally, the Golden Rule may be purely a matter of rational self-interest. To treat others as we would like to be treated is in our long-term self-interest, because we are less likely to be harmed by others, and more likely to get what we want. So viewed, the Golden Rule is gutted of all other-consciousness and reduced to long-term egoism. As such, it does not address the internal conflict between self-interest and other-consciousness, and it does not offer any reason why one would, much less should, act morally when the chances of undesirable consequences are zero. That is, it fails to answer the question, "why be moral?" The clear answer is to resolve the internal conflict, the anxiety and distress, created by other-consciousness.

The next approach to morality is utility, which holds that choices should be guided by choosing the alternative that will produce the greatest benefit, not for the individual making the choice, but for society as a whole. It is often paraphrased as the greatest good for the greatest number.

Utility has many problems, not the least of which is that there is no way to measure or even estimate the relative balance of benefit to society produced by one alternative versus another when compared to the harm each causes. According to utility, it would be the "right" or "moral" choice for a small town without a doctor to kidnap a doctor and force her to stay in town to care for the town's residents. All the town's residents would be healthier. Some people's lives would be saved, and the doctor would not be seriously harmed, just kept from going somewhere else. In this way, utility allows the desires of one individual to be taken for the perceived greater good or happiness of others.

Kidnaping the doctor is merely the correlative of one person enslaving five people to build a house. In both instances, whoever has sufficient power satisfies his desires by taking or depriving others of their desires. Thus, by giving greater value to the consequences for many people over those of a single individual, utilitarianism denies individualism as surely as might makes right does. Utilitarianism simply substitutes the amorphous good of many people for individual self-interest as the objective and justification of might.

Utilitarianism has infected liberal democracy, and especially the American political system. It serves as the moral justification for the progressive income tax, which is nothing more than one group of people using their power through the political system to redistribute wealth through society. Of course, not all taxes redistribute wealth, but no matter how many politicians or well-intentioned people call it "doing the right thing," any taking of one person's property simply to transfer it to another person, although ostensibly for the greatest good of the greatest number, is the same as a common street corner stick up. Until utilitarianism as a moral justification for robbery is exposed for what it is and eliminated from human society, society will never escape the might makes right of biological society. An elaborate republican or democratic political system that fronts for utilitarian robbery does not change that reality.

Moral Progress

It is risky to attribute progress to human history, for progress implies movement toward some higher state of existence. Human political and social history may, in part, and only part, be viewed as the result of expanding the people who see and are seen through the eyes of other-consciousness. Children develop other-consciousness for a widening circle of people beginning with family members and expanding to more distant relatives or members of their immediate social group. That development stops at some point from family, clan, tribe, race, social or economic class, nation and the "brotherhood of man." Even the animal rights movement of today, which traces back at least to the outlawing of bull and bearbaiting in twelfth or thirteenth century England, owes its existence to the extension of other-consciousness to other species.[7]

In 1997, a group of animal rights activists broke into a mink farm and released several thousand babies and young adults who were destined for the coat racks. This was surely a well-intentioned act motivated by other-consciousness for the mink and their loss of anthropomorphized "freedom." Unfortunately, minks have no other-consciousness for their own species. When released they literally fought and killed each other. The rationalization for this terrible outcome–for the mink as well as the activists–was that at least the minks had a chance at freedom. Equating the consciousness of the mink with humans was a tragic mistake. The activists may as well have kidnaped a local kindergarten class and "set them free" in the middle of Yellowstone National Park.

Although the greatest minds of the ancient world, if not of all time, offered justifications for slavery, the ancient world had pagan proponents of the equality of man.[8] The Roman Empire had a few powerful advocates of the humanity of the slave and his entitlement to humane treatment. The Emperor Claudius prohibited killing useless slaves and decreed that an abandoned sick slave who recovered was to be automatically free. The Emperor Antoninus Pius decreed that an abused slave, if he could prove injury, should be sold to another master. Under the *lex petronia*, masters were forbidden to condemn their slaves to fight in the arena without a magistrate's approval. Nero allowed maltreated slaves asylum by his statute and a magistrate to hear their complaints. As late as 1856 in the *Dred Scott* case, the United States Supreme Court refused to allow slaves to be heard in court and moved the nation closer to Civil War. Not until the nineteenth century did the abolition of slavery become widespread. The United States outlawed the importation of slaves in 1808, and tolerated slavery until the end of the Civil War. The British Empire outlawed the slave trade in 1807, and slavery itself in 1833.[9]

Throughout history, women have been treated as inferior, even as beasts of burden and property. Early English common law made the husband and wife as one, and that one was the husband.[10] The wife was his property, and he had the right to punish her by beating her with a stick no bigger around than his thumb. Hence, the "rule of thumb." This was, however, an improvement over the ancient Roman law which gave to the husband the power of life and death over his wife and children. This power was apparently seldom used, although infanticide was prevalent in ancient times. Martin Luther found women good for "childbearing, cooking, praying, and not much else."[11]

Scientific papers in the nineteenth and twentieth centuries pretended to prove that women were intellectually inferior and physically unsuited to the challenging academic curriculum of a university because they could not cope mentally and perform their biological function as mother.[12] Yet Plato advocated equal education and treatment of women. So much for progress being steady or without reverses.

The kingdoms of autocrats who claimed their authority from God have given way to an idea, the idea of the equality of all men and women. The people seen through the eyes of other-consciousness is widening. The democratizing of societies throughout the world is a vote of confidence that every person, man or woman, is entitled to an equal say about profound political decisions, even if they are not equally capable of making them. The modern battle cry of democracy and equality, was the declaration, all men are "endowed by their creator with certain unalienable rights, that among these are the right to Life, Liberty, and the pursuit of Happiness." When this declaration was made, it was not as universal as it seems today. "All men" did not include any slaves, for Jefferson owned slaves and refused entreaties to free them. Nor did "all men" include *any* women. The legal disabilities of black men were removed before they were for white or black women, who were not allowed to vote for nearly 150 years after the Declaration of Independence.

Some evolutionary biologist, steeped in the mathematics of population genetics, will surely explain other-consciousness as merely a epigenetic trait produced by population dynamics. Other-consciousness improves social cooperation and therefore has survival advantages. So be it. The larger question is whether humans have become something more than evolutionary atoms. Have we become individuals? One of the first uses of Darwinian evolution was Social Darwinism which rendered the inequality of people in human society scientific. But are we merely drone bees, who exist for one evolutionary or biological purpose, to fertilize the queen so she can produce more bees, and once that function is fulfilled, a quick death is all that awaits? Of course death awaits us all. Of course we are biological entities that may contribute to the population dynamics of human populations. These are physical constraints we cannot escape. But, is there any value to living beyond one's contribution to population dynamics?

We become individuals when we answer, "Yes!" We cannot answer yes until we have both self-consciousness and to some extent, other-consciousness. By consciously valuing ourselves the same as others, we become individuals. We suffer from the anxiety and distress of the conflict this understanding produces. We acquire moral capacity, and the need for moral rules to guide us in how to live as individuals, not evolutionary atoms. It bears repeating that other-consciousness is not just the capacity for affective, visual and cognitive perspective-taking. It is not just the ability to understand the mental processes of another person or animal sufficient to manipulate those processes to achieve one's will. It is not just the intellectual search for rational consistency between propositions or the rational pursuit of self-interest even considering the possible responses of other equally calculating humans. It is not just resisting an impulse to harm a rival even though one has the power to kill him. All of these abilities and behaviors evolved in other species and in humans are the precursors of other-consciousness, the emergent property from all of these abilities which produce a conscious conviction in the equal value of every other-conscious human.

A morally capable individual is a self-conscious and other-conscious person who is capable of and tries to make choices in creating and achieving his or her volitional will by means that give equal value to all similarly conscious and motivated humans. These people are individuals. *Individualism* is the belief that the ultimate value of life is as a morally capable individual. An *individualistic society,* is one devoted to the ideal of individualism. Its objective is to create the greatest opportunity possible for all morally capable individuals to create and satisfy their volitional will in a real world with all the constraints that world imposes because each and every one is equally valuable. To prefer any one over another is to deny that equality. Thus, an individualistic society may emerge from biological society by conscious design to transcend the mathematics of population genetics.

Enough about other-consciousness as the biological foundation of equality and the need for morality. If it is not clear by now that universal equality is the sole criterion of morality, stop reading. Close this book and turn on the television. If a couple of days of watching television in light of what has been said does not adequately demonstrate the existence of other-consciousness and that some people have it and some do not, and that those who do not are dangerous to a civilized society, then this book is a waste of time.

If other-consciousness does exist, and if universal equality is the goal of morality, how can that ideal be translated into everyday practice? Is there a rule that can guide the choices of other-conscious individuals in Society to adequately resolve the internal conflict between self-interest and other-consciousness and thereby make universal equality an existing state?

Universal Equality as Moral Theory

To translate universal equality into the practice of the morality of equality, a clearer understanding of what it means to satisfy one's desire is required. A sharp distinction must be made between desire and achieved desire. It should be clear by now that desiring something and making that desire an existing state is not the same. A desired state can only become an existing state with the application of sufficient power to cause it to exist.

Possessions

Possessions are all those existing states that have been selected by an organism's will and caused to exist by sufficient power. At any time, each person has various possessions. The most basic possession is life itself, the combination of matter with the property of will and power. Part of the possession of life is health, bodily integrity, that is, having all the usual, working, anatomical parts, and the consciously controlled actions of one's body, also called labor. These possessions are commonly called life and liberty. Liberty is the ability to use one's power to try to achieve one's desire, but it is never absolute because no one has unlimited power. No one can travel backward or forward in time, or travel faster than the speed of light. These and other physical constraints are always present, although they are not relevant to morality. In order to achieve one's desires, one may impose constraints on another person, e.g., make them a slave. The absence of human imposed constraints are generally referred to as freedom.

Possessions also include a person's physical accouterments, which are commonly called property, i.e., clothes, a car, a house, etc. Property is a relationship between a person and a separate physical object that is made an existing state by the person's power. These relationships vary substantially in time, distance, degree and quality. The objects with which the relationship is made an existing state may be as physically close as one's clothes or a wedding ring or as ephemeral as the desk of the chairman of the board of a company in which one owns shares of stock. Property also includes relationships with or to other organisms, e.g., a pet, or livestock, or people such as one's spouse, parents, children, business associates, employer, etc. The other person is not the property, but the existing relationship with that person, is property. Imagine leaving a baseball game and walking into the parking lot where there are hundreds of parked cars. One of them is yours. It is "yours" not because it or you are unique, but because you have established a relationship with that particular car. Chapter VI will discuss in more detail how systems of rights and duties recognize and protect the relationships that are property.

Experiences may also be possessions. Attending a symphony or rock concert, snow boarding down a mountain, falling in love, or having sex, are all existing states any person might desire and achieve with sufficient power. But, these possessions, like all possessions, remain an existing state for only a finite time, though some longer than others. When the experiences end, the memories are all that is left, and life ends in death.

Information, knowledge or skill may be a possession. Knowing how to build a house, how to write a computer program, where to find the best deal on a used car, who will buy a used car another person has for sale, how to run a business, are all possessions. In short, possessions are any objective that can be desired and that power has made an existing state.

We are all born with our basic possessions. Some people are more blessed from birth with intelligence, strength, health, personality, or perseverance, but everyone starts with life, a body, and an ability to move, to learn and to grow. And, everyone starts with parents, unless they were put into a trash bin. From birth to death, life is the process of constantly acquiring, maintaining and disposing of possessions.

Possessions are not limited to humans. All organisms have their life until they die, and many animals establish relationships with various objects that if done by a human would be called property. Birds build nests; beavers build dams and lodges; bees build hives. Some animals mate for life, and remain more faithful to their mates than do many humans. The cheetah that kills its prey makes the prey no less its property than does a human hunter. Many species mark and defend a territory.

Desire alone cannot create a possession. A person may desire an Olympic Gold medal for the marathon and train all her life for that one race, but if someone else crosses the finish line first, the desire is unfulfilled. An inventor may work for years on cold fusion, but if someone else invents it first, no amount of labor can make his desire a possession. The final determiner of whose desires are satisfied is always who has the greatest power.

Possessions are never constant, but ever changing, and must be constantly maintained or they will dissipate. If one learns a language, but never uses it, it will be mostly forgotten. If one has a car and does not service it and put gas in it, it will eventually stop running. If one marries the love of his or her life, but then ignores the other for a career or otherwise, love will likely die. Life begins, and ends.

What part of the life process does universal equality apply to? It cannot be the natural right inherent in all life to try to achieve the will. That would be like an equal right to gravity. We have it whether we want it or not. The biological world operates on power to survive and reproduce. This reality of power means that the strong prey on the weak to survive. The lion eats the gazelle. Humans evolved in the biological world where might makes right, but with the emergence of self-consciousness and other-consciousness, the value of the self inherent in the autonomic will conflicts with the emerging other-consciousness. Thus, morality is about how people choose to use their power to acquire more possessions. Universal equality is in the equal value of all people in achieving their desires with the use of their power. The central problem for morality is to formulate a rule for making choices that gives equal value to the desires of all people affected by one's choice.

Constructive and Destructive Power

Power can be used to acquire or maintain possessions either constructively or destructively. *Constructive power* is power used to satisfy an individual's desires without lessening any other individual's possessions. *Destructive power* is power used to satisfy the individual's will that causes another individual's possessions to be lessened. Physical power, the power of alliance, the power of persuasion, and economic power can each be used either constructively or destructively. The rule of the morality of equality is to always choose to act only with constructive power to achieve one's will so as never to lessen another morally capable individual's possessions. It is impossible to reject this rule without also rejecting other-consciousness and universal equality and advocating might makes right. By applying this rule, the universal equality of other-consciousness can be put into practice so that all internal conflicts between self-interest and other-consciousness will be satisfactorily resolved. This rule will be the founding principle of an individualistic society and the fundamental law of the legal system that governs all relations among private individuals.

The following explanation of constructive and destructive power may seem legalistic, but necessarily so. The principle of constructive power must be easily understandable by all people with moral capacity so they can use it to choose their acts in all situations. It must also be precise enough so that judges can decide cases brought before them involving claims that one person used destructive power. By defining the moral rule as a legal rule, the interpretation of legislators and judges is minimized. Defined originally as a legal rule, no transition from moral theory to legal practice is required. Universal equality is the goal. How it is put into everyday practice is the challenge. How does constructive power put universal equality into practice?

Physical power

We can acquire more possessions in a several ways. First, we can acquire them without any interaction with other people, as when we use our physical power on matter by either transforming its form or changing its location. For example, if I live in a house by a forest, during the winter I can gather wood from the forest to burn to stay warm and cook my food.

No one else is involved in my cutting, gathering and burning it. I use my power to satisfy my desires, that is, to acquire more possessions, and no one else has fewer possessions because of it. The net satisfaction of all human desires in the world is thereby increased. The use of physical power to change matter to a more desirable form or location without lessening another's possessions is the constructive use of power.

If I do not have a forest nearby or it belongs to someone else, and I want to stay warm and cook my food, I can go to my neighbor's house and take the wood I want. I achieve my desire for wood and have more possessions, but my neighbor has less. Therefore, my use of power is destructive. If in the spring, I find some wheat seed and plant and nurture it into more wheat than I can eat, I use my physical power constructively to grow the wheat to satisfy my hunger. I can take my extra wheat to my neighbor or the market and exchange it for the wood I desire to stay warm. My neighbor and I both have chosen to satisfy our desires by exchanging wheat for wood, and both of us use our power constructively to satisfy our desire because both of us have possessions we value more than the ones we had before we exchanged possessions. The total satisfaction of human desires has increased.

In the latter example, there are no more physical possessions created by the exchange. The amount of fire wood and wheat in the world before and after the exchange is the same. Each person satisfies his desire by exchanging one possession for another possession he values more than the one he gives up. This mutual increase in value is presumed because no one will choose to exchange one of his possessions for something he values less than what he already has. This is inherent in the concept of value as the will's desire to cause a particular future state to become an existing state. If I value wheat more than the wood, the future state my will selects is maintaining my relationship to the wheat, not giving it up to create a new relationship with the wood.

None of our possessions are permanent, and neither is the value we place on them. The value of possessions often changes over time. Winter may be mild, fire wood plentiful, and food scarce. I may wish I had kept my wheat, but if I had simply gathered fire wood instead of growing wheat without anyone else involved, I would face the same changed value. Nothing about the exchange changes the value I put on wheat versus wood. These changes of value after an exchange do not change the original overall increase in net satisfaction of desires.

When a thief breaks into a house and takes the owner's television, that is a destructive use of physical power. The thief achieves his will for a television, but he does so by taking the other's television. The same is true when a mugger grabs his victim's purse and runs away with it or when the embezzler transfers the money from one account to his own. And too, when a murderer kills his victim, he satisfies his will by taking his victim's life. Each of these examples involves only a physical use of power, not the power of persuasion or of alliance or economic power. The victim's life or property is simply taken by physical power. These destructive uses of physical power have traditionally been the subject of the criminal law of property crimes and murder, assault, battery and mayhem.

It is not enough, however, to simply say that one may not choose to take another's property to satisfy one's will. Foreseeable consequences, both immediate and remote, and not just intended consequences, must be considered. Adult humans are capable of considerable foresight. The very act of choosing between alternatives requires foresight of at least some of the consequences of each alternative course of action. In order to choose between using destructive or constructive power, one must understand the consequences of each alternative course of action and whether it will lessen another person's possessions. If it will, then choosing that alternative with a consciousness that it will lessen another's possessions is a *conscious use of destructive power*. If the act is done without being consciousness that it will lessen another person's possessions, then it is an *unconscious use of destructive power*. Either way, the consequence of the use of power is destructive. Whether the use of power is destructive, depends solely on whether another person's possessions are lessened by the act, not the consciousness of the person who chose the act that caused it. Whether the destructive power also violates the moral principle to always choose to use constructive power depends on whether the person was conscious or with the exercise of the foresight expected of a morally capable individual he would have been conscious that his chosen alternative would lessen another's possessions. Thus, a conscious use of destructive power is the most blameworthy moral choice. Unconscious uses of destructive power resulting from a failure to foresee the consequences of one's chosen alternative are less blameworthy, but still destructive power. The degree of blame attached to those acts depends both on whether the destructive power was used consciously or unconsciously and the magnitude of the lessening of others' possessions.

When persuasion is not involved and a purely physical act is judged as either constructive or destructive, only the consequences of the act are considered. Were another person's possessions lessened? A beneficent or malevolent motive for the act is irrelevant. The person who consciously uses destructive power ordinarily is punished as a criminal.

The person who unconsciously causes harm with destructive power ordinarily is required to compensate the other for the loss of his possessions as in the civil law of torts and contracts.

The need to consider unintended consequences when choosing one's actions can be illustrated by a person who wants to shoot his rifle at targets. He needs no one else to satisfy his will. He has the rifle, the cartridges and a farm where he can set up his target. If he tacks his target on a fence next to his neighbor's front porch and commences to shoot, any fool can foresee the neighbor's house will be damaged. If he consciously expects shooting at the target will lessen the neighbor's possessions, then shooting is the same as choosing to lessen the neighbor's possessions to satisfy his desire, which is a conscious use of destructive power. It does not matter that the shooter does not intend or desire to damage his neighbor's house. This would be especially true if the shooter had an alternative of placing the target in front of a high dirt bank on his own property where there would be no chance of the bullet lessening another's possessions. Choosing between alternative means of satisfying one's desires is, after all, the purpose of morality.

To the other-conscious person, the desire to shoot at targets is as valuable as the neighbor's desire to have his house or his head *sans* bullet holes. Constructive power requires that one may not act to satisfy a desire–that is, acquire a possession–by lessening another's possessions. To do so is to claim that one's desires are more important than the other person's, which is a reversion to might makes right. One alternative that is always available is not to act at all. If one lives in an apartment complex, there is no place to shoot a rifle without lessening another's possessions, so the act must not be done.

It is not enough, however, to avoid consciously lessening another's possessions when one acts. Instead of a fence, suppose the shooter puts his target on a hedge and he cannot see the house on the other side, or he does not look, but he is conscious the bullet will travel beyond the hedge. If he shoots at the target, he consciously expects the bullet will strike something before it stops, but he is unconscious whether it will lessen another's possessions. There are, unfortunately, cases of people who shoot at a target in their yard; the bullet kills someone a great distance away; and the person who shot the gun was never conscious of the person killed. One cannot set in motion a force, be it a bullet, a pesticide applied to a field, or a gene inserted into a plant or animal, or a drug with side-effects such as thalidomide, that will go beyond the horizon of his consciousness of consequences and may lessen another's possessions.

One must make a reasonable effort to determine what the consequences will be.

Anglo-American common law has dealt with these questions of what a person knows or a reasonable person in the same circumstances should know by the exercise of reasonable foresight. These concepts would generally apply in the interpretation of the quality of uses of destructive power. In short, a person must use his best foresight to avoid lessening another's possessions when choosing his acts. When the circumstances are such that one expects that the consequences of one's acts will go beyond the horizon of foresight, the person must choose a different alternative or she acts at her peril that her act will lessen another's possessions.

In summary, to avoid the use of physical destructive power, each person must use his best foresight of the consequences of his choice of alternatives to avoid his acts lessening another's possessions. If one's foresight predicts another's possessions will be lessened by an act, either another means to achieve the same end must be chosen or the act must not be done. If one's best foresight fails to produce a reasonable assurance that one's acts will not lessen another's possessions, then the act must not be done or the actor is morally and legally responsible for all consequences that lessen others' possessions.[13]

Power of Persuasion

Exchanges result from the use of the power of persuasion. An *exchange* occurs when one person gives another one of his possessions and receives one of the other's possessions in return. Possessions may be exchanged immediately or by the promise to perform in the future. The contemporaneous relationships established between people by exchanges is the basis of contract law. The promise to transfer one's possession in the future is itself an existing relationship between the participants in the exchange and thus a possession.

Under traditional contract law, many different kinds of promises create legally enforceable contracts, but not all promises create a contract. A legally enforceable contract must be supported by what the law calls consideration. Consideration is the transfer of a possession by one participant in the exchange in order to obtain from the other one of his possessions. The promise to transfer a possession in the future creates the relationship between the participants that becomes the possession of the person to whom future transfer is promised. If a person says to a stranger on the street, "I promise to put your children through college," this is not an exchange because the stranger has given none of his possessions in order to receive the promise. There is no "consideration" for the promise, and it is not legally enforceable.

As defined in Chapter I, persuasion is the power a person uses to satisfy his will by inducing another to choose to act in a way that will satisfy the persuader's will. In other words, persuasion is the power of getting one person to choose to transfer one of his possessions to another person. Persuasion may be either unconscious or conscious. When the person persuaded is unconscious of the other or his acts intended to persuade or the act the other desires to be done, the persuasion is unconscious. A political issue ad that does not identify who is trying to persuade the audience to vote a certain way would be an attempt at unconscious persuasion. An ad intended to produce a choice opposite from the one specifically argued for would also be unconscious persuasion because it uses "reverse psychology" to induce viewers to choose to do the opposite of what the ad asks them to do. The use of a specific product in a movie to persuade viewers to buy it when they are unconscious of the attempt to get them to buy the product is another example.

Conscious persuasion occurs when the person who is the object of the persuasion is conscious of (1) the identity of the one trying to persuade him, (2) the other's acts to persuade him, and (3) the act the other desires to be done. When a panhandler holds out his hand to a person on the street, he uses conscious persuasion to try to persuade the other to satisfy his desire for money by the other choosing to give him money. Most important, persuasion may be either voluntary or involuntary. *Voluntary persuasion* requires that

(1) the person persuaded is conscious
- (a) of the identity of the persuader;
- (b) of the persuader's acts to persuade him;
- (c) of all the alternative courses of action of which the persuader is conscious;
- (d) (i) of all the information available to the persuader from which to understand each alternative and the consequences of each; or
  (ii) that some information is being intentionally withheld; and

(2) the person persuaded chooses to act as the persuader desires motivated solely by a belief that by so doing he will have more valuable possessions than by selecting any other alternative course of action.

Involuntary persuasion is persuasion with any one of the elements of voluntary persuasion missing from the person's choice to act as the other desires. It may be achieved in many ways. The persuader may make the other's alternatives appear limited or may limit the information from which the other can understand the consequences of each alternative so that the act the persuader desires the other to choose appears to be the most desirable alternative and therefore more likely to be chosen. At the battle of Cannae, the Carthaginian general Hannibal ordered the center of his army's line to give way when engaged by the Romans. The Romans alternatives were to either maintain their line or pursue the retreating enemy, and they chose to continue to press the center. When they did, exactly as Hannibal desired, the flanks of Hannibal's army enveloped the Roman army and slaughtered them. Through his battle tactics, Hannibal persuaded the Romans to march into the trap that won him the victory he desired.

The Romans were not voluntarily persuaded to be surrounded by Hannibal's army and slaughtered. They may or may not have been conscious of all the alternatives that Hannibal was conscious of, and they certainly were not aware of all the information available to Hannibal to understand the consequences of each alternative, nor did they make their choice motivated by a belief they would have more valuable possessions. This is, however, an example of conscious persuasion as the Romans knew Hannibal was trying to persuade them to act in a way that they would lose the battle. The Romans chose to act as Hannibal desired, and he won the victory he desired.

In World War II, during the Battle of the Bulge, the Germans surrounded the 101st Airborne Division in the town of Bastogne. The Germans made it appear that resistance was suicide and demanded surrender. In his famous reply, "Nuts!" Gen. McAuliffe, the commander of the 101st, was unpersuaded.

Persuaded acts are acts of choice, and thus free will. If one has no alternatives or no understanding of his alternatives, then there can be no choice. *Persuasion* is inducing another to choose to act in a desired way. The alternatives may be very limited; the consequences of each may be so one-sided that no choice seems available; but if there is a choice, the person's consciousness selects the alternative. Even when a robber puts a gun to his victim's head, as the Germans did to Gen. McAullife, and demands, "your money or your life," that is a choice, and the resulting act is one of free will, but not voluntary persuasion. Within the limitations of our alternatives and our power to achieve our desires, we do choose our own destiny.

Every exchange resulting from voluntary persuasion will, at the moment of the exchange, necessarily produce a distribution of possessions more valuable to all participants, but that increase is not guaranteed to last forever. Mistaken judgments about the value of possessions exchanged will always occur both in exchanges and when people act without involving others. Everyone who has bought a stock that went down in price has certainly changed his opinion about the value of owning the stock. One may be totally wrong about the eventual value of his chosen alternative, but that is irrelevant so long as each element of voluntary persuasion was present when the exchange occurred. Who can decide what is in one's self-interest, what is more valuable, better than oneself?[14] If a person has moral capacity, how can another person substitute his judgment about what possessions are most valuable without denying the equality of the other's will and resort to might makes right?

A benevolent motive cannot change the fact that preventing another morally capable person from choosing what she values most is an exercise of destructive power. One person satisfies his desire by preventing another from satisfying her's. Parents often make such choices, and rightly so, before their children become morally capable individuals. The motive for lessening another morally capable person's possessions is, however, simply irrelevant to whether destructive power has been used.

Information, skill and know how are possessions. Voluntary persuasion does not require that A give up one of his possessions to *try* to persuade B to act to satisfy A's desire. But, if A withholds information to avoid losing one of his possessions, A must tell B that A is withholding information that may be important to B in choosing whether to satisfy A's desires. If B goes to a used car lot and negotiates with A, the used car salesman, to purchase a car, voluntary persuasion requires that A either tell B all the information he has about the car that could be of any importance to B in deciding whether to buy the car or A must tell B that A is specifically withholding from B important information. It would likely be important to B to know how much A paid for the car, as B would want to pay as little as A would take. A could tell B that he has that information, but he will not tell B, and B must make his decision whether to buy and for how much without it. The same applies to other types of information such as the mechanical condition of the car, whether it has a blown head gasket etc. B then can make his choice knowing that some important information is being withheld, but A must tell B that A is withholding information and the general nature of the information withheld so B can understand his alternatives and choose whether he will have more valuable possessions by satisfying A's desire to sell the car.

The current odometer disclosure laws require the disclosure of the true mileage of the car as important information any car buyer would want.

The last element of voluntary persuasion, whether a person's choice is motivated solely by a belief that one will have more valuable possessions as a result of the exchange, deserves a fuller explanation. As a rule of morality, when using the power of persuasion one may use others to satisfy one's desires but only if the other person chooses to do so because she believes that by doing so she will increase the value of her own possessions. Universal equality means that both parties to an exchange, based on equal information about available alternatives and their consequences, choose to exchange their possessions because they both believe they will have more valuable possessions. If this is not true, then one person must satisfy his desire by lessening the other person's value of his possessions.

If constructive power becomes the basic rule of law for all relations between morally capable individuals, one question might be whether a person can claim he was the victim of involuntary persuasion because the possessions he received were less valuable than what he gave up. The answer depends on whether a person is allowed to refute his own motive of self-interest when entering into the exchange. The motive of pure self-interest is irrefutable if in viewing the situation one can say that there is a way to explain how the person believed he would have more valuable possessions as a result of the exchange rather than less. Thus, the person who watches a telethon for a charity and then sends a check for $1 million cannot later ask for the money back claiming she did not get as good a feeling from the donation as anticipated. There is a view of this situation that the person believed she would have more valuable possessions by giving the money.

This is not to say that the donor can never complain. The charity must use voluntary persuasion to get the donation. If one of the elements of voluntary persuasion is missing, such as information about the charity was withheld or misrepresented, that would render the persuasion involuntary, because all this information is necessary for the donor to reach the best possible judgment of the value of giving the money to charity.

If there is a possible explanation of how the person could have believed she would have more valuable possessions, then the exchange can be shown to be the result of involuntary persuasion. If the robber says, "your money or your life," since the person has his life and money, the only possible outcome of the exchange is for the person to have less valuable possessions if he either gives up his money or loses his life. When the person persuaded cannot have more valuable possessions under any view of the events, and his choice is which of his possessions to give up, the persuasion cannot be voluntary.

Another way to look at this is whether one of the available alternatives involves a risk of loss of one's possessions created by the other person. When the robber says, "your money or your life," one of the alternatives is to refuse and resist. Maybe the robber will flee, or can be overpowered, but that alterative risks the loss of one's life. If instead, a panhandler sticks out his hand and asks, "Can you spare a dime," or if the Paralyzed Veterans Association asks for a donation, one alternative is to say no. One could, as many people do, give the panhandler or the charity money with no other expectation of having more valuable possessions than a good feeling from helping someone who needs it. The good feeling is more valuable than the money given away to get it. But, the panhandler could have a gun in his waistband or otherwise convey an implied threat of the loss of one's possessions. Any circumstance that conveys an explicit or implied threat of loss of one's possessions is sufficient to constitute a destructive use of the power of persuasion, or involuntary persuasion.

When all the other elements of voluntary persuasion are present, the choice of whether one will have more valuable possessions as a result of the exchange, cannot be second guessed. The value of the possession one gives up versus the value of the possession received is uniquely in the consciousness of the person making the choice. If a morally capable individual is responsible for the destructive consequences of his chosen acts on others, then he must be responsible for the same consequences to himself.

All exchanges involve reciprocal uses of the power of persuasion. There are thus, three possible combinations of constructive and destructive power in every exchange: each person uses voluntary persuasion; one uses voluntary persuasion and the other uses involuntary persuasion; or both use involuntary persuasion. Each person's use of persuasion must be examined separately to determine whether she used voluntary persuasion. When an exchange occurs through involuntary persuasion, one person may end up with less valuable possessions. After learning what made the persuasion involuntary, one may still believe that she has more valuable possessions and choose to do nothing, or she may not have made the same exchange and demand a return of her possessions given up for the exchange.

Voluntary versus involuntary persuasion is not entirely new. For a long time, the law has considered what information is available when people choose whether to exchange their possessions and on what terms.

Although stated differently, choices made with equal information have been a part of the civil law for a very long time.

Ancient Roman Law had the maxim *caveat emptor,* buyer beware, but it also had *caveat venditor*, which required sellers, of slaves or cattle for example, to disclose any physical defects to the buyer, and held the seller accountable despite a plea of ignorance of the defect.[15] Modern society abounds in laws about truth-telling. Today a person who obtains another's property by deceiving him with false information or omitting to disclose material information is liable civilly in damages and criminally for fraud. A used car buyer does not need to ask whether the mileage on the car is accurate or whether the odometer has rolled over. Car dealers are required by federal law to disclose the correct odometer readings.

Fraud is in essence a choice to exchange possessions when one person has unequal information material to the exchange. Absent a mind swap before each exchange, both people can never have exactly the same information. For persuasion to be voluntary, each person persuaded must have all of the information that is relevant *to him* to choose how to act. In the law of fraud, that information must be material, which means it could influence a person's choice whether to exchange one of his possessions. How the adequacy of the information provided would be determined by a court is discussed in more detail in Chapter X.

Some information is so basic to certain exchanges that disclosure of truthful and complete information is required by statutes. Numerous laws prohibit false advertising. Securities laws require disclosure of information about the companies and their business. There are labeling laws for foods, drugs, cosmetics, and products that can be dangerous if not used properly. Nearly every aspect of civilized society depends on truthful information for people to choose what is most valuable to them. Common to all these laws is the essence of voluntary persuasion: no one should satisfy his desire by inducing another to choose to satisfy that desire based on false or incomplete information.

The importance of sufficient, and accurate information also finds expression in the legal doctrine of mutual mistake of fact as a basis for rescinding or undoing a contract that the parties entered into believing certain facts to be other than they really are. Neither party is blamed or called upon to pay damages, and the contract or exchange could have resulted from voluntary persuasion, but the contract may nevertheless be undone because of the mistake.

The power of persuasion is not limited to economic exchanges. How many times has one person said to another, "I love you," just for sex, and in the morning everything looks different? With the advent of HIV and other sexually transmitted diseases, laws have been passed that make it a crime to fail to disclose to a sex partner one's health status. For instance, Florida has a statute[16] that provides:

> It is unlawful for any person who has chancroid, gonorrhea, granuloma inguinale, lymphogranuloma venereum, genital herpes simplex, chlamydia, nongonococcal urethritis (NGU), pelvic inflammatory disease (PID)/acute salpingitis, syphilis, or human immune deficiency virus infection, when such person knows he or she is infected with one or more of these diseases and when such person has been informed that he or she may communicate this disease to another person through sexual intercourse, to have sexual intercourse with any other person, unless such other person has been informed of the presence of the sexually transmissible disease and has consented to the sexual intercourse.

The moral principle of constructive power governs choices about the most intimate personal relationships. Rape, battery and other physical acts not consented to that lessen another's possessions involve the use of physical destructive power. Relationships such as marriage and sex as shown by the above statute may result from either voluntary or involuntary persuasion. All personal relationships between morally capable adults must result from voluntary persuasion so that each person will have more valuable possessions as a result. Remember that experiences, services, labor, and affection may be as much possessions as a car. They may or may not last very long, but they are possessions–particular future states selected by the will and caused to exist with the organism's power.

Suppose an unmarried man and a married woman are attracted to each other. The marriage relationship of the woman and her husband is a possession of the husband. Does the unmarried man or married woman use destructive power by having sex? The answer depends upon the exact nature of the husband's possession in the marriage. If the husband and his wife have agreed that either may have sex with others, then the wife does not lessen her husband's possession in the marriage relation by having sex with her lover. If the wife has promised to be faithful, and she knows her husband will be hurt by her affair, as opposed to knowing that he does not care or even approves, then having an affair would be a destructive use of power against her husband, because even if the husband does not know about the affair, his possession in the marriage will be lessened. The next time the wife and husband have sex, the woman must disclose the affair as that information is relevant to the husband's choice whether to have sex with his wife because of the risk the wife has contracted a sexually transmitted disease. If the wife conceals the affair, she uses destructive power. If the wife refuses to have sex with her husband to avoid telling him about her affair, then he has lost that part of his marriage.

If the husband asks his wife to be faithful, but she refuses, neither she nor her lover uses destructive power by having sex. The husband's unsatisfied desire for his wife's fidelity is not a possession. The husband does not possess his wife's fidelity unless and until she chooses to gives it to him as a result of voluntary persuasion. Otherwise, he would have a possession simply by desiring it. The wife would be required to satisfy her husband's desire simply because he desires it and against her will. To have a possession in a relationship with another person,[17] that relationship must result from an exchange with all parties using voluntary persuasion. Perhaps John Hinckley is distressed by the fact that Jodie Foster has male friends and a child, but Hinckley has no possession in anything Foster may do with whomever she desires. Wanting something, no matter how badly, does not make it a possession, and neither does needing it. Need, want and desire are all synonyms.

If the woman's lover knows she has promised fidelity to her husband, and has not ended that promise by divorce or otherwise, and he has sex with her, he uses destructive power by lessening the husband's possession in his marriage and by causing the woman to use destructive power against her husband. To do an act conscious that it will lessen another's possessions is a conscious use of destructive power. It does not matter whether a gun or another person is the means used to lessen the other's possession.

King David fell in love with Bathsheba and impregnated her, while she was married to the loyal Uriah. David ordered Joab to "[s]et Uriah in the forefront of the hottest battle, and retire you from him, that he may be struck, and die."[18] Joab did as ordered. David used destructive power, the same as if he had killed Uriah with his own sword.

Suppose the lover is not conscious that the woman is married[19] or she tells him she has not promised fidelity to her husband when, in fact, she has. If he has sex with her, does he use destructive power? Yes, but it is unconscious destructive power and not a conscious use of destructive power. Unless the lover is conscious of the husband's possession in his wife's fidelity, he does not choose to satisfy his desire by lessening the husband's possession. Nor is lessening the husband's possession a foreseeable consequence.[20] Rather, the married woman uses involuntary persuasion to satisfy her desire for sex with the man by failing to inform him of her promise of fidelity or by misrepresenting that she has not promised fidelity. That information is necessary for the man to choose not to use destructive power. Thus, the married woman uses conscious destructive power against both her lover and her husband.

Similar situations involving commercial or business relationships are known in the law as the tort of intentional interference with a contract. A owns a house, and B is a real estate broker. A enters into a listing agreement with B to pay B a commission for the sale of the house. A potential buyer, C, learns A's house is for sale from a newspaper ad placed by B. B introduces C to A, but they do not enter into a contract. Unbeknownst to B, C goes directly to A and buys A's house without A paying B any commission.

The law provides that C has intentionally interfered with A's contract with B by persuading A to breach his contract with B by not paying B a commission. Both C and A use destructive power because A lessens B's possession in the contract, i.e., A's promise to pay B a commission, and A uses destructive power by satisfying his desire to sell the house, but by breaching his promise to pay B a commission.

If the contract between A and B is an exclusive listing agreement, that is, A promises to pay B a commission only if B procures the buyer, and B does not introduce A to C, and a sale results, then neither A nor C uses destructive power because B does not have a possession in obtaining a commission if A sells to someone B has not introduced to A. It does not matter whether A and C both know of the listing agreement between A and B, the same as if the unmarried man and married woman both know of the marriage but the wife has not promised fidelity. Possessions in relationships with other morally capable persons can only be achieved by voluntary persuasion. One who knows of the relationship and chooses to lessen it to satisfy his desire, acts with destructive power, whatever form of power he uses.

The variety of relationships created with voluntary persuasion is limited only by the imagination. They can be as formal as written contracts, or as informal as unspoken understandings evidenced by a period of conduct conforming to commonly understood expectations. Government often makes laws that define when a relationship is a possession, how long the possession will last and how it can be ended. An example is the Uniform Commercial Code, which is a set of rules for contracting to buy and sell goods. The contracting parties may change most of the rules if they choose to, but otherwise the rules govern.

If B uses involuntary persuasion to get A to sell his house to B, B uses destructive power against A but not C. Unless C's desire for a house is a possession in the house itself, C's failure to achieve her desire when competing with others cannot lessen C's possessions.

What does the moral principle of constructive power offer for choosing between alternatives in a society where some people are other-conscious and some do whatever they have the power to do? First, moral rules are meaningless to people who cannot or will not choose to act morally, e.g., Crusoe's cannibals. Second, moral rules resolve the internal conflict between conscious self-interest and other-consciousness. The moral rule of constructive power resolves this conflict when the consequences of one's acts affect another who is viewed with other-consciousness. A society with nonmoral animals or immoral humans in it produces choices like the following examples.

When the Nazi SS officer came to the house where Anne Frank was hiding and asked if there were any Jews inside, was the family morally obligated to tell the truth and turn Anne over to the SS? Most people say no. Some say lying in this situation represents a conflict of moral principles. Others say that the rule of telling the truth must always be judged in context, and in this context the rule requiring telling the truth does not apply. Still others say that moral principles must be prioritized. Instead, the family was not required to tell the truth because the SS officer was himself using conscious destructive power. When faced with destructive power, one need not use only constructive power in response. When the SS Officer, or anyone, uses conscious destructive power, he denies the equality of individuals upon which moral rules are founded, and thus repudiates the need to choose one's acts considering the consequences on other individuals. As the SS Officer is a known immoral human who claims the value of his will is superior to all others, everyone involved is left with only his natural right to try to do anything to achieve his will. The moral rule of constructive power governs only the relations of morally capable individuals.[21] But what of Crusoe's own moral dilemma of killing the cannibals? His ultimate resolution was rational self-interest, i.e., self-preservation, because the cannibals lacked other-consciousness for him, like the SS Officer, they left him no alternative from which to choose.

If the SS Officer were instead a grizzly bear approaching a campsite where a group of boy scouts were sleeping around a campfire and the scoutmaster created a diversion to draw the bear away from the children or failing that killed the bear, no one would question the morality of the deception or the killing any more than the deception of the American Avocet or black-necked stilt. The fact that a human uses conscious destructive power to take and kill a child, only makes the moral choice easier, not more difficult. By choosing to prevent or reduce the risk of another morally capable individual or child losing her possessions or her life as a result of another person or animal using destructive power, the power used is constructive power because it increases, not lessen, the other's possessions. That destructive power is used against an immoral human or a nonmoral animal to accomplish this does not change the constructive use of power toward another morally capable individual. Choosing to achieve one's own will by selecting an alternative that does not lessen another morally capable individual's possessions is constructive power.

The Necessities

If individualism is the ultimate objective of human society, that objective, that state of physical existence, presupposes the integration of the subsystems of complexity necessary for individualistic society to emerge. First, individual humans must have the mental complexity necessary to become other-conscious, and second, human society must fulfill its biological function, not for some, but for every single individual. Each individual for whom biological society fails has no choice but to try to do anything to survive or die.

An individualistic society must maintain the order of complexity necessary for all morally capable individuals to choose to use only constructive power. Therefore, Society must guarantee that the conditions necessary for every individual to choose to act solely on the moral principle of constructive power will be provided to any individual who cannot provide his or her own with constructive power.

In a society of 280 million, if even one citizen cannot survive without resorting to destructive power, Society fails for that individual, whose autonomic will impels him to try to do anything to survive. Whether to use destructive power to survive is a nonmoral choice because the complexity necessary for a moral choice does not exist. Thus, if any member of Society must choose to use destructive power to survive, the moral basis of Society will be destroyed. The necessities are thus those possessions without which a person must use destructive power to survive. There are two kinds of necessities, physical and civil.

Physical Necessities

The physical necessities are food, clothing and shelter. Without these, life cannot continue. Medical care for life threatening conditions must be added to the other three necessities because when the choice is life or death, there is no moral choice. One will do what one can and must to try to survive.

There is, in fact, always a choice, but no one can be expected to choose death over violating a moral rule. Surely some people choose death rather than violating a deeply held belief, e.g., Socrates, but to insist that Jean Valjean[22] choose death rather than steal a loaf of bread to feed his family, is to ignore the objective of an individualistic society. Any law that punishes such a choice is a raw reversion to might makes might. And, it is contrary to the "prime directive" of the autonomic will.

The physical necessities are the minimum needed to sustain life. When Society must provide the necessities, only the minimum necessary to maintain life is required. The minimum does not mean half-starved, half-naked people living in tents or tar paper shacks clinging to life by the barest thread. It does mean, however, that the necessities are just that and no more. Comfort and pleasure are not necessities. They are desirable, not necessary. One way Society might actually provide the necessities is discussed in Chapter XI.

Another necessity is protection from destructive power. Society is a power of alliance against all destructive power, and by guaranteeing the physical necessities for life, Society removes all possible need to choose to ever use destructive power. When others use destructive power, destructive power is generally the only way to successfully oppose it. Therefore, to prevent members of Society from having to choose to use destructive power, Society must prohibit all uses of destructive power against any member and use its power of alliance to prevent it. Only when Society fails in this obligation, may an individual choose to use destructive power in self-defense. The prohibition and prevention of the use of destructive power are physical necessities.

By guaranteeing the physical necessities of life, Society removes any need for its members to choose to use destructive power.[23]

Civil Necessities

The objective of Society is to create the greatest opportunity for individual happiness. Having fulfilled all the necessities of biological society, Society must, as a last resort, also provide the civil necessities, which are the things necessary to allow every citizen the opportunity to participate fully in Society.

The civil necessities are educational opportunity and legal counsel when necessary to vindicate or enforce one's legal rights. Opportunity does not equal success. Opportunity is the chance for an education.

Society guarantees no one that he will be a doctor or lawyer or physicist or tool and die maker. Society does guarantee that if a person has the ability to meet the standards set for a job or profession, then no lack of economic means or artificial barriers will prevent him from getting the necessary education.

Legal counsel is a civil necessity, not because lawyers need jobs, but for the same reason that no one is expected to perform an appendectomy on himself. Although the law would be greatly simplified in a Society in which the morality of equality is the fundamental law, the rules of procedure and evidence designed to produce the most consistently true and correct results will inevitably be more detailed than an average person will be able to master without specially trained assistance. No trial is fair if one of the parties does not have the benefit of a lawyer. As long as there are courts to enforce their legal rights, a lawyer will be a necessity.

The necessites are discussed in more detail in Chapters X and XI.

Non-Necessities

Every possession that is not necessary to choose to use only constructive power is a non-necessity. The non-necessities may contribute greatly to individual happiness, but they are not necessary to maintain the moral foundation of Society. Likely, a Society freed of restrictions other than the prohibition of destructive power will produce an abundance of non-necessary goods and services never before seen. If acquiring and consuming non-necessities is a measure of happiness, an individualistic society will likely be the happiest in history.

Chapter V

Reflections on Human Nature

At this point I want to pause and reflect a bit on what science has been able to tell us about human nature, because political philosophy is generally founded on a particular view of human nature. Before the scientific revolution and the advent of the social sciences, the description of human nature was essentially the realm of philosophers and theologians. The rise in the "scientific" study of human nature has produced a new authority for opinions about not only what human nature is, but also how society *ought* to be organized as a consequence. As we shall see, science since at least Darwin, has offered justifications for everything from racism to eugenics to immorality. Today, every social issue seems to require a sociological study as the authority for how to establish social policy. Recent sociological studies address whether children are adversely affected by mothers going back to work shortly after giving birth or by being raised by gay couples. The statistically significant conclusions from these studies then provide the irrefutable proof for the advocates of one or the other side of the political debate over the issue. If children are not adversely affected, then the feminists crow that they have been right all along and government must support greater child care. If science has "proven" that children as a group are not adversely affected, how can anyone contradict the irrefutable truth of science?

Until the last three hundred or so years, there was little doubt that human nature was real. The enlightenment of the eighteenth century, Marx in the nineteenth century and the development of sociology, anthropology and psychology in the twentieth century raised serious doubts about whether human behavior is fixed or can be shaped into any form. The famous behavioral psychologist, John B. Watson, went so far as to claim that given any twelve healthy infants he could take one at random and train him into any occupation, regardless of his "talent, penchants, abilities, vocations and race of his ancestors."[1] B.F. Skinner nearly succeeded with a pigeon.[2]

The dominant problem for sociologists, anthropologists and evolutionary biologist in the nineteenth and twentieth centuries was to explain the apparently huge differences between European and primitive people of different races and without civilization. With typical cultural superiority, many European and American social scientists claimed that primitive peoples and Negroes were biologically "inferior" in intellect and morals.

Although Charles Darwin is most often credited with the theory of evolution through natural selection, another British naturalist, Alfred Russel Wallace, first published the theory.[3] Wallace also first claimed that evolution applied to humans, but within five years he changed his mind, and argued that "some higher intelligence directed the process by which the human race . . . developed."[4] At the same time, he converted to spiritualism and thus slipped into Darwin's shadow.

Darwin waited twelve years after publishing his theory of evolution in *Origin of the Species* to publish *The Descent of Man* in which he too argued that evolution applied to humans. Despite great controversy, Darwin remained steadfast in explaining the physical differences in races[5] and the sexes in terms of sex selection. Differences in culture and civilization of primitive people, however, he attributed to superior biological capacities of some people over others. His hierarchy of people thus opened the door for scientific racism.

In Darwin's wake, some scientists and intellectuals advocated hereditary explanations for all kinds of behavior. William James, the father of modern psychology, and William McDougall, another early psychologist, wrote extensively about human instincts for acquisitiveness, gregariousness, jealousy, constructiveness, honesty, trustfulness, kindness, sociality, parentalism, etc. From 1900 to 1920, over 600 books and articles appeared in the United States and England advocating the instinct theory.[6] Some of Darwin's disciples even claimed they could identify criminals from their physical characteristics.[7]

The advent of intelligence testing made feeblemindedness the watchword for inherited defects of human behavior. Herbert Goddard traced one family's history to show the effect of inherited feeblemindedness and the need to stop it. Kallikak, a soldier in the American Revolution, had an affair with a "mentally defective" tavern girl. Goddard identified 480 descendants of this union, of which 143 were said to be feebleminded, 46 normal, and the rest unidentifiable. Goddard concluded that the defectives were due to the tavern girl because

Kallikak had married a good Quaker girl and produced morally upright children.[8]

This belief in inherited behavior, especially its role in criminal and immoral behavior, led to the eugenics movement as the way to improve the human race by eliminating the offspring of bad genes. While this movement found its most odious expression in Nazi Germany, by 1915 thirteen states had laws authorizing the sterilization of criminals and the mentally retarded. By 1930, thirty states had such laws. In *Buck v. Bell*,[9] the United States Supreme Court reviewed a Virginia statute that allowed the feebleminded to be sterilized. Justice Holmes, normally an astute observer of human nature, described the girl ordered sterilized:

> Carrie Buck is a feeble-minded white woman who was committed to the State Colony [for Epileptics and Feeble Minded] ... in due form. She is the daughter of a feeble-minded mother in the same institution, and the mother of an illegitimate feeble-minded child.[10]

In a now infamous, passage, Holmes wrote, "Three generations of imbeciles are enough."[11] It turned out, however, that Carrie Buck was not an imbecile and neither was her child.[12] When science errs, the law often follows.

In 1923, Princeton psychologist Carl Brigham published *A Study of American Intelligence,* which relied heavily on intelligence tests given to every person inducted into the U.S. Army in Word War I, to conclude that the "race hypothesis" was true, that is, the Nordic races are superior to all other groups, and the further south a race originated, the more inferior it is. He never explained how the Egyptians became the first great civilization and builders of the Pyramids. Brigham's study also coincided with widely held prejudices and a great immigration from Eastern and Southern Europe. The next year, Congress severely restricted immigration from areas with inferior or undesirable races.[13]

Sex did not escape "scientific scrutiny," either. Darwin argued at length that women were not just different but inferior for anything physical or intellectual, except childbearing and rearing. In 1871, Dr. Edward Clarke of Harvard Medical School wrote *Sex in Education* about the dangers of higher education for girls. He claimed that women could do college work, but it would seriously injure their physique in the long run and those who completed college "almost invariably succumbed to physical and mental breakdowns." The famous educator, John Dewey, cited statistics showing that of the women who received higher education, fewer had children and more died in childbirth and concluded, "these figures speak for themselves." James Cattell argued against higher education for women because of the lower birth rate and because with greater economic opportunity the American family must suffer because women "can conveniently leave their husbands should it so suit their fancy."[14]

Fortunately for women–and men–such scientific studies did not pass for gospel. By the early 1900's, scientists who doubted heredity's power over human behavior, produced "scientific studies" to prove culture and environment, not heredity, were responsible for human behavior.[15] The tide began to turn against heredity when studies failed to correlate delinquency and criminal behavior with intelligence tests scores or that of parents, but did correlate with the social situation of parents.[16] In the early 1920's, one study found the intelligence of criminals approximately equal to the distribution of the general population, and in one prison 75% higher than the prison guards.[17]

The usefulness of intelligence tests was severely criticized. Goddard continued to believe intelligence was inherited, but accepted environmentally induced mental deficiencies and became one of the first to propose that delinquency should be solved not by punishing but by treating and training children and that delinquents should be admitted, not committed, to a school, not an institution, until they graduated. The accumulated evidence for environmental and cultural influences on human behavior led to cultural determinism and the belief that any kind of society can be planned and created with the right conditioning.

In his book, *In Search of Human Nature,* from which the above summary has been taken, Carl Degler discusses how the advocates of heredity and the advocates of culture used science as a front for their personal beliefs about the human condition, what makes us behave the way we do, and more importantly how society *ought* to be. The heredity advocates assumed biology and race mainly determine both physical characteristics and behavior in order to justify the status quo. All too often their "science" reinforced very intolerant and hateful beliefs about other races and women. The nurture advocates used science to support their assumption that culture and environment determine behavior because it offered hope for rapid change, not change at the snail's pace of natural selection, if just the right conditions were created in society. They rejected heredity as too much like predestination and determinism which produces a fatalism that no one can be any more than the sum total of his genes.

The nurture advocates, however, produced their own version of determinism, which has also become a host spreading the virus of utilitarianism. The seemingly inevitable consequence of the emphasis on environment and culture as the cause of behavior has been the erosion of responsibility for one's acts, especially in the criminal law. Lawyers always push an idea to its logical extreme, hence the TV intoxication, twinky, and TV wrestling imitation defenses. If culture and environment determine later behavior, no one is responsible for his acts because they are caused by conditions over which one has no control?

Any determinism, but especially environmental and cultural determinism, is the social equivalent of the Ichneumonidae wasp's larva eating the core of a paralyzed society until it consumes and kills it. Cultural determinism is an atavistic rejection of the very emergent capacity that enables humans to become more than the sum total of their genetic pool, culture and environment, more than a datum in the formula of population genetics. By denying the capacity for the choice of, and thereby responsibility for, one's acts, cultural determinism condemns man to the very animal automatism from which moral choice allows escape. It denies the moral capacity of man. As such, it is as destructive of human hope as any other determinism.

Jacob's observation is helpful:

> Complex objects are produced by evolutionary processes in which two factors are paramount: the constraints which at every level control the systems involved; and the historical circumstances which control the actual interactions between the systems.[18]

The more complex the system, the more its history influences it behavior. Thus, history is nurture, and constraint is nature. As the most complex known objects, humans are the most influenced by their history, but they cannot escape the constraints of their component systems of complexity, both individual and social.

The true constraints of human nature also constrain an individualistic society. Humans are animals in a material world like every other biological organism. Humans differ from other animals, but most of these differences are differences of degree not of kind. If Jacob is right about the relative influence of history and constraints on complex systems, humans probably have the least specific biologically determined behavior, and thus the most behavior that can be chosen. But, as the pioneering psychologist Abraham Maslow[19] observes, humans do have certain basic, i.e., autonomic, desires that must be satisfied and therefore constrain human behavior. Maslow categorizes these basic desires as the physiological ones necessary to maintain life and homeostasis, the safety ones of security, stability, protection and absence of fear, anxiety or chaos, and the social and psychological ones of belonging, love, self-esteem, and self-actualization. Many specific behaviors to achieve these desires are consciously controlled and chosen, yet autonomic motivations always shape these behaviors.

Consciously created objectives also motivate behavior. Maslow also describes how the basic desires overlap to provide complex motivations for behavior. No conscious motivation can be separated entirely from the unconscious, autonomic motivations. Humans differ in kind from the other animals primarily in our ability to become partially conscious of our autonomic will and its source and within the constraints permitted by our complex systems, to create a volitional will and to choose moral means to satisfy both our autonomic and volitional will. The whole nature vs. nurture debate overlooks the human capacity to make moral choices.

Suppose the race hypothesis is true. So what! If humans are individuals instead of evolutionary data, the objective of an individualistic society is for every individual to have the greatest possible opportunity to achieve whatever his will is with constructive power. The point of individualism is that statistically significant sociological correlations or averages are irrelevant to individuals, even though they may be the engine of evolution. None of the supposedly scientific explanations for the differences in humans makes one *iota* of difference in an individualistic society. Whether the average Negro has an average IQ of twenty points less than the average Caucasian, Asian or Hispanic tells us nothing about an individual Negro, Caucasian, Asian or Hispanic man or woman. What is important is whether a person has moral capacity and whether he uses destructive power to achieve his desires, whatever they may be.

In his *Rhetoric*, Aristotle observes that people expect to be specially respected by their inferiors in birth or other capacity.[20] In Aristotle's time, it was self-evident that men, and certainly women, were born and remain unequal and should be treated differently because of their natural inequality. Jefferson made no attempt to prove that all men are created equal. He simply asserted, "We hold these truths to be self-evident." Aristotle and all the sages of antiquity surely were not too stupid to recognize that all men are created equal, nor did they all decide to deceive the rest of humanity into believing what they knew to be false. Nor was Jefferson blind to the natural inequalities of men from birth. Although Aristotle found men self-evidently unequal in their physical abilities and character, and Jefferson found men self-evidently equal in the way they deserved to be treated in relation to other men, both ideas were the basis upon which each believed society *ought* to be organized.

If morality emerges as the need for rules to resolve the internal conflicts between conscious self-interest and other-consciousness, and if the rule of constructive power adequately resolves these internal conflicts by giving equal value to every person's achieved desires, the question remains, how is constructive power transformed from a rule of individual choice to a rule of social obligation? How does an individualistic society emerge from a human biological society in which some, but not all, of its members are morally capable individuals?

PART II

Translating the Morality of Equality into the Political Theory and Political Practice of an Individualistic Society

Chapter VI

The Origin and Purpose of Rights

In his *Second Treatise on Government*,[1] Locke referred extensively to various rights of people and government. A short list of "natural" rights Locke asserted is as follows:

Every man has a right
- of self-preservation, and to preserve all mankind;[2]
- of freedom of his person and to inherit his father's goods;[3]
- of war against an aggressor;[4]
- to his labor and to property acquired with that labor;[5]
- to demand compensation from anyone who causes him damage;[6]
- to free himself from government until he consents to it;[7]

By the right of nature, captives taken in a just war are slaves;[8]
In a body politic, the majority have a right to act and conclude the rest;[9]
Government has the right to make laws with penalties of death and all lesser penalties.[10]

Israeli Prime Minister Ariel Sharon said about the resumption of peace talks with the Palestinian Authority, "I am profoundly aware that Israel and its citizens possess the basic right–which is the right of every nation–to live in security and peace."[11]

Hardly a day goes by without someone claiming a right to something or other. So what are these things called rights that people so freely claim? They cannot be natural rights, "which cannot be denied its possessor," because all of them *can* be denied. The "right" of self-preservation is referred to as a "natural" right. As discussed in Chapter VII, Hobbes, makes self-preservation the theoretical basis for human political society and justice, although, as everyone knows, life is easily extinguished. If the right of self-preservation is qualified as the right *to try* to preserve one's life, which cannot be denied, then it may be considered a natural right, but then the qualification swallows the whole because a natural right is the undeniable ability of every living organism *to try* to achieve any objective its will selects.

Artificial Rights and Duties

All human created rights are an attempt to separate might from right and to create a world, at least the human part of it, in which achieving one's desires is independent of the power necessary to achieve it. These rights exist only in human society. They can be denied, though some people may believe they *ought* not be denied.

To distinguish human created rights from the one natural right to try to do anything, I shall call all human created rights *artificial rights*. The dictionary defines "artificial" as "made by human skill; produced by humans (as opposed to *natural*), . . . [and an] imitation or simulation of the real thing;" that is, of the undeniable natural right to try. Artificial rights are "based on arbitrary and superficial characteristics," selected by the conscious will of humans. They are also an "artifice," which is defined as "a skillful or artful contrivance or expedient."[12] The adjectives "artificial" and "artifice" distinguish these rights from the one natural right and suggest how artificial rights alter the natural order of biological society. Artificial rights separate the social order of biological society produced by unconscious processes and those aspects of human society consciously chosen and caused to exist by humans which are artificial, or non-natural. Thus, artificial rights are an emergent property of a biological society composed of individuals with sufficient complexity to consciously alter the natural or unconscious order of their biological society.

Artificial rights originate as behavioral patterns created by a conscious desire about how people *ought* or *ought not* to use their power. The verbal expressions of these desires are often stated negatively, "Thou shalt not kill," because they express a desire that a person with the power and the desire to kill another *ought* to refrain from doing it. As history and the evening news continually show, however, every murder victim's artificial right to life can be and is denied. The victim has a natural right to try to do anything to prevent his death, and an artificial right to life. The murderer has a natural right to try to kill his intended victim, but an artificial duty not to use his power to kill his victim. The author of the artificial right to life, the person or group who says how power ought or ought not to be used, threatens to use his power to try to prevent the killing, or if too late, to try to punish the murderer.

The label "artificial" is purely descriptive and does not imply any particular right now recognized is deserving or undeserving of being accepted as how people *ought* to use their power. On the contrary, a system of artificial rights and duties is essential to establishing an individualistic society that operates on the morality of equality. The first step in creating an efficacious system of artificial rights and duties, however, is to understand exactly what these artificial rights are and how they are created and enforced. Only then we can distinguish between the deserving and undeserving claims.

Humans have tried to separate might from right since at least the beginning of civilization by consciously creating systems of artificial rights and duties to govern human social relations. Under these systems, each person has an artificial right to certain possessions which means that those possessions may not be taken away from even the person who lacks sufficient power to prevent another person from taking it. There are also artificial rights to have certain possessions whether one has insufficient power on her own to obtain them. Finally, each person has an artificial duty not to use his power to take a possession to which another has an artificial right: "Neither shall you commit adultery. Neither shall you steal. Neither shall you covet your neighbor's wife; neither shall you desire your neighbor's house, his field, or his man-servant, or his maid-servant, his ox, or his donkey, or anything that is your neighbor's."[13]

A system of artificial rights and duties supposedly separates might from right by making the possessions to which one has an artificial right independent of the power necessary to acquire or keep them. The artificial right to free speech, means that one can say what he wants; the government may not use its power to prevent the person from speaking even if the government has the power and the will to prevent it. Anyone with the power and will to prevent it has an artificial duty not to use her power to achieve her will by preventing the other from speaking. The artificial right to life, means that no one may use his power to kill another, even if he has sufficient power and the will to do so.

A system of artificial rights and duties created outside of or preexisting human society is traditionally called a "natural" rights theory. Locke and Hobbes created "natural" rights systems which are summarized in Chapter VII. These theories are called "natural" rights theories because the rights and duties they assert are derived from nature and not the conventions, customs, or habits of any particular human society. Hobbes "natural" rights theory began with the premise that the most basic nature of humans is a desire for self-preservation and the fear of a violent death. Accordingly, all humans have a "natural" right to self-preservation. Everything necessary to exercise the "natural" right of self-preservation is therefore a derivative "natural" right. Locke also took self-preservation to be a "natural" right, but added to human nature, a desire for happiness achieved through the pursuit of property, which was therefore also a "natural" right.

For both Hobbes and Locke, the "natural" right to self-preservation spawned a law of nature that commands all men to use the most rational and efficacious means of achieving their "natural" right of self-preservation and property. Both Hobbes and Locke realized, however, that any law without the power to enforce it is a nullity. As Locke put it:

> And that all men may be restrained from invading other's rights and from doing hurt to one another, and the law of nature be observed which willeth the peace and preservation of all mankind, the execution of the law of nature is, in that state [of nature], put into every man's hands, whereby everyone has a right to punish the transgressors of that law to such a degree as may hinder its violation; for the law of nature would, as all other laws that concern men in this world, be in vain, if there were nobody that in the state of nature had a power to execute that law and thereby preserve the innocent and restrain offenders...[14]

Locke also acknowledged that despite the "natural" right to punish transgressors, one might not have sufficient power to punish or exact damages from the transgressors of his "natural" rights:

> ... In the state of nature, there often wants power to back and support the sentence [for the violation of a "natural" right] when right, and to give it due execution. They who by any injustice offend will seldom fail, where they are able, by force, to make good their injustice; such resistance many times makes the punishment dangerous and frequently destructive to those who attempt it.[15]

In other words, the frail second grader has a "natural" right to his lunch money, but he cannot enforce that right against the fifth grade bully who takes it every day.

When a system of artificial rights and duties is created within a society by the customs, culture or conscious agreement of its members, it is traditionally called a conventional or legal rights theory, since the artificial rights and duties are created by society.

The Origin and Purpose of Rights

No system of artificial rights, "natural" or conventional, actually separates might from right. An artificial right helps only the people without sufficient power to achieve their will. A person with sufficient power to achieve his will gains nothing by his artificial rights, unless others refrain from using their power because of their respect for their artificial duty. The fifth grade bully agrees that although he can take the second grader's lunch money, he *ought* not to take it, so he chooses not to take it. If the artificial rights of the society mandate respecting the property of others, all people would be helped in achieving their will to keep their property if everyone respects the artificial right and chooses not to take another's property.

All systems of artificial rights and duties must have an enforcing authority, which is the people who augment the power of those people with insufficient power to achieve their will. These people use their power to restrain anyone from taking the possessions to which another has an artificial right. In other words, they enforce the artificial duty not to take another's possessions. They may also augment another's power so he can obtain possessions to which he has an artificial right, but which he has insufficient power to obtain on his own.

A child in our society has an artificial, legal, right not to be abused or neglected by a parent. A three-year-old child obviously does not have the physical power to prevent a parent from beating, starving or sexually abusing it. If the state children's services agency receives information that a child has been abused, it has an artificial, legal, duty to take the child from the parents and protect it from future abuse. A seventeen-year-old, 6' 4", 230 lb. linebacker whose 120 lb. father threatens to beat him does not need the children's services agency's additional power to avoid a beating.

In the United States, every person has an artificial, legal, right not to be held against his will. If the police learn that this has happened, they have a legal duty to free the person imprisoned. The police have an artificial, legal duty to add their power to the person imprisoned to achieve his will to be free of the imprisonment.

When the U.S. Supreme Court ordered an end to segregation, black children had an artificial, constitutional, right to attend the University of Alabama. When George Wallace stood in the school doorway, federal troops and marshals were there to augment the black students' power to enter the building and attend classes. The white students who had the same constitutional right did not need the federal troops or marshals to attend the University of Alabama.

Any system of artificial rights and duties without the power necessary to enforce them is nothing more than a statement of will, a verbal expression of a desire for a particular future state to become an existing state. Consequently, an artificial right, like any other desire, must have the power necessary to cause that future state to become a reality or it is simply an unsatisfied desire. The U.S. Supreme Court's decision that black children had a right to attend the University of Alabama was a statement of will. Without the federal troops to open the school house door and let them in, the Supreme Court's decision was as meaningless as an order declaring every black child has a right to be white. It does not matter whether the statement of will is that of one person or an entire society. Without the necessary power, the artificial right cannot become an existing state. Will cannot be separated from power.

The people who augment the power of other people who have insufficient power of their own to acquire or keep the possessions to which they have an artificial right are the enforcing authority. Without the Children's Services agency, the police or the federal troops to enforce the artificial rights of those without sufficient power to obtain or protect their possessions, an artificial right is "in vain."

A few historical examples will further illustrate how these systems of artificial rights and duties try to separate might from right and how they have evolved through history. In many monkey and ape societies, there is a social hierarchy with a dominant male at the top. Numerous social behaviors are organized around the social hierarchy. One such behavior often involves mating. Dominant males try to reserve the females for themselves to mate with. They maintain a vigil over subordinate males and threaten and intimidate and even attack and injure them for attempting to breed with females. The threats and intimidation communicate the behaviors that the dominant male does not want the others to engage in even though they have the physical power to do so, and retaliation usually follows when the threat is ignored. In some ape societies, two or three individuals who could not alone be dominant, sometimes form an alliance against another more powerful individual and by their alliance become the dominant individuals.

As human societies grew larger, they developed ever more sophisticated ways to communicate the behaviors and possessions the most powerful individuals permitted. The number of individuals with sufficient power of alliance to dominate a society has varied widely. Hammurabi's Code,[16] as one of the first written code of laws, notified Hammurabi's subjects of the behaviors he permitted and protected, and the punishment he would exact for violating his commands.[17] The people protected by the Code had artificial rights. The rest had an artificial duty not to interfere with the other's artificial rights.

Hammurabi's Code provides: "If a man has struck his father, his hand shall be cut off." In this example, the father has an artificial right not to be struck by his son. The son has an artificial duty not to strike his father. Since Hammurabi and his soldiers could not stay in every house and restrain every son who raised his hand to strike his father. A method of responding to violations of artificial rights after they occurred was necessary.[18]

If the son violated the father's artificial right not to be struck, Hammurabi would exact the penalty stated in the Code. Punishment after the fact has always been a method of enforcement, as it is in monkey and ape societies. The punishment threatened is supposedly so terrible that it will deter anyone from violating the artificial right. Threats of punishment are, of course, a form of physical power. If the violation occurs despite the threat, execution of the punishment serves to equate one loss with the loss inflicted by the punishment and to further deter future violators.

A more complex example from Hammurabi's Code is as follows: "If a man has harbored in his house a male or female slave fugitive from the palace or from a commoner, and has not produced them at the demand of the police, the owner of that house shall be put to death." This section creates a right of the master over the slave, and a duty to produce a fugitive slave. Again, the Code employs the threat of a terrible punishment to try to enforce the right.

These ancient examples show two of the earliest recorded attempts to prohibit some people from using their power to achieve their will. In each, Hammurabi states how power *ought* to be used and prohibits those uses undesirable to him and those he wants to protect. The son has the power to strike his father, even kill him, but Hammurabi says he *ought* not to do it. The house owner had the power to hide another's slave and refuse to turn it over upon demand.

Hammurabi's system of artificial rights and duties would not have existed without his power to enforce it. If someone had been more powerful than Hammurabi, he would have established the artificial rights and duties and punishments, as happened whenever one ancient kingdom conquered another, e.g., William the Conqueror.

In 1066, William the Conqueror invaded and conquered England. He rewarded his favorites with privileges and large estates of land previously the property of English Lords. He also ignored the earlier English laws that had come down from Edward the Confessor placing numerous restrictions on the absolute power of the king. Succeeding Norman Kings followed William's example. In the one hundred and fifty years following the Norman Conquest, a power struggle developed between the Norman Kings and the English Barons who wanted a return of the Saxon laws. The Norman Kings also abolished numerous rights of the church which the English ecclesiastics wanted restored.

In 1215, the English Barons surrounded King John with their armies on the fields of Runnymede.[19] After years of trying, the barons finally succeeded in forcing King John to sign the Great Charter of King John, otherwise known as the Magna Charta. Upon threat of death, King John signed the charter and thereby established the liberties, the artificial rights, of the English people.[20] The Magna Charta contained forty-nine articles. Among these artificial rights was perhaps the most famous:

> XXIX. No free-man's body shall be taken, nor imprisoned, nor disseised, nor outlawed, nor banished, nor in any way be damaged, nor shall the King send him to prison by force, excepting by the judgment of his Peers and by the Law of the land.

One could hardly find a more direct statement of how one person may not use his power against another who lacks adequate power to resist. Many free men lacked the power to prevent the king from arresting and imprisoning, outlawing or banishing them, or from taking their property. By Magna Charta, the English Barons declared the artificial right of all free men, again, not women and not slaves, not to have the superior power of the king imprison, outlaw, or banish them or take their property.

Other examples from Magna Charta of the artificial restriction of the king's power include:

> XX. No Sheriff nor Bailiff nor the King nor any other, shall take horses or carts of any Free-man, for carriage, unless it be by his own will.

> XXI. Neither the King nor his Bailiffs shall take another man's timber for castles or for any other uses, unless it be by the will of him to whom the timber was belonging.

John's oath and the great seal of England on the charter were not, however, sufficient to insure these artificial rights. As soon as John or his successors' fortunes changed, the charter would be ignored or disavowed, as it, in fact, was when John appealed to the Pope who decreed it void as given under duress, which, of course, it was. To enforce King John's faithful administration of the charter according to its terms,[21] the Barons formed a council of twenty-five. The Barons extorted and then enforced the artificial rights of Magna Charta with the allied power of their swords.

The English Barons continued their power struggle for the artificial rights in the Magna Charta through three succeeding kings before those rights were so firmly established that they became the bedrock of English law and society. The power struggle did not end there, however, as the rights granted in Magna Charta applied only to Freemen. The struggle continued with the expansion of the group of people who claimed and received the benefit of the rights in Magna Charta and to establish other rights as Parliament and the king battled for supremacy. The seventeenth century witnessed more than its share of this struggle with the English Civil War, the beheading of Charles I, the Protectorate of Oliver Cromwell, the restoration of the monarchy in Charles II, and the glorious and bloodless revolution that put William III on the English throne and established constitutional monarchy in England.

Another great political step in th expansion of artificial rights occurred with the American Declaration of Independence, the American Constitution, and the Bill of Rights. The great change from 1215 to 1789, is evident from a comparison of excerpts from Magna Charta, the Declaration of Independence, and the American Constitution:

MAGNA CHARTA:

John, by the Grace of God, King of England, Lord of Ireland, Duke of Normandy and Aquitaine, and Earl of Anjou, to his Archbishops, Bishops, Abbots, Earls, Barons, Justiciaries, Foresters, Sheriffs, Governors, Officers, and to all Bailiffs, and his faithful subjects,–Greetings. Know ye, that We, in the presence of God, and for the salvation of our own soul, and of the souls of all our ancestors, and of our heirs, to the honour of God, and the exaltation of the Holy Church and amendment of our Kingdom, by the counsel of our venerable fathers, ...; have in the First place granted to God, and by this our present Charter, have confirmed for us and our heirs for ever:– ... We have also granted to all the Freemen of our Kingdom, for us and our heirs for ever, all the underwritten Liberties, to be enjoyed and held by them and by their heirs, from us and from our heirs. – ...

DECLARATION OF INDEPENDENCE:

A Declaration By The Representatives of the United States of America in Congress Assembled, July 4, 1776.

When, in the course of artificial events, it becomes necessary for one people to dissolve the political bands which have connected them with another, and to assume, among the powers of the earth, the separate and equal station to which the laws of nature and of nature's God entitle them, a decent respect to the opinions of mankind requires that they should declare the causes which impel them to the separation.

We hold these truths to be self-evident, that all men are created equal; that they are endowed by their Creator with certain unalienable rights; that among these are life, liberty, and the pursuit of happiness. That, to secure these rights, governments are instituted among men, deriving their just powers from the consent of the governed; that, whenever any form of government becomes destructive of these ends, it is the right of the people to alter or to abolish it, and to institute a new government, laying its foundation of such principles, and organizing its powers in such form, as to them shall seem most likely to effect their safety and happiness. . . . when a long train of abuses and usurpations, pursuing invariably the same object, evinces a design to reduce them under absolute despotism, it is their right, it is their duty, to throw off such government, and to provide new guards for their future security. . . . The history of the present King of Great Britain is a history of repeated injuries and usurpations, all having, in direct object, the establishment of an absolute tyranny over these states. To prove this, let facts be submitted to a candid world:

* * *

He has dissolved representative houses repeatedly, for opposing with manly firmness, his invasions on the rights of the people.

* * *

He has constrained our fellow-citizens, taken captive on the high seas, to bear arms against their country, to become the executioners of their friends and brethren, or to fall themselves by their hands.

* * *

We, therefore, the representatives of the United States of America, in general Congress assembled, appealing to the Supreme Judge of the world for the rectitude of our intentions, do, in the name, and by the authority of the good people of these colonies, solemnly publish and declare, that these united colonies are, and of right ought to be, free and independent states; that they are absolved from all allegiance to the British, Crown, and that all political connection between them and the state of Great Britain is, and ought to be, totally dissolved; and that, as free and independent states, they have full power to levy war, conclude peace, contract alliances, establish commerce, and to do all other acts and things which independent states may of right do. And, for the support of this declaration, with a firm reliance on the protection of Divine Providence, we mutually pledge to each other our lives, our fortunes, and our sacred honour.

AMERICAN CONSTITUTION:

We, the people of the United States, in order to form a more perfect union, establish justice, insure domestic tranquility, provide for the common defense, promote the general welfare, and secure the blessings of liberty to ourselves and our posterity, do ordain and establish this constitution of the United States of America.

From these examples can be seen the thread of artificial rights in a system of rights and duties throughout human history. Such systems are the commands of those individuals with sufficient power to enforce their will throughout the society. These individuals are the enforcing authority, the government. At first, tribal chieftains and monarchs and their class enforced their will upon weaker people. In ancient times, however, societies developed that expanded the numbers of people allied together to form the dominant power necessary to create and enforce the artificial rights and duties within society. In some societies, many people allied together and created a process for selecting individuals to act for the alliance to enforce the artificial rights and duties they established. The Greek democracies and oligarchies, and the Roman Republic are but a few examples. English history from the Norman Conquest to Magna Charta to the American Revolution and American Constitution reflects a steady increase in the number of people allied together to establish the power of alliance to create the society's artificial rights and to form the enforcing authority to enforce those artificial rights and duties.

Since Hammurabi, the formulation of artificial rights has been extended to a greater number of members of society and the enforcing authority has become more responsive and subject to its citizens, but the process itself has not changed. It cannot be changed because every system of artificial rights and duties must have its Hammurabi or English Barons or Continental Army. Without them, any system of artificial rights and duties can exist only as a statement of will, a dream in someone's consciousness, or ink spots on a page. This book sets out a system of artificial rights and duties, but there is no power to enforce it.

The *Ought* of Artificial Rights and Duties

Where do the statements of will, the *ought* of artificial rights, come from? First, a statement of will must be the will of someone. A theist may say it is a statement of the will of God: "Thou shalt not kill." Still, it must be uttered by a person. The religious skeptic will say that making

God the author is an appeal to authority and an invocation of eternal damnation as a punishment to try to enforce it. None of the great minds of the ancient world believed in the Olympian Gods except as a ruse to control the ignorant, superstitious mob that made up the majority of society. In Enlightenment France of the eighteenth century, Voltaire and the other philosophes mercilessly attacked religion. The most telling reply was that law, morality and social order would collapse without the fear of eternal damnation provided by religion. Why else would anyone obey the law or choose to be moral? The horrific punishments of an omniscient and omnipotent God were necessary inducements to social stability.

A religious justification for a system of artificial rights may be persuasive to followers of the religion that system is based on, but not to other religions. No large society can avoid divergent religious faiths. Thus, a secular system that avoids competing religious doctrines is preferable, especially if it is consistent with the tenets of religious morality and artificial rights. Such a system could unite people of all faiths.

For the human author of statements of will, *ought* comes from perceiving reality and imagining a state of reality more desirable than the present one. It is merely the process by which the conscious will selects an objective. Any perception of reality may be more or less accurate because the senses and human understanding are fallible. Humans also form judgments from their perception and understanding of the world that are generally divided into labeling things as good, e.g., pleasurable, useful or desirable, or bad or evil, e.g., painful, harmful or undesirable. (Neutrality or indifference is not so much a judgment as the absence of judgment.) Each person judge's his or her own good or bad.

Some imagined states of reality can be achieved with adequate power, and some cannot. Fortunately, the difference between the possible and impossible is not always clearly marked, or else human adventure, discovery and invention might come to a halt. For thousands of years, people thought it was impossible for a man to fly, but it is not. When Jules Verne wrote *From Here to the Moon,* no one thought a trip to the moon was possible, yet it is. This is true in the social as well as the physical or scientific sphere. The recent collapse of the major communist states in the world was a failed attempt to make an imaginary state of social existence, communism, a reality. But, the imagination of a communist society as better and more desirable led to the attempt to make it a reality, as a similar desire led to the American Revolution.

Ought is then simply a statement of the will or desire for an imagined future state. One who says that the future state "A" *ought* to exist, has said no more than, "I want 'A' to exist." "I desire 'A' to exist." If "A" becomes an existing state, it may be better or worse than the present state or other alternatives depending on the accuracy of the perception and understanding of the consequences of causing "A" to exist. Soviet communism turned out not to be what Marx had imagined.

People are often the means other people use to achieve their will. The powerful use the weak to achieve their will. This is how purely biological society operates. The weak imagine a future state in which the strong cannot satisfy their desires by taking the possessions of the weak. They imagine a state in which they can acquire or keep their possessions regardless of whether they have the necessary power. They value this imagined state as better than when the strong take their possessions. This imagined state of reality thus *ought* to exist. Fundamentally, *ought* is nothing more than an emphatic declaration of desire: I am hungry; I want a hamburger; I need a hamburger; I ought to have a hamburger; I have a right to a hamburger. I am alive; I want to stay alive; I need to stay alive; I ought to stay alive; I have a right to life. Thou shalt not kill–me. An artificial right is a statement that even if a person lacks the power to achieve his will, that lack of power *ought* not prevent him from achieving his will. Thus, an artificial right is a self-contradiction.

The artificial right cannot be an existing state without the power necessary to cause the desired future state to become an existing state. The English barons' statement of the liberties of the English people did not make them artificial rights. Rather, the baron's armies compelled the king to sign Magna Charta, and then the barons' power enforced it. If the king imprisoned a freeman after 1215 without judgment of his peers according to law, the barons' armies had to use their power to free him or the right granted in Article XXIX of the Magna Charta was no right at all. The Continental Congress that adopted the Declaration of Independence knew its statements of unalienable rights were meaningless dreams without the Continental Army, as shown by all signors pledging their lives, fortunes and sacred honor to make it a reality. Without the power to enforce those artificial rights they are as meaningless as Congress passing a law that a girl in an iron lung has a right to dance. Congress does not have that power. This contradiction can only be resolved by accepting that artificial rights are nothing without the power necessary to make them a reality.

An artificial right augments the power of a person without the power to achieve his desire. A person in a wheelchair may have the money to buy a hamburger, but she cannot climb the stairs to get it. If the person has an artificial right to access, e.g., the Americans with Disabilities Act, the restaurant owner has an artificial duty to remove the barrier. Before desegregation, Lester Maddox stood in the doorway of his Pickrick restaurant with a pick handle to prevent blacks from entering. Desegregation laws gave blacks the artificial right to eat at Maddox's restaurant. These laws are just another way of saying, "I want a hamburger at the Pickrick. I ought to have a hamburger at the Pickrick. I do not want anyone to prevent me from having a hamburger at the Pickrick. I have a right to have a hamburger at the Pickrick."

A slight rewording of this last statement of will transforms it into an artificial duty:[22] "Thou shalt not use your power to prevent me from having a hamburger." An artificial duty is a statement that one person must act or refrain from acting as directed by the will of another person. As such, a duty is simply a rewording of the statement of will about how other people *ought* to act. Thus, some people have an artificial duty to use their power to supplement another's power so he can achieve his will: "Thou shalt give me a hamburger." Food stamps, Medicaid, and other government entitlement programs create these kinds of artificial rights and duties.

If artificial rights are simply statements of individual will, then no individual or group's statement of will has any claim to superiority any more than any individual's will is superior. All wills are equally valuable. Only power gives one statement of will superiority over another. This is as true for an entire system of artificial rights and duties that is the legal system of a nation as it is for "I have a right to a hamburger." Systems of artificial rights and duties are the powerful competing to achieve their will, as King John learned at Runnymede and Hitler and Tojo learned in World War II. But, this is precisely the condition a system of artificial rights and duties is supposed to eliminate: might makes right.

To give greater authority and remove the source of artificial rights from the individual or group, the creators of artificial rights have often appealed to an authority superior to humans as the source of artificial rights. This authority falls generally into two classes: religion and reason, and more recently science, which is a specific form of reason. In most religious based systems, and certainly Christian ones, the source of artificial rights, what *ought* to be, is what God wills. They use eternal damnation as an added threat to induce obedience in this life. The appeal to reason, natural law, or natural justice as the source of artificial rights is less effective than religion because it has no threat of eternal retribution for disobedience, and because the most reasonable people often become irreconcilable enemies.

All human societies with which I am familiar have a social hierarchy that enforces the artificial rights of the society. In all but the most primitive human societies, there is an institution known as government, which is the enforcing authority. Artificial rights are enforced by government, and they can also be created by government. Except for artificial rights created against the government, e.g., the Magna Charta, the American Constitution, and the Bill of Rights, government always makes and enforces the artificial rights of society because government is the most powerful or dominant group in society.

If there has been any progress in human history, it has been the expansion of other-consciousness, manifested not only in moral philosophy and religious teachings, but also in the formation of alliances to create a society in which other-consciousness is the source of the statements of will of the artificial rights. Progress has been made toward making the conscious objective of society the creation of the conditions in which all other-conscious members of society have the greatest possible opportunity to discover and achieve their volitional will. This is an enormously difficult task because not all people have other-consciousness, and those who do not are often the most powerful, partly because they do not have the internal conflicts that other-consciousness produces. They have no qualm about killing and taking the possessions of other-conscious individuals, like the cannibals of Crusoe's island. Before an individualistic society can emerge, enough other-conscious people must form a power of alliance sufficient to make it an existing state.

Human history is a progression of increasing complexity. When humans learned to use fire, tools, agriculture and domesticated animals, each new system increased the complexity of human society. When humans began to consciously try to understand the world, they became philosophical creatures and the complexity of human society increased further. Rational morality is a part of that conscious search to understand. There are evolutionary precursors to conscious morality, and humans almost certainly have not escaped the evolutionary processes that reward moral behavior by natural selection. Other-consciousness is, I believe, the current apex of both the unconscious evolutionary processes and the conscious search to understand and to create the world we desire. The religious and secular expressions of universal equality are the precursors of other-consciousness. The morality of equality is a self-organizing principle for a human society of other-conscious individuals. When a number of other-conscious persons form a power of alliance sufficient to enforce the morality of equality as the artificial rights and duties of a human society, an individualistic society can emerge.

If all people were other-conscious and acted solely by the morality of equality, artificial rights and an enforcing authority would be unnecessary. Until then, other-conscious individuals must form a power of alliance to enforce the morality of equality as the artificial rights of Society. As more people adopt the morality of equality as the rule to guide their choices, the enforcing authority, government, may wither, but it will not disappear.

The spread of other-consciousness in human history has not been steady. We regressed as in the Middle Ages and Nazi Germany. The emergence of an individualistic society is no more inevitable than the evolution of the human species. Liberal democracy is a step toward an individualistic society, but it is not an individualistic society because it still allows some people to use their power to satisfy their desires by taking the possessions of other people who do not have the power to prevent it. Universal equality may be the statement of will, the ideal, of liberal democracy, but it is not the reality of an individualistic society.

The fallacy of liberal democracy is the tautology of utilitarianism wedded to universal suffrage which creates a false equality between the will of a majority and the moral objective of society as the greatest good for the greatest number, which is a majority. As long as this fallacy persists, an individualistic society cannot emerge from liberal democracy. Democracy as a form of government by majority must be uncoupled from moral authority before an individualistic society can emerge. Only if a majority of other-conscious voters make constructive power the moral and legal basis for all rights can an individualistic society emerge. Since liberal democracies do not distinguish between those with and without other-consciousness in granting the franchise, other-conscious members of a liberal democratic society may be a distinct minority. A majority in a liberal democracy can and do violate universal equality as easily as an absolute autocrat, perhaps easier, because liberal democracy disguises every act of an electoral majority with the moral imprimatur of utilitarianism.

Liberal democracy is a form of government, not an existing state in which the morality of equality becomes the artificial rights and duties. Liberal democracy may be a means of creating and maintaining the power of alliance necessary for other-consciousness people to create and enforce the artificial rights of an individualistic society, but democratic political institutions can and often are used to take a minority's possessions. Locke's assertion of the right of the majority to bind the minority because that is the only way a group can make a decision[23] only reinforces might makes right through democracy. The specific limits on the federal government's powers in the Constitution are better than the law of nature but still inadequate protection for the minority of a single individual. This inadequate protection of the individual from a majority's use of destructive power is why liberal democracy, even with enumerated, constitutionally protected individual rights, is not, and cannot be the end of political history.

Before the Civil War, the Constitution permitted one man to possess and compel the labor of another human being. The master and slave's statements of will about slavery undoubtedly differed. The masters' power was, however, greater than the slaves' power. Thus, slavery was an artificial right. During and after the Civil War, the abolitionists freed the slaves and passed the Thirteenth Amendment outlawing slavery. Their power made it an artificial right not to be enslaved.

Before 1919, adults could legally purchase, possess and consume alcoholic beverages. Then the Eighteenth Amendment made alcohol illegal. In 1933, a more powerful political alliance passed the Twenty-first Amendment which repealed the Eighteenth Amendment. Possession of alcohol is an artificial right. No it isn't. Yes it is.

In pre-Khomeini Iran, women could show their faces or other parts of their bodies in public without fear of punishment. Expressing an unorthodox view of Islam or Mohammed was not likely to result in a death sentence for Islamic heresy. Of course, Christian societies executed many heretics and witches, just not as recently as in Iran.

Might does make right because only power can make and enforce artificial rights. Power cannot be separated from will without ending life; nor can power be separated from will in creating artificial rights. The job of political philosophy is to choose the *ought* of artificial rights that society will use its power to create and enforce. Will that society be an individualistic society?

The United States seems to be the closest to an individualistic society to exist so far. We will examine next the political philosophy that lead to the creation of the constitutional form of government in the United States to see how it approaches the *ought* of an individualistic society, but still falls short.

Chapter VII

The Social Contract in Theory

The prevailing political theory before the adoption of the American Constitution was the theory of society as a social contract between all members of society who agreed to become a collective whole. The social contract is generally understood through the writings of its three chief modern architects, Thomas Hobbes (1588-1679), John Locke (1632-1704), and Jean-Jacques Rousseau (1712-1778). Since the political theory of each of these writers[1] contributed significantly to the times and thought that produced the American Revolution and Constitution of the United States, before examining the American experiment in universal equality, a brief review of the lives and theories of these philosophers will help illustrate why as only a political theory the social contract is insufficient to create an individualistic society.

Thomas Hobbes

Hobbes lived through the political turmoil of the struggle between the Stuart Kings, James I and Charles I, and Parliament over monarchical absolutism versus parliamentary supremacy. That struggle culminated in the English Civil War, the beheading of Charles I, the protectorate of Oliver Cromwell, and the restoration of Charles II, all of which Hobbes witnessed. He died before the Glorious Revolution that replaced the Stuart monarchy with the constitutional monarchy of William and Mary. Throughout this period, religious intolerance and competition for religious supremacy infused, if not overrode, other political motives. The advances of modern science with its materialistic rather than godly explanations of the world further contributed to the dehiscence of English society.

Hobbes was educated at Oxford, served as an assistant to Francis Bacon, met Galileo, and corresponded with Descartes. As with many intellectuals of his day, Hobbes was drawn to Bacon's experimental natural philosophy or science. In his many writings, Hobbes proposed a materialistic theory of the biological world from which he derived his political theory.

After an extended period on the continent, Hobbes returned to England in 1637 to continue his writing. He soon returned to Paris, however, fearing imprisonment when his theory of absolute sovereignty satisfied neither side of the political crisis of 1640 between Parliament and the royalists. He then became a tutor to the future Charles II, and returned to England in 1651 after losing favor with the royalist exiles who considered him a "rabid Protestant."[2]

With the progress of the Reformation, the divine right of kings as the justification for absolute monarchy was under attack. According to divine right, kings are God's representatives on earth. Since God's power is absolute over men throughout the universe and time, the king, as God's earthly representative, has absolute power over men on earth. Hobbes famous work, *Leviathan*,[3] provided a secular justification for absolute authority, whether of a single person or an assembly, which suited Cromwell and his Protectorate, but Cromwell's authority did not last, and Charles II returned to the throne, temporarily restoring divine right to the monarchy.

In *Leviathan*, Hobbes begins his political theory by describing a state of nature as the pre-social condition of man in which all men were born equals. Though he acknowledges natural inequalities in strength and intellect, etc., he states that the weakest man can always kill the strongest, either alone through cunning or in combination with others. In this state of nature, whatever a man produces or possesses, others come to kill him to take it for themselves. All men are enemies and try to destroy or subdue one another in "a perpetual and restless desire of power after power that ceases only in death."[4] In an often quoted passage, Hobbes describes the state of nature as a constant state of war in which men have the "natural" right to do anything:

> ... where every man is the enemy of every man, ... men live without other security than what their own strength and their own invention shall furnish them withal. In such condition there is no place for industry, because the fruit thereof is uncertain: and consequently no culture of the earth; no navigation nor use of the commodities that may be imported by sea; no commodious buildings; no instruments of moving and removing such things

as require much force; no knowledge of the face of the earth; no account of time; no arts; no letters; no society; and, which is worst of all, continual fear and danger of violent death; and the life of man solitary, poor, nasty, brutish, and short.[5]

Whether this state of war ever actually existed for all men, Hobbes maintains that it does exist among all kings and nations.

In this state of nature, nothing is just or unjust because there can be no law without a common power superior to all men to enforce it and therefore no justice, or right or wrong. In this state, there is no property except what a man can take and hold with force against all who try to take it. But, men prefer peace because they fear death. They want to gain by their efforts those things that make life pleasant. From this state, Hobbes deduces the Right of Nature, which is each man's liberty to use his power to do anything he thinks best for his self-preservation, and the law of nature,[6] which is "the absence of external impediments." The law of nature is a general rule discovered through reason, which forbids doing anything destructive to one's life and commands doing whatever seems best to preserve it.[7]

Hobbes states the fundamental law of nature is to seek peace when possible and when not, to use all means of self-defense. In other words, survival is the primary goal of life. From this, Hobbes deduces the second law of nature, the Golden Rule, which he states as:

> ... that a man be willing, when others are so too, as far forth as for peace and defense of himself he shall think it necessary, to lay down this right to all things, and be contended with so much liberty against other men as he would allow other men against himself.[8]

From these two fundamental laws, he also derives an extensive list of additional laws of nature such as the law of justice, of equity, of equal use of things in common, of primogeniture and first seizing, and of submission to arbitrement. The "science" of these laws of nature he calls moral philosophy. Thus, for Hobbes, morality is the science of the rational pursuit of self-interest, i.e., egoism. The Golden Rule is one of rational self-interest. Cost-benefit analysis is the ultimate moral principle.

To provide a common power superior to all men to enforce the laws of nature, men agree with their fellow men to give up completely to the sovereign, their "natural" right in a state of nature to do anything. The sovereign may be one man or an assembly, but this covenant–a Puritan concept that fit Hobbes' religious views–of men in a state of nature to transfer absolutely their "natural" right to do anything to the sovereign, is Hobbes' social contract.

Hobbes argues that the sovereign must have absolute power because without it, men will not have adequate assurance that all members of society will perform their part of the social contract. With this power superior to all others, the sovereign makes and enforces whatever laws he, in his sole discretion and wisdom, deems appropriate. Though Hobbes advises the sovereign to make laws for the good of the people, the people are obligated to obey bad laws as well as the good, because no matter how bad the bad laws are, they are better than the state of nature. Justice, he says, is following this agreement, the social contract. Injustice is breaking it or the laws made by the sovereign.

Fear of the sovereign's absolute power, not eternal damnation by an omnipotent, vengeful God, most effectively holds society together. Only this absolute power makes private contracts possible. It allows one man to perform his part of an ordinary contract before another does, confident that if the other does not perform, the sovereign will force him to perform by a punishment much worse than any advantage gained by not performing, e.g., cutting off the hand of the son who strikes his father. Thus, each man is more likely to perform without the necessity of force because he fears worse consequences if he fails. Hobbes never explains, however, why the death penalty for petty theft has never been sufficient to deter the destitute from stealing bread.

Although Hobbes' theory supports absolute arbitrary power in the sovereign as necessary to create and maintain society, the ultimate source of the legitimacy of that absolute power comes from the consent of members of society in transferring their "natural" right to do anything to the sovereign, not from divine right. And, the purpose of the social contract is to create peace and prosperity for the self-interest of consenting individuals, not for the fulfillment of a religious objective.

John Locke

Locke, like Hobbes, was also well-educated and lived through much of the political turmoil of seventeenth century England. He too retreated to the continent when his friend and patron, the Earl of Shaftesbury, former chancellor of England, was accused of conspiracy. From his writings, Locke appears to have been a deeply religious man, though some of his philosophical positions seem to directly contradict religious doctrine.

His interests were broad. His well-known works besides his magnum opus on political theory, *Two Treatises of Civil Government*, include his

Essay on Human Understanding, a groundbreaking work in psychology, *Letters on Toleration*, which advocated religious toleration, and *Thoughts Concerning Education*, about reforms in education.

Also like Hobbes, Locke proposes a political theory of "natural" rights and a law of nature as preexisting political society. His view of human nature and his purpose are, however, entirely different from those of Hobbes. Hobbes provides a secular, consensual justification for the absolute authority of government and the injustice of all opposition to the sovereign, whereas Locke set out to justify a revolution against just such absolutism.

As the philosophical leader of the Whigs, Locke provided a justification for the revolution of 1688 that put William III on the English throne as a constitutional monarch, thus replacing the Stuart line. The express purpose of his *Two Treatises of Civil Government* was "to establish the throne of our great restorer, our present King William." But Locke's theory transcended the historical moment and the need to justify current events. In less than 100 years it became an integral part of the unwritten British Constitution.[9]

In his *First Treatise,* Locke refuted Sir Robert Filmer's arguments for the unchallengeable divine right of kings from God's supposed grant to Adam of authority over his children. In the *Second Treatise,* Locke addressed the necessity for and the limited purpose of government.

Locke begins his *Second Treatise* by asking, if there is no divine authority for government, and it is not simply the result of might makes right "by no other rules but that of beasts," then what is the origin of political power. To distinguish political power "from that of a father over his children, a master over his servants, a husband over his wife, and a lord over his slave," Locke defines what he means by political power:

> Political power, then, I take to be a right to make laws with penalties of death and, consequently all less penalties for the regulating and preserving of property, and of employing the force of the community in the execution of such laws, and in the defence of the commonwealth from foreign injury, and all this only for the public good.

Having refuted divine right in the *First Treatise*, Locke, like Hobbes, describes a state of nature, in which men are equal in their possession of certain "natural" rights. This equality is again a variant of the Golden Rule. But unlike Hobbes, Locke maintains that the state of nature is not a state of chaos and constant war and strife, where might makes right. In Locke's version of the state of nature, that is, the true nature of man uncorrupted or conditioned by existing social institutions, men are free and equal. They all possess natural reason which dictates that men live together in mutual respect with common universal, or natural, rights by the law of nature, which *is* reason.[10] As equals in a state of nature, the law of nature commands that equals "ought not harm another's life, health, liberty or property." Further, as equals, they ought not use other people as they would an animal, so they must refrain from invading others' "natural" rights.

In the state of nature, each person possesses natural reason and is thus knowledgeable of the law of nature. He can interpret his own natural rights and has the natural right to punish violators of his natural rights. Without this natural right to punish violators and enforce the law of nature, it would "be in vain." If one murders another, he violates the law of nature and declares himself an enemy of all who recognize the law of nature. They thus have a natural right to kill him as they would a lion or tiger. On his own authority, Locke asserts that the natural right to punish is not absolute. Punishment must be proportional to the violation and only enough "to make it an ill bargain to the offender, give him cause to repent, and terrify others from doing the like."

Unlike Hobbes, Locke argues the state of war is not the same as the state of nature. Rather, a state of war exists only when a person declares by word or deed that he does not recognize the law of nature and the equal rights of all people, and that he intends to use force against another. For Locke, the state of nature is one of peace except for when some individuals violate the law of nature. Nevertheless, the state of nature is imperfect, and to remove these imperfections, people consent to political society.

In the state of nature, each person has the natural right to judge for himself when another has wrongfully violated his natural right.[11] No one can be disinterested and objective, however, in interpreting the law of nature because everyone is biased toward his own self-interest. Even if one reaches a legitimate judgment that his natural rights have been violated, his natural right to punish the violator and obtain compensation from him may be insufficient to vindicate his natural right. To furnish a means of unbiased arbitration of disputes over natural rights and to provide a collective power to enforce them, people consent to the formation of the political state and a government as the recipient of everyone's natural right to interpret and enforce the law of nature. Thereafter, only the government has the right to interpret natural rights, to punish violators without favoring any person or group, and to use the state's collective authority to enforce its interpretation. This agreement is Locke's social contract.

The purpose of political society and government is given by the purpose of the social contract to protect each person's natural rights that exist independent of the state. These natural rights are life, liberty and individual property. In this way, natural rights and the law of nature limit the proper scope of legitimate government, and its use of force. Statutes passed by a legislature are supposed to be a disinterested interpretation of the law of nature that facilitate and enhance the citizens' preexisting natural rights, they do not create new rights.

Locke's social contract ultimately rests on majority rule and tacit acquiescence, not actual individual consent.

> ... [T]hat which begins and actually constitutes a political society is nothing but the consent of any number of freemen capable of a majority to unite and incorporate into such a society. And this is that, and only that, which did or could give beginning to any lawful government in the world.[12]

Locke states that unanimous, individual consent is a practical impossibility that would lead to governmental impotence and instability, which was probably true in seventeenth century England. He states that all men agree to the initial social contract, but once created, the majority determines the form of the government, not a Hobbesian absolute monarch or assembly. The consent must be for each person, since government has no authority without the consent of the individual. Although he states express consent is sufficient for all purposes, he does not give an example of express consent in the *Second Treatise*. Rather, individual consent is tacit consent. For instance by entering the country, a foreigner "consents" to the social contract and the government. If born in the country, one consents simply by staying when he comes of age. By accepting an inheritance, one consents to the same government that bound the deceased.

Locke states that majority rule is limited by (1) the purpose of the social contract–to interpret not to limit natural rights, (2) periodic elections, (3) the legislator's sense of community and shared interest in the purpose of the contract, and (4) the right of revolution. Should the legislators act contrary to the purposes of the contract, they become tyrants or rebels against society. The ultimate insurance against these abuses of power is the right of revolution.

Jean-Jacques Rousseau

Rousseau was born in Calvinist Geneva. His father neglected his parental duties, but managed to "introduce his son to Plutarch and the classics as well as some novels."[13] Without a formal education, Rousseau educated himself. At an early age, he was apprenticed to an engraver. Sparked by a disgust for engraving and a fear of another beating by his master, at thirteen he ran away and began a lifelong journey as a nonconformist bordering on revolutionary, if not as a participant, certainly as one whose ideas fomented it.[14]

He converted to Catholicism, had numerous occupations including "lackey, music-teacher knowing nothing of music, secretary to a somewhat fraudulent Greek Archimandrite seeking alms for the restoration of the Holy Sepulchre, lover of Mme. Warens (twelve years his senior), clerk in a survey office, tutor, inventor of a revolutionary system of numerical musical notation, secretary to the French ambassador to Venice, composer, secretary to a wealthy tax-collector, etc." In 1744, he moved to Paris, where he lived with a woman with whom he had five children, all of whom he admitted abandoning to a foundling home at birth. He fled Paris in 1762 when his *Emile* was condemned by the Paris parliament, but returned in 1770 and died there in 1778.

Rousseau lived during and contributed to the French Enlightenment. There were three currents running through his time, political, intellectual and religious. One was the progress of constitutional limitations on otherwise absolute monarchs. While England had a constitutional, monarchy after William and Mary, France and other European nations still clung to the absolute, arbitrary power of divine right, which would ultimately fall in the democratic revolutions to come. Another was the erosion of faith and religious orthodoxy under the relentless criticism produced by advances of natural philosophy–science. The third was the emerging idea of the individual as educable and capable of making crucial decisions for himself and society.

Rousseau summarized his political philosophy in *The Social Contract*.[15] The foundation for that work was, however, laid in his First and Second Discourses.[16] Like Hobbes and Locke before him, Rousseau begins with a state of nature in which he says all humans were equal, happy and good, like other animals, without foresight, pride, or fear of violent death. In the state of nature, humans never harmed each other or other animals except out of self-preservation, which was moderated by a natural compassion for all animals. Some argue Rousseau's state of nature adopted an evolutionary view of humans so primitive that they were not yet human.

He claims that humans developed from established families building huts to using language, crafts, the arts, metallurgy and agriculture, and deception. This development finally led to social cooperation, which in turn produced a need to divide land and segregate each person's work from each other, caused men to realize that they were unequal, and created a violent competition for material goods. In his romantic view of humans, the study of the sciences and philosophy that grew out of the socialization process created the inequality that never existed in the state of nature.

The development of inequality produced a crisis of self-preservation. Men therefore joined together to aggregate their forces to act in concert to solve this problem:

> Where shall we find a form of association which will defend and protect with the whole common force the person and the property of each associate, and by which every person, while uniting himself with all, shall obey only himself and remain as free as before.

Rousseau's answer was the social compact, which is necessary to restore the natural equality that existed before society, not the other way around as Hobbes and Locke postulated. The terms of the social compact are simply, "the total alienation of each associate, and all his rights to the whole community," not to a king or assembly or government, so everyone is in the same condition with a common, coextensive interest in society. The terms are the same everywhere and tacitly understood by everyone even if never formally announced.

The body politic the social compact creates is a moral, collective body, composed of all those who can vote in the assembly. The act of civil association gives society unity, a common self, life, and will. In this way all people become equal and subject to the "general will" of society. Without this prior unanimous, though tacit, agreement, no minority has any obligation to submit to a decision of the majority. Like Locke, however, remaining in society is sufficient tacit agreement.

As the title of Rousseau's book makes clear, this tacit agreement is called a social contract, but it is not a contract in any traditional sense. It is not enforceable within society, and it may be changed whenever the general will of society deems it in the common interest. The civil state formed by the social contract substitutes justice for instinct and gives actions their moral character. The common interest of all society, not the self-interest of the individual, is the moral standard. "Instead of destroying the natural equality of mankind, the fundamental compact substitutes, on the contrary, a moral and legal equality for that physical inequality which nature placed among men, and that, let men be ever so unequal in strength or in genius, they are all equalized by convention and legal right." Rousseau is no communist or utilitarian. He defends the unequal distribution of private property by arguing that the social contract makes society the master of all wealth, without changing its possessors. Society gives the possessors a title and protects it with the collective power of society.

The "general will" is Rousseau's term for the spirit and will of the body politic. Even in Rousseau's hands, the general will is a morphing concept. The general will is the common interest of all society, and therefore can never be wrong. It is the sovereign and resides in the people as a whole. It applies to all citizens alike without distinction. It is expressed by majority vote of all the people assembled periodically, but the vote of a majority does not express the general will when society is dominated by individuals and factions who vote for only their own private interests and not the common interest. Then a majority vote produces a "will of all" that can be wrong.

Rousseau's distinction between the general will that cannot err and the will of all that can has a neat logic to it, but it is incapable of practical guidance on difficult political decisions, and because the general will is the moral standard, and can be expressed by a minority, all political debate takes on overtones of moral superiority that rarely conduces to understanding and consensus.

Although Rousseau speaks often with near reverence of "the people," he also says they are often too dumb to understand ideas that cannot be expressed in "vulgar language,"[17] and they sometime must be deceived for their own benefit, as when wise men create the state by disguising their own wisdom as that of God. And, though he advises regular periodic assemblies of the people, he does not advocate democracy as the best form of government, but rather says the best and wisest should govern the multitude.

What can we make of the philosophy of the social contract? It has been essentially an elaborate statement of will upon which to construct a system of artificial rights and duties. The essential difference between Hobbes and Locke's social contract theory is seen in their different purposes. Hobbes uses it to justify a secular, unchallengeable absolutism, while Locke uses it to refute absolutism and justify revolution against absolute, arbitrary, tyrannical power. That both Locke and Hobbes appeal to reason and call it the law of nature to reach opposing views of human nature, the source of morality, and the proper use of power in political society, proves the inadequacy of reason and the law of nature as the ultimate authority for human society or the restraint of the power reposed in government. Reason is a tool to reach a conscious objective, not the means of identifying that objective. Ironically, the American revolutionaries used Locke's theory to justify their revolution against the monarchy that very theory put in power. It also served as the basic framework for constitutional government. The French used Rousseau to justify their revolution and all of its excesses of the guillotine in the name of "the people."[18]

As just a philosophy, the social contract cannot give real substance to specific relationships within society. Hobbes, Locke and Rousseau were other-conscious, as evidenced by their agreement on the equality of all men, though not women or slaves. Their accomplishments are not diminished because their theories did not completely transcend the attitudes of their times. They were each partly right in identifying the source of human equality, of other-consciousness, and they each made equality the goal of morality and liberty the goal of polity.[19] Hobbes and Locke found it in reason, while Rousseau found it in the "natural" emotion of sympathy and pity for other creatures. Without both reason and emotion other-consciousness cannot emerge.

For all their disagreements, Hobbes, Locke and Rousseau agree on three essential points: the equality of individuals, the necessity of the power of alliance to equalize the power of individuals in some respects, and the agreement or consent of the individual as the legitimate source of authority in society. Whether called the morality of equality, the law of nature, natural rights or natural justice, the statements of will that *ought* to govern human society without the power to enforce them are mere "wishful thinking," in this world or the next.[20] Hobbes claims that without a common power superior to all men there is no justice. Locke states that the lack of power of individuals to enforce their natural rights is one of the conditions of the state of nature that drives men to enter into the social contract. Rousseau states that when individual men no longer have sufficient power to preserve themselves, their only recourse is to join together and aggregate their power in society, and that the conventions of that agreement transform the force of might into the justice of right.

The philosophy of the social contract is not a justification of human society. Society needs no justification. Rather it is a justification for how power *ought* to be used in society. Universal equality, whether stated in the religious terms of the Golden Rule or the secular terms of a law of nature, natural rights, natural justice or the categorical imperative, is the objective of an individualistic society.

Any doubts about whether the political philosophy of the social contract as an expression of the ideal of the universal equality of all individuals and the political theory upon which the American republic was consciously designed are removed by the Declaration of Independence. Still, the Declaration of Independence and the victorious Continental Army did not translate universal equality and political theory into a reality. How well did the founding fathers translate the ideal and theory into reality is the next question.

Chapter VIII

The American Experiment

From Colonies to Constitution

The same historical pressures that molded English political and legal history in the 1600s and 1700s had similar effects in the American colonies leading up to the American Revolution. The first steps in making universal equality a political reality was, of course, the Declaration of Independence and the American Revolution, but in the years following the American victory at Yorktown, the idea that a people could govern themselves was severely tested. A severe postwar economic depression in, and competition among, the thirteen newly independent states created irresistible forces for the abuse of majority rule. The chaos of self-government eventually cried out for order and stability, and the Constitution[1] and Bill of Rights.

Even before the Revolution, the English law was a part of colonial government. Well before Hobbes and Locke, the Virginia Charter of 1606, granted "all liberties, franchises and Immunities within anie of our other dominions to all intents and purposes as if they had been abiding and borne within this our realme of Englande or any other of our saide dominions." This charter provision had perhaps been reviewed by the famous jurist Lord Edward Coke, who in 1610 claimed in *Dr. Bonham's Case* that "when an act of Parliament is against common right and reason, . . . the common law will controul and adjudge such act to be void." Coke later wrote that any statute contrary to Magna Charta, "shall be void." Magna Charta Chapter 40 required commissioners to "doe equall right, to poore and to the rich."[2] In 1620, the Puritan colonists signed the Mayflower Compact, and on January 14, 1639, the Fundamental Orders of Connecticut established the government of the colony. Both very much resemble a social contract.[3]

In the colonial debate over parliamentary supremacy versus colonial autonomy, the arguments divided between Lockean natural rights and Coke's view of the common law. In time, the differences tended to merge.[4] Samuel Ward of Rhode Island describes in his diary the debate in the Continental Congress in 1774 over the colonial case against British policy:

> Richard Henry Lee of Virginia asserted that colonial rights rested on *four* foundations–'on Nature, on the British Constitution, on Charters, and on immemorial Usage.' John Jay, delegate from New York, agreed that resort should be had to the law of nature and to the British Constitution to ascertain colonial rights, but James Duane of New York thought the constitutional argument sufficient; ... without recurring to the Law of Nature–because this will be weak support.... Committee of congress 'agreed to found our rights upon the laws of Nature, the principles of the English Constitution, and charters and compacts.'"[5]

The June 1776 Virginia Revolutionary Convention Declaration of Rights contained a mixture of the political theory of natural rights and the traditions of English law. The basic problem was how to limit arbitrary power to secure individual rights. Power tended to expand, and the need to defend liberty was then "one of the leitmotifs of English history." Foreshadowing the Declaration of Independence, the Virginia Declaration stated:

> That all Men are by Nature equally free and independent, and have certain inherent Rights, of which, when they enter a State of Society, they cannot by any Compact, deprive or divest their Posterity; namely, the Enjoyment of Life and Liberty, with the Means of acquiring and possessing Property, and pursuing and obtaining Happiness and Safety.[6]

Also included was the right of revolution if the peoples' representatives, as their servants and trustees, failed to perform properly. New Hampshire and Maryland's Bill of Rights declared, "The doctrine of non-resistance, against arbitrary power and oppression, is absurd, slavish, and destructive of the good and happiness of mankind."

Once the colonies declared independence, the security of individual liberties became the province of state constitutions.[7] Without a king and lords, two of the checks the English mixed form of government put on an unrestrained popular majority were removed. Republicanism transferred their power to the people acting through their representatives. State constitutions gave the real power to assemblies and legislatures, and little to executives or the judiciary. Some included bills of rights, but most state bills of rights were adopted by state legislatures, not by ratifying conventions or popular vote. "Natural" rights existed without written bills of rights, but written bills of rights seemed to remove any doubt and gave a measure of comfort.

After the Revolution, a severe postwar depression set in. The Continental Congress was impotent. Some state legislatures were too conservative to act while others went to radical excesses "that threatened the very foundations of private property." In September 1786, mobs of angry farmers surrounded the New Hampshire legislature demanding the abolition of all debts and the issuance of paper money to be loaned to the farmers to help them weather the depression. Violence or threat of it spread throughout the country. Some state legislatures succumbed to the farmers' demands. When the Massachusetts' legislature failed to respond, the farmers closed the county courts to try to stop the foreclosures. In the same year, the Country Party of farmers in Rhode Island won a large majority in the state legislature and elected the Governor and Lt. Governor. The legislature considered proposals to transfer ownership of most private property to the state government or to "redistribute real estate equally among heads of households every thirteen years."[8]

America was in imminent danger of losing her hard won universal equality and unalienable rights to the chaos of anarchy and the tyranny of the majority. The overriding problem for the Constitutional Convention was to create a stable, strong national government, not to protect individual liberties.

The July 1787 Northwest Ordinance included the first United States Bill of Rights. The ordinance created the first United States officers with power directly over people and included the rights to *habeas corpus,* trial by jury, representative government, due process as under common law, bail, no cruel and unusual punishments, no excessive fines, just compensation for taking of private property or services, sanctity of contracts, and religious liberty. And, it banned slavery.

The Constitutional Convention was in session when the Continental Congress passed the Northwest Ordinance. Some delegates to the Convention supported including a bill of rights while others argued that a federal bill of rights would be superfluous to the states' bills of rights, which would not be repealed. And, the Constitution included some specific protections against both the federal and state governments: a prohibition against *ex post facto* laws, bills of attainder, and the state's impairment of the obligation of contracts.

When the proposed Constitution was sent to the Continental Congress, Richard Henry Lee proposed sending it to the states with a bill of rights from the Continental Congress because experience showed they were necessary to protect rights and liberties against those who govern:

> In conformity with these principles, and from respect for the public sentiment on this subject it is submitted that the new Constitution . . . be bottomed upon a declaration, or Bill of Rights, clearly and precisely stating the principles upon which this social compact is founded.[9]

Unpersuaded, the Continental Congress sent the Constitution to the states for ratification without comment on a bill of rights, and even struck the debate on a bill of rights from the journal of Congress to hide the issue from the states.

On October 6, 1787, in the first public explanation of the new federal Constitution and the difference between it and the state constitutions, James Wilson, a delegate to the Constitutional Convention from Pennsylvania, argued that unlike the state constitutions that granted to government all powers not expressly reserved, the federal constitution delegated only those powers expressly stated.[10] Wilson also thought a federal bill of rights would imply that the federal government had a power over rights protected even though the Constitution conferred no such power. Madison and Hamilton agreed.[11] Others, including Jefferson, opposed this interpretation, pointing out that the Constitution did not grant Congress the power to pass *ex post facto* laws, or bills of attainder, but it nevertheless prohibited them. Several states ratified the Constitution with a demand for a bill of rights.

The issue carried over into the election of the first Congress.[12] In the Constitutional Convention, Madison opposed a federal bill of rights, but in his campaign against James Monroe for a Virginia congressional seat, Madison changed his mind because of North Carolina's insistence on amendments before ratifying the Constitution, and because of the apparently increasing popular sympathy for the Anti-federalists. Once elected, Madison felt duty bound to propose a bill of rights, although both Federalists and Anti-federalists generally opposed it.

The House committee that considered Madison's proposed amendments deleted much of his language about natural rights, the right of the people to reform their government whenever adverse or inadequate, and statements about the purpose of government. How quickly rebels become rulers. Without George Washington's support, the amendments would have failed in the House of Representatives for lack of the necessary two-thirds majority. In the debate over the amendments, Federalist Samuel Livermore declared his constituents in New Hampshire would view them as of no more value "than a pinch of snuff; they went to secure rights never in danger."[13] The Bill of Rights was, however, quickly ratified.[14]

Ironically, the Bill of Rights, which now holds a place in the pantheon of legal declarations perhaps more sacred than the original Constitution, was virtually an afterthought. Locke's idea of political society created by a majority that create a government limited in its purposes and powers had been put into practice in the state constitutions, but more importantly in the federal Constitution. The unanswered question, however, is whether the founding fathers succeeded in adequately defining the purposes for which government may use coercive force.

The founding fathers erected several defenses against the abuse of power by the federal government. Two that require no further explanation are the dispersion of governmental power across a federal system[15] between the national and state governments and the separation of powers among the three branches of the federal government. The most important one, however, is a written constitution. The ambiguity between limited, delegated powers, and the purpose of the federal government to "promote the general welfare," among other things, was surely a necessary political compromise, but it was nevertheless a weakness that the creeping incrementalism of ambition, necessity and time have exploited.

The Constitution and Bill of Rights specifically limit government power. But, as a law, the Constitution, like any law, must be enforced when violated or it is "in vain." The only method to enforce it is a court of law,[16] which requires judges and lawyers. As unpleasant as the thought may be, there can be no rule of law without lawyers, because only in the courts can the wishful thinking of political philosophy become political and legal reality. In the continual defense of the Constitution, lawyers are the foot soldiers. How well lawyers and the courts have held the government to its delegated powers and limited purposes is the next topic.

The Supreme Court as Enforcer of Limited Government

The Early Years

The Supreme Court very early addressed whether the Constitution embodied a natural rights philosophy and the natural law which the Court could enforce against the federal or state governments or whether the

Court could only interpret and apply the specific text of the Constitution. In 1798 in *Calder v. Bull*,[17] Justice Chase argued:

> ... The people of the United States erected their Constitutions, or forms of government, to establish justice, to promote the general welfare, to secure the blessings of liberty; and to protect their persons and property from violence. The purposes for which men enter into society will determine the nature and terms of the social compact; and as they are the foundation of the legislative power, they will decide what are the proper objects of it: The nature, and ends of legislative power will limit the exercise of it. ... There are certain vital principles in our free Republican governments, which will determine and over-rule an apparent and flagrant abuse of legislative power; as to authorize manifest injustice by positive law; or to take away that security for personal liberty, or private property, for the protection whereof of the government was established. An ACT of the Legislature (for I cannot call it a law) contrary to the great first principles of the social compact, cannot be considered a rightful exercise of legislative authority. ... The genius, the nature, and the spirit, of our State Governments, amount to a prohibition of such acts of legislation; and the general principles of law and reason forbid them. ... To maintain that our Federal, or State, Legislature possesses such powers, if they had not been expressly restrained; would, in my opinion, be a political heresy, altogether inadmissible in our free republican governments.

Locke would have approved. Government was limited by the purposes for which it was created by the social compact, but to what source could a judge look to for the terms of the social compact other than the text of the Constitution without substituting his own reason for that of the people expressed through their legislature? Without some limit to legislative authority, there was no limited government, but without some limit to judicial authority, one unlimited master is substituted for another.

Justice Iredell disagreed with Chase and treated the text of the Constitution as the limit of the Court's power to invalidate a state or federal law, and his view, at least initially, prevailed:

> If any act of Congress, or the Legislature of a state, violates ... constitutional provisions, it is unquestionably void; though, I admit, that as the authority to declare it void is of a delicate and awful nature, the Court will never resort to that authority, but in a clear and urgent case. If, on the other hand, the Legislature of the Union, or the Legislature of any member of the Union, shall pass a law, within the general scope of their constitutional power, the Court cannot pronounce it to be void, merely because it is, in their judgment, contrary to the principles of natural justice. The ideas of natural justice are regulated by no fixed standard: the ablest and the purest men have

differed upon the subject; and all that the Court could properly say in such an event, would be, that the Legislature (possessed of an equal right of opinion) had passed an act which, in the opinion of the judges, was inconsistent with the abstract principles of natural justice.

Other justices of the court sought textual support for Justice Chase's view. In 1825, Justice Washington argued that the privileges and immunities clause in Article IV, § 2, clause 1, supported the protection of all citizens' *fundamental* rights,[18] and this view had its adherents at least into the twentieth century.[19] Other justices looked to other provisions of the Constitution and amendments to it for similar authority. Of course, the word "fundamental" does not appear in the text of the Constitution.

From 1798 to the Civil War, the Supreme Court held only two acts of Congress unconstitutional. In *Marbury v. Madison* (1803),[20] just before leaving office, President Adams appointed Marbury to be a justice of the peace for the District of Columbia, but Madison, the new Secretary of State, refused to deliver Marbury's commission to him. The Supreme Court, through Chief Justice Marshall, held that Madison could not legally or constitutionally withhold the commission, but Marbury had made a fatal mistake when he petitioned the Supreme Court to issue a writ of mandamus, which is a court order commanding a person to perform a specific act, i.e., to deliver Marbury's commission. The Court held that the statute passed by Congress authorizing the Supreme Court to issue a writ of mandamus was unconstitutional because it conferred original jurisdiction on the Supreme Court that the Constitution did not. Marshall supported the decision with several arguments on the construction of the language of the Constitution, but most importantly he based the decision on the role of a written constitution in limiting the powers of the government it created:

> That the people have an original right to establish, for their future government, such principles as, in their opinion, shall most conduce to their own happiness, is the basis on which the whole American fabric has been erected. The exercise of this original right is a very great exertion; nor can it nor ought it to be frequently repeated. The principles, therefore, so established are deemed fundamental. And as the authority, from which they proceed, is supreme, and can seldom act, they are designed to be permanent.
>
> *   *   *
>
> The powers of the legislature are defined and limited; and that those limits may not be mistaken or forgotten, the constitution is written. To what purpose are powers limited, and to what purpose is that limitation committed to writing; if these limits may, at any time, be passed by those intended to be restrained? . . .

Having claimed the power of judicial review, which the text of the Constitution does not confer, the Marshall Court did not again declare an act of Congress void. In the contract clause cases, however, the Marshall Court invalidated several state laws that interfered with the free use of property by corporations or individuals because they impaired the obligation of contracts and the inherent rights of individuals to be free of legislation interfering with vested rights. Before the Civil War, with only a few exceptions, the federal government did not try to limit individual "natural" rights. Not until fifty-four years later did the Supreme Court hold another act of Congress unconstitutional when it declared the Missouri Compromise void in *Dred Scott v. Sandford* (1857).[21]

The faith that many of the founders placed in the state governments to protect individual rights when they dismissed a federal bill of rights as unnecessary proved ill-founded. Before the Fourteenth Amendment was ratified after the Civil War, the Bill of Rights applied only to the federal government, not the states, which were free to, and at times did, ignore the Bill of Rights.[22] Even after the Fourteenth Amendment was adopted, the Bill of Rights have been applied to the states only piecemeal, in what can only be charitably described as an intellectually dishonest means to a necessary end.[23] While the Court rejected natural rights theory as an overarching, unwritten authority for judicial protection of individuals from government, natural rights theory is not dead.

The Civil War Amendments

Whether or not the founding fathers intended for the Constitution to embody a natural rights philosophy, it did not abolish slavery as a violation of the natural rights of slaves or the law of nature. On the contrary, the Constitution enshrined slavery with the three-fifths compromise for determining representation of the slave states in the House of Representatives, the limit on Congress abolishing the slave trade, and the fugitive slave clause.[24] The extension of universal equality to all men required another, much bloodier revolution, the Civil War. The legal outgrowth of this revolution was the ratification of the Civil War Amendments to the Constitution. The Thirteenth Amendment prohibits slavery. The Fifteenth prohibits the states from denying the right to vote because of race, color or previous condition of servitude. The next hundred plus years with the Fourteenth Amendment has given further evidence of the as yet unresolved conflict between natural rights theory and the text of the Constitution as the founding social and legal document of the United States.

Due Process, Equal Protection and Economic Freedom

The Fourteenth Amendment, in part, provides:

> No State shall make or enforce any law which shall abridge the privileges or immunities of citizens of the United States; nor shall any State deprive any person of liberty or property without due process of law, nor deny to any person within its jurisdiction the equal protection of the laws.

The Fourteenth Amendment does not expressly apply the Bill of Rights to the states. When presented with this contention, the Supreme Court repeatedly rejected it, convinced Congress did not intend the amendment to be so radical a shift in the balance of power between the states and the federal government.[25] The incorporation of many of these rights is discussed further below regarding the Court's civil liberty cases.

After the Civil War, a tremendous economic expansion occurred, and the states tried to regulate the expanding industries. Many of these laws were challenged as a violation of due process or equal protection of the law. At first the Supreme Court allowed many of these regulations as a use of the state's police power, that is, the power to protect the health, safety, welfare and morals of the public, which were held unconstitutional only if they violated specific provision of the Constitution or were found to be arbitrary. Later, any law found to be inconsistent with a majority of the justices' view of appropriate restraints on liberty was invalidated.

1874 to 1900

From 1874 to 1900, even as the Court upheld a law as within a state's police power, it sometimes suggested limits beyond which the state legislature could not go. In *Munn v. Illinois*[26] (1877), the Illinois Constitution explicitly declared grain elevators to be "affected with a public interest," and a statute implemented that provision by setting maximum rates grain elevator operators could charge for storage. The Court upheld the statute as within the state's police power because grain elevators were "affected with a public interest." The Court alluded to what would become the doctrine of liberty of contract when it said, "Undoubtedly, in mere private contracts, relating to matters in which the public has no interest . . . the legislature has no control over such a contract."[27] The Court did not decide whether a private contract becomes one "in which the public has [an] interest" simply by the state constitution or state legislature declaring it to be or whether there is some limit that prevents a private contract from being constitutionally or legislatively turned into one "affected with a public interest." The ultimate question is, however, in what territory is a constitutional or legislative majority forbidden to exert its power.

In *Barbier v. Connelly*[28] (1884), the Court upheld a San Francisco ordinance requiring laundries to obtain a health certificate that the business could be operated without injury to the neighborhood by unsanitary conditions or fire. The Court stated the limits imposed on state governments by the Fourteenth Amendment:

> The fourteenth amendment, in declaring that no state 'shall deprive any person of life, liberty, or property without due process of law, nor deny to any person within its jurisdiction the equal protection of the laws,' undoubtedly intended not only that there should be no arbitrary deprivation of life or liberty, or arbitrary spoliation of property, but that equal protection and security should be given to all under like circumstances in the enjoyment of their personal and civil rights; that all persons should be equally entitled to pursue their happiness, and acquire and enjoy property; that they should have like access to the courts of the country for the protection of their persons and property, the prevention and redress of wrongs, and the enforcement of contracts; that no impediment should be interposed to the pursuits of any one, except as applied to the same pursuits by others under like circumstances; that no greater burdens should be laid upon one than are laid upon others in the same calling and condition; and that in the administration of criminal justice no different or higher punishment should be imposed upon one than such as is prescribed to all for like offenses.
>
> But neither the amendment–broad and comprehensive as it is–nor any other amendment, was designed to interfere with the power of the state, sometimes termed its police power, to prescribe regulations to promote the health, peace, morals, education, and good order of the people, and to legislate so as to increase the industries of the state, develop its resources, and add to its wealth and prosperity.

While acknowledging the intent to enshrine universal equality, the Court nevertheless, states that when due process and equal protection conflict with the state's exercise of its police power, the police power wins because due process and equal protection were not intended to limit the state's police power. This is in spite of the fact that the Constitution nowhere mentions the state's police powers and the Fourteenth Amendment explicitly applies to the states.

In *Mugler v. Kansas*[29] (1887), the Kansas Constitution and an implementing statute prohibited the sale of intoxicating liquor and required all businesses that made or sold alcohol to be closed as a public nuisance. The Court upheld the acts as within the state's police power, but again noted that a state's police power is not unlimited, stating:

> . . . As was said in *Munn* . . . while power does not exist with the whole people to control rights that are purely and exclusively private, government may require 'each citizen to so conduct himself, and so use his own property, as not unnecessarily to injure another.' But by whom, or by what authority, is it to be determined . . . [what] will injuriously affect the public? Power to determine such questions, so as to bind all, must exist somewhere; . . . Under our system that [police] power is lodged with the legislative branch of the government . . . to determine, primarily, what measures are appropriate or needful for the protection of the public morals, the public health, or the public safety.
>
> . . . [But] the courts must obey the constitution rather than the law-making department of government, and must, upon their own responsibility, determine whether, in any particular case, these limits have been passed. . . . If, therefore, a statute purporting to have been enacted to protect the public health, the public morals, or the public safety, has no real or substantial relation to those objects, or is a palpable invasion of rights secured by the fundamental law, it is the duty of the courts to so adjudge, and thereby give effect to the constitution.

As Chief Justice Marshall pointed out, the consequence of a written constitution is that judges must decide when a law is inconsistent with the Constitution. The Fourteenth Amendment's prohibition against deprivation of life, liberty or property without due process or equal protection of the law requires judges to answer a basic question. Does due process of law require only that a political majority follow fair procedures when it makes laws, or does it also limit the purposes and means used no matter how scrupulously fair the procedures followed in passing it are? Following fair procedures is usually referred to as procedural due process, while the objects and means are substantive due process. If due process is only a rule of procedure, it offers no protection whatsoever to an individual against the power of a political majority exercised following fair procedures. All possessions are held by the grace of a majority's refusal to take it. But, written constitutions are intended to limit the power of government, so merely requiring fair procedures offers little protection from an abuse of power. The drafters of the Fourteenth

Amendment certainly did not intend to require the states merely to use fair procedures when enacting laws that denied former slaves the civil rights that whites had always enjoyed. There must be some substance to due process of law and equal protection of the law, but the Constitution itself does not provide it.

If the due process and equal protection clauses of the Fourteenth Amendment are to have any substance, then the Supreme Court must create and enforce a jurisprudence of natural justice, i.e., due process and equal protection. The drafters of the Civil War Amendments have in essence said, "We want universal equality, but we want you, the Court, to make it a reality." The Court's Fourteenth Amendment and Bill of Rights decisions are the tortured birth of universal equality into the world of legal rights. The Bill of Rights and Fourteenth Amendment are natural justice reduced to writing and made the law of society, like the liberties of Magna Charta were reduced to writing. Putting these principles in writing gives natural justice the imprimatur of the consent implicit in positive law.

The dichotomy between individual rights, which the government may not infringe, but is, in fact, required to protect, and the scope of the police power to promote morals–a political majority's morals–increase industries, develop resources and add to the welfare and prosperity of society, is the basic social conflict that requires artificial rights founded on the morality of equality to resolve.

The statement in *Barbier* "that there should be no arbitrary deprivation of life or liberty, or arbitrary spoliation of property," and the slightly more specific statement in *Mugler* that the law must have a "real or substantial relation" to it objects and not be a "palpable invasion of rights secured by the fundamental law" appear as attempts to state a "fixed standard" of natural justice. They are all part of the attempt to adequately state and enforce universal equality. The Court's search for the principles of natural justice was evolving by including new interests or relationships of individuals that it would protect from the power of a political majority.

In *Allgeyer v. Louisiana* (1897),[30] the Court struck down a Louisiana law invalidating a marine insurance policy because it deprived the defendant of his liberty without due process.

> ... [W]e think the statute is a violation of the fourteenth amendment of the federal constitution, in that it deprives the defendants of their liberty without due process of law. ... The 'liberty' mentioned in that amendment means, not only the right of the citizen to be free from the mere physical restraint of his person, as by incarceration, but the term is deemed to embrace

the right of the citizen to be free in the enjoyment of all his faculties; to be free to use them in all lawful ways; to live and work where he will; to earn his livelihood by any lawful calling; to pursue any livelihood or avocation; and for that purpose to enter into all contracts which may be proper, necessary, and essential to his carrying out to a successful conclusion the purposes above mentioned.

The following year in *Holden v. Hardy* (1898),[31] the Court upheld a Utah statute that limited miner and smelter's working hours as within the state's police power upon concluding the Utah legislature adequately demonstrated the ill effects on the health of miners addressed by the statute.

> We have no disposition to criticise the many authorities which hold that state statutes restricting the hours of labor are unconstitutional. . . . It is sufficient to say of them that they have no application to cases where the legislature had adjudged that a limitation is necessary for the preservation of the health of employees, and there are reasonable grounds for believing that such determination is supported by the facts. The question in each case is whether the legislature has adopted the statute in exercise of a reasonable discretion, or whether its action be a mere excuse for an unjust discrimination, or the oppression or spoliation of a particular class.

The Court continued its struggle to state a first principle of natural justice to limit the power of a political majority. After *Holden* there were two criteria. One is the object of the law, e.g., protecting the morals, health, safety or welfare of workers, which the court says is within the state legislature's police power. The second is what evidence will satisfy the Court that the law actually protects the health, safety or welfare. The outcome of a case can rest on either ground. The law is invalid if its objects are outside the police power, or if the evidence shows "no real or substantial relation to those objects" or a "mere excuse."

1900 to 1937

From 1900 to 1937, the Court further expanded the substance of due process to protect individuals from legislation that used means the Court considered not reasonably related to a legitimate governmental end. The Court struck down labor regulations, price controls, and other economic laws considered illegitimate objects of legislation. With the dual test of legitimate objects and evidence to support them, substantive due process continued to be "regulated by no fixed standard, [and] the ablest and the purest men" disagreed. Yet now the Court could and did say when "the Legislature (possessed of an equal right of opinion) had passed an act which, in the opinion of the judges, was inconsistent with the abstract principles of natural justice."

In *Lochner v. New York*,[32] (1905), the Court again confronted the conflict between the individual and the power of a political majority, and the Court's role in resolving that conflict by reference to the Constitution. In *Lochner*, the Court struck down a New York statute that prohibited bakers from working more than sixty hours per week or ten hours per day. The majority stated the constitutional issue as follows:

> The statute necessarily interferes with the right of contract between the employer and employees, concerning the number of hours in which the latter may labor in the bakery of the employer. The general right to make a contract in relation to his business is part of the liberty of the individual protected by the 14th Amendment of the Federal Constitution. [citation omitted] Under that provision no state can deprive any person of life, liberty, or property without due process of law. The right to purchase or to sell labor is part of the liberty protected by this amendment, unless there are circumstances which exclude the right. There are, however, certain powers, existing in the sovereignty of each state in the Union, somewhat vaguely termed police powers, the exact description and limitation of which have not been attempted by the courts. Those powers, broadly stated, and without, at present, any attempt at a more specific limitation, relate to the safety, health, morals, and general welfare of the public. Both property and liberty are held on such reasonable conditions as may be imposed by the governing power of the state in the exercise of those powers, and with such conditions the 14th Amendment was not designed to interfere. [citations omitted]
>
> The state, therefore, has power to prevent the individual from making certain kinds of contracts, and in regard to them the Federal Constitution offers no protection. If the contract be one which the state, in the legitimate exercise of its police power, has the right to prohibit, it is not prevented from prohibiting it by the 14th Amendment. . . . [W]hen the state, by its legislature, in the assumed exercise of its police powers, has passed an act which seriously limits the right to labor or the right of contract in regard to their means of livelihood between persons who are sui juris (both employer and employee), it becomes of great importance to determine which shall prevail,–the right of the individual to labor for such time as he may choose, or the right of the state to prevent the individual from laboring, or from entering into any contract to labor, beyond a certain time prescribed by the state.

The majority admit they cannot state a fixed standard of natural justice, i.e., due process, but the Constitution compels them to decide when a state law is a "legitimate exercise" of the police power. Thus, the Court defaults to an *ad hoc* intuitionism to declare the New York statute an unconstitutional restriction on the liberty of contract.

Justices Holmes in dissent accused the majority of imposing its theory of economic policy on the states:

> This case is decided upon an economic theory which a large part of the country does not entertain. . . . I strongly believe that my agreement or disagreement has nothing to do with the right of a [political] majority to embody their opinions in law. It is settled by various decisions of this court that state constitutions and state laws may regulate life in many ways which we as legislators might think as injudicious, or if you like as tyrannical, as this, and which, equally with this, interfere with the liberty to contract. Sunday laws and usury laws are ancient examples . . . The liberty of the citizen to do as he likes so long as he does not interfere with the liberty of others to do the same, . . . is interfered with by school laws, by the Postoffice, by every state or municipal institution which takes his money for purposes thought desirable, whether he likes it or not. . . . [W]e sustained the Massachusetts vaccination law, . . . statutes and decisions cutting down the liberty to contract by way of combination . . . prohibition of sales of stock on margins, or for future delivery . . . [and] an eight-hour law for miners. . . . Some of these laws embody convictions or prejudices which judges are likely to share. Some may not. But a Constitution is not intended to embody a particular economic theory, whether of paternalism and the organic relation of the citizen to the state or of laissez faire.
>
> It is made for people of fundamentally differing views, and the accident of our finding certain opinions natural and familiar, or novel, and even shocking, ought not to conclude our judgment upon the question whether statutes embodying them conflict with the Constitution of the United States.
>
> . . . I think that the word 'liberty,' in the 14th Amendment, is perverted when it is held to prevent the natural outcome of a dominant opinion, unless it can be said that a rational and fair man necessarily would admit that the statute proposed would infringe fundamental principles as they have been understood by the traditions of our people and our law. . . .

The last sentence is Justice Holmes' attempt at a first principle of a jurisprudence of natural justice. His references to "natural" events, whether unconscious or intentional, and fundamental principles, not the text of the Constitution because it does not provide an answer, demonstrate the natural justice foundation of his opinion. What makes "opinions" or the "outcome of a dominant opinion" natural? Like Hobbes and Locke, Holmes appeals to reason as the final arbiter when he makes the test of constitutionality "a rational and fair man." Such references always remind me of one of my favorite questions to ask prospective jurors in a trial: "How many of you are biased and prejudiced?" I have never had a juror answer that question, and I have never met a judge who thought he or she was not rational and fair.

In *Muller v. Oregon*,[33] (1908) the Court upheld a statute regulating the working hours of women as reasonably related to the welfare of women. The famous Brandeis Brief convinced the Court that there was sufficient evidence of a proper exercise of the police power. When *Muller* was decided, women still could not vote.

In *Nebbia v. New York*[34] (1934), Nebbia was convicted of the crime of selling milk for less than the minimum price set by law. A five to four majority of the Court, through Justice Roberts, upheld the law as a legitimate exercise of the police power and rejected a claim that the milk industry was not "affected with a pubic interest." Echoing Justice Holmes' dissent in *Lochner*, the majority said, "A state is free to adopt whatever economic policy may reasonably be deemed to promote public welfare, and to enforce that policy by legislation adopted to its purpose." One can only wonder whether the solutions to economic depression proposed in the Rhode Island, New Hampshire and other state legislatures in response to the post-Revolutionary War depression would have passed this constitutional test.

Nebbia was decided in the depths of the Great Depression, and the four dissenters pointed out that the New York statute expressly stated it was temporary and in response to a legislatively declared emergency involving the supply of milk. The four dissenters argued:

> The argument advanced here would support general prescription of prices for farm products, groceries, shoes, clothing, all the necessities of modern civilization, as well as labor, when some Legislature finds and declares such action advisable and for the public good. This Court has declared that a state may not by legislative fiat convert a private business into a public utility. [citations omitted] And if it be now ruled that one dedicates his property to public use whenever he embarks on an enterprise which the Legislature may think it desirable to bring under control, this is but to declare that rights guaranteed by the Constitution exist only so long as supposed public interest does not require their extinction. To adopt such a view, of course, would put an end to liberty under the Constitution.

The dissenters were right.

The New Deal Cases

When Franklin Roosevelt was elected president, his New Deal created numerous federal programs intended to relieve the misery of the Great Depression and to get the economy going again. These programs ran up against the limited powers delegated to the federal government in the Constitution and a Supreme Court still committed to the liberty of contract. The Court struck down most of the New Deal legislation, often because it violated the powers reserved to the states in the Constitution. Other programs were found to be beyond the power granted to Congress in the Constitution.[35] When the legislation did not involve state's interests, and was within the federal government's powers, it was usually upheld.[36]

In 1937, President Roosevelt tried to change the Constitution by changing the judges on the court. His plan to pack the court with judges sympathetic to his New Deal failed, but Justice Roberts, who authored *Nebbia* and had voted with the majority in striking down the New Deal cases, had a change of heart and switched sides.[37] After 1937, the Court rejected all substantive due process challenges to economic and social welfare legislation.

In *Lincoln Federal Labor Union v. Northwestern Iron & Metal Co.* (1945),[38] the Court overruled *Allgeyer* and *Lochner* and held that a state may legislate against what it considers injurious internal commercial and business practices if the laws do not violate a specific federal constitutional prohibition or valid federal law. The pendulum of constitutional interpretation thus swung back to Justice Iredell's side, at least for economic and social welfare laws.

In *Williamson v. Lee Optical Co* (1955),[39] the Court went even further in rejecting a due process and equal protection challenges to an Oklahoma statute that prohibited opticians from fitting or duplicating eyeglasses. The Court found no specific constitutional prohibition to the Oklahoma statute, but it went even further by suggesting hypothetical reasons that would support the regulation even if the legislature never considered or relied upon them.[40] By 1975, with different justices and a better economy, numerous restrictions on commercial activity fairly recently upheld were substantially invalidated on anti-trust[41] and First Amendment[42] grounds as the Court extended the anti-trust laws and the First Amendment's protection of free speech from political or ideological speech to some "commercial speech."[43]

The Civil Liberties Cases

In 1908, in *Twining v. State of New Jersey*[44] the Court again rejected a claim that the Due Process Clause of the Fourteenth Amendment made any of the Bill of Rights, specifically the right against self-incrimination, applicable to the states, and instead restated the test of due process[45] that had not been violated:

> ... Is it a fundamental principle of liberty and justice which inheres in the very idea of free government and is the inalienable right of a citizen of such a government? ... In approaching such a question it must not be forgotten that in a free representative government nothing is more fundamental than the right of the people, through their appointed servants, to govern themselves in accordance with their own will, except so far as they have restrained themselves by constitutional limits specifically established, ...

Twining's refusal to apply the Bill of Rights to the States began to erode until finally the dam burst. In 1917, the Court relied on due process in protecting property rights to strike down a Louisville city ordinance prohibiting blacks from moving into areas where the residents were primarily white.[46] In 1923, a law prohibiting teaching in a language other than English was held to violate the liberty to make educational decisions.[47] In 1925, the Court upheld a conviction under a criminal anarchy statute, but assumed that the Due Process Clause in the Fourteenth Amendment protected freedom of speech under the First Amendment of the Bill of Rights.[48] By 1936, the Court held a state may not deny a criminal defendant counsel or use a forced confession in violation of the Sixth or Fifth Amendments of the Bill of Rights.[49]

In *Rochin v. California* (1952),[50] the question before the Court was whether the police violated Rochin's right to due process under the Fourteenth Amendment. Without a warrant, the police forced open Rochin's Door. When he tried to swallow two capsules on his night stand, they unsuccessfully tried to forcibly remove the capsules from his mouth. They then took him to a hospital and directed a doctor to pump his stomach against his will and retrieved the two capsules. Rochin was convicted of drug possession for the two capsules.

Justice Frankfurter wrote the opinion of the Court reversing the conviction, but the opinion was more a labored self-defense of the Court, than an explanation of why the police violated due process of law. This can be explained in part by Justice Frankfurter's longstanding,[51] vehement, even contemptuous, rejection of the idea that the due process clause is simply "a compendious expression of the original federal Bill of Rights." In reversing Rochin's conviction as a violation of due process, he cited the lower court's decisions calling the forced regurgitation of evidence "shocking" and self-incrimination as surely as a "verbal confession." But, he did not recognize the Fifth Amendment prohibition against self-incrimination as applying to the states. He explained at length that although "due process of law, . . . is not to be turned into a destructive dogma against the states in the administration of their systems of criminal justice," the Court must decide whether the police offended "those canons of decency and fairness which express the notions of justice of English-speaking peoples even toward those charged with the most heinous offenses.'"

He admitted that there is no fixed standard for deciding the case other than "those personal immunities . . . 'so rooted in the traditions and conscience of our people as to be ranked as fundamental, . . . or are 'implicit in the concept of ordered liberty,'" but he claimed this formulation was a "settled conception of the Due Process Clause" and that in dealing "with human rights, the absence of formal exactitude, or want of fixity of meaning, is not an unusual or even regrettable attribute of constitutional provisions." With this glib statement, Justice Frankfurter transmuted the lead of no fixed standard of natural justice into constitutional gold. He countered Justice Iredell, without mentioning him, with a litany of supposed protections against judicial abuse: "[t]he vague contours of the Due Process Clause do not leave judges at large" because judges are limited by "the whole nature of the judicial process," and "considerations deeply rooted in reason and the compelling traditions of the legal profession," and "the duty to exercis[e] a judgment, within the narrow confines of judicial power in reviewing State convictions, upon interests of society pushing in opposite directions," and "established standards of judicial behavior," and "requisite detachment" and "sufficient objectivity" and the judges' "habit of self-discipline and self-criticism, incertitude that one's own views are incontestable and alert tolerance toward views not shared" and "an evaluation based on disinterested inquiry pursued in the spirit of science, on a balanced order of facts exactly and fairly stated" and being "duly mindful of reconciling the needs both of continuity and of change in a progressive society." In a phrase that has become indispensable to the lexicon of every imagination-challenged trial lawyer, he concluded, "This conduct shocks the conscience."

Justice Black concurred in reversing Rochin's conviction but accused Justice Frankfurter of using natural law:

> What the majority hold is that the Due Process Clause empowers this Court to nullify any state law if its application 'shocks the conscience',

offends 'a sense of justice' or runs counter to the 'decencies of civilized conduct.' . . .

Justice Douglas concurred in the judgment but pointed out a contradiction in the Court's holding:

> [W]e cannot in fairness free the state courts from that command [Fifth Amendment] and yet excoriate them for flouting the 'decencies of civilized conduct' when they admit the [self-incriminating] evidence. That is to make the rule turn not on the Constitution but on the idiosyncrasies of the judges who sit here.

It did not take much longer before the Court held all but a few of the Bill of Rights were fundamental rights applicable to the states by way of incorporation into the Fourteenth Amendment due process clause.[52] Now any state regulation of these rights must further a compelling state interest and use means least restrictive of those rights or it is unconstitutionality. If a fundamental right is not affected, the state law does not violate due process or equal protection unless it arbitrarily deprives a person of life, liberty or property, or is not rationally related to a legitimate state interest.

The Court has, however, gone beyond the Bill of Rights in holding some rights to be fundamental. In 1961, Justice Harlan, Jr., advocated in a dissent the right of privacy for married persons to possess and use contraceptives.[53] In *Griswold v. Connecticut* (1965),[54] the Court recognized that "fundamental" right, and found it not in the text of the Constitution or Bill of Rights, but in the "penumbras" of the Bill of Rights. Justice Goldberg relied on the Ninth Amendment: "The enumeration in the Constitution, of certain rights, shall not be construed to deny or disparage others retained by the people." He cited the maxim of constitutional and statutory interpretation that no "clause in the constitution is intended to be without effect," and concluded that liberty includes fundamental rights, not just, nor all, those in the Bill of Rights. These nonenumerated fundamental rights are the "liberties that are 'so rooted in the traditions and conscience of our people as to be ranked as fundamental.'"

In 1972 in *Roe v. Wade*,[55] the Court extended the fundamental right of privacy to include a woman's right to an abortion. When the "ablest and purest" differ, political strife will surely follow. The report of the combatants' artillery often echoes across the political landscape. No other case since *Dred Scott* has forced the opposing views of Justices Chase and Iredell out of the Court and into the political arena in the debate over the qualifications, or rather judicial philosophy, of federal judicial appointees. Should they be disciples of Chase or Iredell?

Twenty years after *Roe,* the Court decided *Planned Parenthood of Southeastern Pennsylvania v. Casey* (1992).[56] The Pennsylvania Abortion Control Act of 1982 placed several restrictions on a woman seeking an abortion, including some specifically intended to dissuade women from having an abortion. The Court was sharply divided, and like the three preceding abortion cases,[57] no majority opinion emerged. Although each side offers many pragmatic reasons, the crux of the division is simply whether the right to an abortion is properly modified by the adjective "fundamental." If so, *Roe* should be reaffirmed. If not, it should be overruled.

In a plurality opinion, Justices O'Connor, Kennedy and Souter argue that a woman's decision to terminate her pregnancy is a "liberty" protected by the "substantive component" of the Due Process Clause of the Fourteenth Amendment. They recognize that neither the Bill of Rights nor state laws when the Fourteenth Amendment was adopted supported a right to an abortion. They claim, however, that substantive due process claims require the Court to exercise "reasoned judgment" to set the scope of individual liberty "within the demands of organized society." They rely on cases extending constitutional protection to personal decisions relating to marriage, procreation, family relationships, child rearing and education, contraception, and whether to bear or beget a child.[58] *Roe,* they argue, followed the reasoning and tradition of these precedents. Further, society has not rejected *Roe,* (the plurality does not say how society could reject *Roe,* short of a constitutional amendment) and a majority of the Court has expressly reaffirmed it in later cases.[59] Furthermore, as a rule of personal autonomy and bodily integrity, like cases limiting government's power to require or bar rejecting medical treatment, post-*Roe* decisions accord with *Roe's* view that a state's interest in protecting life, much less the potential life of a fetus, does not override individual liberty

Justice Blackmun, the author of *Roe,* argues that the Court correctly applied past precedents on bodily integrity and privacy to include a woman's right to choose to have an abortion as fundamental. He levels his most acerbic criticism at the four justices who advocate overruling *Roe,* accusing the Chief Justice of a "stunted conception of individual liberty," within which "a woman considering whether to terminate a pregnancy is entitled to no more protection than adulterers, murderers, and so-called "sexual deviates.'" He ridicules the notion that the democratic process will fill the void left by an overruled *Roe*: "[O]ur country since its founding has recognized that there are certain fundamental liberties that are not to be left to the whims of an election. A woman's right to reproductive choice is one of those fundamental liberties. Accordingly, that liberty need not seek refuge at the ballot box."

Justice Stevens joins most of Justice O'Connor's plurality opinion.[60] He reiterates *Roe's* holding that an unborn fetus is not a person entitled to constitutional protections, a holding he states no justice of the Court has disagreed with. The state's interest in potential human life is therefore not of constitutional dimension, i.e., not fundamental; however, a woman's interest in bodily integrity is and must be respected. Furthermore, any state opposition or regulation must have a legitimate purpose consistent with the First Amendment, and not a theological or sectarian purpose.

Chief Justice Rehnquist, joined by Justices White, Scalia, and Thomas, argue *Roe* should be overruled. Their pragmatic reasons included confusion and uncertainty created by the Court's inability to produce a majority opinion, or state clearly the constitutional standard for judging when a state statute affecting abortion is unconstitutional. On the crucial issue, however, Chief Justice Rehnquist argues that the *Roe* Court was wrong when it relied on pre-*Roe*, "right of privacy" cases[61] to hold the right to abortion is fundamental. The decision to purposefully terminate a potential life is different in kind from the decision to marry, have children or use contraceptives. A woman's right to have an abortion is a form of liberty within the Due Process Clause, but American historical traditions evidenced by the English common law and American abortion statutes when the Fourteenth Amendment was adopted and when *Roe* was decided do not support the conclusion that the right to terminate a pregnancy is "implicit in the concept of ordered liberty." . . . [or a] principle of justice so rooted in the traditions and conscience of our people as to be ranked as fundamental." Therefore, any rational relationship between the statute and the state's legitimate interests in protecting the potential life of a fetus will sustain the statute. Since the majority concedes protecting potential life is a legitimate state interest, a ban on abortion would be constitutional. With *Roe* overruled, the Court could thus quit the abortion battlefield, or as Justice Scalia calls it, "the abortion-umpiring business," the same as the Court quit the field of social and economic welfare legislation when it overruled *Lochner*.

Justice Scalia, joined by the same minority, argued that the issue was not whether the right to abortion was a liberty, even an important one. He agreed it is. Rather, it is whether that liberty is protected by the Fourteenth Amendment to the Constitution:

I am sure it is not. I reach that conclusion not because of anything so exalted as my views concerning the "concept of existence, of meaning, of the universe, and of the mystery of human life." Rather, I reach it for the same reason I reach the conclusion that bigamy is not constitutionally protected–because of two simple facts: (1) the Constitution says absolutely nothing about it, and (2) the longstanding traditions of American society have permitted it to be legally proscribed.

... [Abortion rights should] be resolved like most important questions in our democracy: by citizens trying to persuade one another and then voting.

Echoing Justice Douglas in *Rochin*, Justice Scalia criticizes the plurality's "reasoned judgment" by quoted Justice Curtis's dissent in *Dred Scott*:

[W]hen a strict interpretation of the Constitution, according to the fixed rules which govern the interpretation of laws, is abandoned, and the theoretical opinions of individuals are allowed to control its meaning, we have no longer a Constitution; we are under the government of individual men, who for the time being have power to declare what the Constitution is, according to their own views of what it ought to mean.

Is Justice Scalia's view any less theoretical when he agrees that the right to an abortion is a liberty, just not one protected by the Fourteenth Amendment? The Fourteenth Amendment protects "life, liberty and property." It does not qualify these objects with adjectives such as fundamental, important or run-of-the-mill. Neither the *Chasers* nor the *Iredellites* explain why such non-textual modifiers decide constitutional questions. Professor John Nowak states, "fundamental rights analysis is simply no more than the modern recognition of the natural law concepts first espoused by Justice Chase in *Calder v. Bull.*"[62] Amen.

The Thirteenth Amendment

The Thirteenth Amendment prohibiting slavery is unique in the Constitution. It is the only provision that addresses the relations between private citizens. The rest of the Constitution addresses the structure of, the powers granted to, and the limits imposed on the state and federal governments. The omission of any principle to govern the relations of private individuals, and thus the laws Congress and state legislatures may pass governing private legal rights, is one of the great weaknesses of the Constitution. Ignoring for the moment government's purpose to protect society from foreign threats, according to Locke, the only purpose of government is to protect the individual's natural right to life, liberty and property in accordance with to the law of nature. Government is supposed to be the disinterested arbiter and the power equalizer between private individuals, but the Constitution does not even include this vague notion as a limit on the use of coercive force by government.

Constitutional Authorization of Force and Individual Rights

The adoption of the Sixteenth Amendment authorizing an unapportioned personal income tax, and the Eighteenth Amendment prohibiting alcoholic beverages illustrates how a political majority can constitutionally take property and do with it as it wishes. What a constitutional majority protects, it can take away. As utilitarianism spread its infection in the psyche of the electorate with each new generation, the moral justification and political expediency for taking one person's property to give it to another who "needs" it more, has become virtually irresistible to politicians pandering to an indifferent electorate. The bidding war in the 2000 presidential election over a prescription drug benefit for senior citizens is uncomfortably reminiscent of the Praetorian Guard selling the imperial throne of Rome to the highest bidder. Even accepting, as I do, the righteous motives of both bidders, the parallel is nevertheless foreboding.

Imposing a tax to confer a private benefit on another was once against the fundamental law.[63] In 1657, a Massachusetts magistrate held void a town of Ipswich tax to give the local minister a house. "[T]o take from Peter to give it to Paul,' is against the fundamental law. 'If noe kinge or Parliament can justly enact or cause that one man's estate, in whole or in part, may be taken from him and given to another without his owne consent, then sure the major part of a towne or other inferior powers cannot doe it.'"[64] In *Calder v. Bull,* Justice Chase gave an illustration of the natural justice limits on legislative authority when he said that "taking from A and giving to B" would violate natural justice.

In 1900, the Supreme Court restated the problem as one of democratic utilitarianism when it upheld a progressive inheritance tax:

> Lastly, it is urged that the progressive rate feature of the statute is so repugnant to fundamental principles of equality and justice that the law should be held to be void, even although it transgresses no express limitation in the Constitution. . . .
>
> . . . [T]axes imposed with reference to the ability of the person upon whom the burden is placed to bear the same have been levied from the foundation of the government. So, also, some authoritative thinkers, and a number of economic writers, contend that a progressive tax is more just and equal than

a proportional one. In the absence of constitutional limitation, the question whether it is or is not is legislative and not judicial. The grave consequences which it is asserted must arise in the future if the right to levy a progressive tax be recognized involves in its ultimate aspect the mere assertion that free and representative government is a failure, and that the grossest abuses of power are foreshadowed unless the courts usurp a purely legislative function. If a case should ever arise, where an arbitrary and confiscatory exaction is imposed bearing the guise of a progressive or any other form of tax, it will be time enough to consider whether the judicial power can afford a remedy by applying inherent and fundamental principles for the protection of the individual, even though there be no express authority in the Constitution to do so. . . .[65]

Doubtless, the "authoritative thinkers" and "economic writers" the Court referred to were utilitarians. The likelihood of any judicial remedy evaporated with the adoption of the Sixteenth Amendment. Like the American Tories after the American Revolution who condemned the Declaration of Independence as treason, or the doctor kidnapped by a town without a doctor, the adoption of the Sixteenth Amendment by a super-majority following constitutional procedures is no comfort at all for those who oppose it.

The time "to consider whether the judicial power can afford a remedy" came in the Great Depression,[66] but rather than provide a remedy, the Supreme Court adopted Stalin's logic when he quipped that one man's death is a tragedy, while a million men's death is a statistic. In 1937, when the Supreme Court upheld the Social Security Act it said that taxing for the needs of the millions of unemployed is in the general welfare.[67]

Suppose instead of adopting the Sixteenth Amendment, the Thirteenth Amendment had been repealed and all persons descended from slaves at the time of the Emancipation Proclamation were declared to be slaves of their former master's descendants? Hopefully, no majority would ever again attempt such a legalized atrocity, but only the power of alliance of those who oppose it could prevent it as the original Constitution's sanction and protection of slavery proves. We must never forget that the Final Solution was cloaked in legality. The Sixteenth Amendment pales in comparison to the repeal of the Thirteenth Amendment or the Final Solution, but it surely illustrates the conundrum of the role of democratic institutions and majorities, even constitutional super-majorities, in making decisions about the use of coercive force against a minority, if only, if especially, a minority of one.

With limits, a personal income tax may be the means of supporting government most consistent with universal equality. It is, however, the absence of any real limits on how a majority can wield this "power to destroy" that makes it so dangerous. Nothing prevents a political majority from passing a "Billionaire's Tax"[68] of one hundred percent on all income and property of all citizens with a net worth of more than one billion dollars, and use all the proceeds for an "earned income tax credit" for all people below the "poverty line." Who could successfully defend the multi-billionaires of the United States, the wealthiest one-thousandth of a percent, and their *need* for more than a billion dollars against the utilitarian moral imperative of the greater good for the greatest number?[69] Social Security retirement and Medicare are precisely this kind of scheme, but billionaires are not the only ones taxed. All working people pay the tax.

The Social Security tax is, in fact, a regressive tax, not a progressive tax, since the income subject to the tax is capped. The billionare pays the least tax as a percentage of income. The person who has paid a lifetime of Social Security taxes now has a justified sense of having paid for his Social Security benefits when he reaches retirement age, and the courts have labeled the benefits entitlements. As is well known, however, Social Security is not a savings account, but a tax like any other tax. The earnings of "A" are transferred to "B."

Again, Social Security is not evil. Its purpose is a part of the complexity necessary for an individualistic society to emerge. But, the current Social Security system is another example of the virtually unlimited power of a political majority. The same is true of Medicare, Medicaid, welfare, etc. Each of these programs, perhaps in the same, perhaps in a different form, would be a substantial part of an individualistic society's obligation to provide the necessities to all citizens and wards who cannot provide their own with constructive power.

Roe did not begin the divisions on the Supreme Court about its role as the interpreter and enforcer of the fundamental law of the United States. Nor did *Roe* begin, or resolve, the conflict between the power of a political majority and the right of individuals to be free of that political power. The justices of the Court have continually clashed over the appropriate interpretation of the Constitution, but those battles are not the justices' fault. Nor is the President who nominates them, nor are the political majorities who elect the President nor the Senators who confirm them to blame. The conflict persists because the Constitution does not resolve it. The Constitution embodies many noble sentiments that after more than 200 years of judicial interpretation the Court has been unable to turn into specific, understandable and predictable legal rules that can be followed by the ablest and purest men or the brightest lawyers, much less the average citizen. Due process, liberty, and equal protection, are just a few of these noble sentiments. But, to paraphrase Justice Douglas in *Rochin,* we cannot in fairness give the Justices of the Supreme Court no fixed standard of natural justice yet excoriate them for differing about how to turn the abstract principles of natural justice into law.

Locke's law of nature is his version of the morality of equality. The general will is Rousseau's. Although the formulation of the morality of equality in Chapter IV is different from Locke's and Rousseau's, hopefully it is more specific, easy to understand and capable of being consistently applied by courts and individuals. It is a fixed standard of justice that perhaps all people who subscribe to universal equality can agree on. Because human political society is consciously designed, the necessity of a moral basis, of the *ought,* for the interaction of individuals is the very essence of civilized society.

The Constitution left the rights between private individuals entirely to the vagaries of political majorities. Given the historical period and the entrenched institution of slavery, this omission is understandable. Nor does it diminish the founding fathers' accomplishments. Nevertheless, the Constitution's silence on the moral basis of society leaves the individual at the mercy of a majority. As American society has absorbed more diverse religious and cultural groups, and rational moral philosophy has been sucked into the maelstrom of utilitarianism and relativism, the ship of state is left to moral dead reckoning with many navigators fighting for the tiller.

The Constitution is a monument to the genius of humans as much as the Great Pyramids, but neither is perfect. Absent a power superior to the Constitution, a majority sufficient to amend the Constitution can change it to deny individual (artificial) rights just as surely, and more permanently than, any legislative majority. And, the constitutional majority is worse because it assumes a moral authority proportionate to its size. If universal equality is to protect the individual from any political majority, that guarantee must not be subject to denial even by a constitutional majority.

The philosophy of the social contract which rests the legitimacy of government on individual consent, even if only tacit, is a significant step toward an individualistic society. A written constitution with some specific legally enforceable limits on the people who are government is another. But, the idea of the social contract governing the relations between individuals and between the individual and government, though conceived nearly four hundred years ago has lingered in the longest possible gestation. To accomplish the next step to a truly individualistic society, the Social Contract must become a real, legally enforceable contract that governs the relations of all members of society, private citizens and government officials, like a written constitution governs the structure, powers and operation of a government within society.

What is needed is a written Social Contract.

Chapter IX

Creating an Individualistic Society

American politicians frequently wrap their position on drug policy, prayer in schools, or social programs, in the deliberately vague but morally suggestive "right thing to do." But, everyone has his own view of the "right thing." If an individualistic society is to emerge from liberal democracy, the morality of equality must become Society's "right thing." This chapter will address why and how this can be done with a written social contract.

The Complexity of an Individualistic Society

We began with the conceptual framework of life as a complex physical system with the emergent properties of will, power and right. Life is the order of complexity that selects a particular future state of all possible future states and causing it to become an existing state. This is the order of complexity of an individual organism. Some individual organisms evolved more complex systems that produce the cooperative behaviors with survival advantages that are animal societies. Animal societies can exist only as long as the cooperative behaviors of individual animals increase the survival and reproduction of the social group, though not necessarily of each individual. This is the order of complexity of biological society.

Apart from necessarily cooperative social behaviors, individual organisms evolved ever more complex systems from which emerged the properties of conscious will, self-consciousness, other-consciousness and ultimately volitional will. These emergent properties of individuals certainly co-evolved with other cooperative social behaviors necessary for biological societies. Without digressing too much, many animals developed systems to inhibit behaviors that could result in members of the same social group killing others members of the group. At first these inhibitors were surely not consciously controlled, and perhaps only humans evolved conscious control of such inhibitions. The internal conflict between conscious self-interest and other-consciousness is likely the order of complexity of the unconscious systems that inhibited behaviors destructive of human biological society from which evolved the more complex, consciously controlled system of inhibition which are the rules of moral choice.

As we have seen, moral rules emerge to consciously resolve the internal conflict other-consciousness produces. If other animals' are an indication, however, the unconscious inhibited behaviors extend only to the social unit not to the species. Lions will attack and kill a member of another pride that enters its territory. Coyotes and wolves will do the same thing. Humans, from primitive tribes to civilized nations, frequently do the same. Thus, is seems likely that as other-consciousness emerges it includes only the members of the immediate social group. The brotherhood of man and universal equality emerge as a property of individual human consciousness only when all humans are seen through the eyes of other-consciousness. But, this is an emergent property of individuals, not of society.

From human biological society emerges human political society when human society is consciously designed to operate other than by the unconscious social behaviors of individuals using their power to try to achieve their individual will. The humans with the greatest power consciously design their society by creating artificial rights and duties that state how individuals *ought* to use their power. These artificial rights and duties are meaningless unless someone or some group with the power of alliance and the will enforces them. When artificial rights and duties are enforced, they become the law.

Various ideas compete as the statement of will upon which the power of alliance is formed to choose the *ought* of the artificial rights and duties of any particular human political society. Might makes right, divine right, communism, fascism, theocracy, liberal democracy and universal equality are each statements of will of the *ought* of a system of artificial rights and duties. Each has served as the statement of will of a power of alliance that created the artificial rights and duties of one or more human societies.

Part I of this book makes the case for universal equality as the political philosophy, the *ought*, of human political society. The morality of equality and its first principle of constructive power within the complexity of the success of human biological society for every individual is the *ought* of the artificial rights and duties of an individualistic society and the statement of will upon which is formed the power of alliance to enforce constructive power as the law of an individualistic society. Constructive power gives equal value to every individual and resolves the internal conflict of other-consciousness by requiring that no individual use his power to satisfy his desire by taking another individual's possession.

Let us now consider how this power of alliance of other-conscious individuals is created to make and maintain the morality of equality as the artificial rights and duties of an individualistic society.

From Liberal Democracy to Individualistic Society

The Declaration of Independence, the American Constitution and the spread of liberal democracy suggests that universal equality is the emerging consensus on the *ought* of artificial rights. But as has also been shown, the social contract and even the American Constitution falls short of making the morality of equality the artificial rights and duties of a political society. For that to happen, several events must occur.

The morality of equality and constructive power as the fuller expression of universal equality in the Declaration of Independence and the American Constitution must be realized. A power of alliance of other-conscious individuals must be formed whose objective is to make the morality of equality the artificial right and duty of every person in Society. Constructive power must become the fixed standard of justice that that Justice Iredell said does not exist and which the Supreme Court has been searching for ever since. Constructive power must become the foundation of all law. It defines the *ought* of the relations of all members to each other in an individualistic society. There is no separate standard for private individuals and for government. Government is nothing more than the mechanism for enforcing the artificial rights and duties of constructive power between private individuals. Might makes right is a physical fact. But, if might does make right, then might can make universal equality right. Only then can the serpent, might makes right, be made to swallow its tail.

The social contract to date has been only a theory of political philosophy, not a real contract. While that theory is preferable to the divine right of kings and other statements of will as the *ought* of political society, Hobbes and Locke's opposing uses of social contract theory show how easily manipulated and abused it is as merely a statement of will for political society. To correct this weakness of social contract theory, I propose the social contract become a real contract that is the statement of will upon which is formed the power of alliance dedicated to making the objective of an individualistic society a reality. The New Social Contract does not necessitate a particular form of social organization or government; however, it must provide the means to create and maintain the order of complexity necessary for the human animal to live socially, to become a morally capable individual, and to choose to act only with constructive power. Without this order of complexity, an individualistic society cannot emerge or continue.

Not all humans are morally capable. Therefore, an individualistic society can emerge only if a sufficient number of morally capable individuals form a power of alliance powerful enough to create and maintain their individualistic society.

A Written Social Contract

There are many theoretical and practical reasons why the New Social Contract must be a real written contract. An express contract is better than a contract implied from the tacit acquiescence of an unspoken understanding between the parties. A written contract is better than an oral contract. Both are legally enforceable, but the parties to a written contract can more clearly know their legal–artificial–rights and duties under the contract and more accurately predict what a court will do in deciding a dispute over the performance or breach of the contract. And, a written contract is less subject to after-the-fact selective or creative memory of its terms.

Written statutes are better than the common law. Anyone can find and read most statutes and usually have a fair idea of what is legal and what is not. The common law is difficult to find in the hundreds, even thousands of cases decided over many years. And, common law rules often conflict and are subject to judicial interpretation, misinterpretation, and change even after the events have already occurred. Courts also do exactly what they declare unconstitutional for the legislature to do, i.e., rewrite the law and apply it retroactively.[1] Perhaps more important, because common law rules so frequently conflict, judges can and do use them as mere rationalizations to support a result they intuitively think is "right." The persistent myth that the law is the one result that right reason would dictate, was finally put to rest in the twentieth century. When this happens, the rule of men is merely disguised with the rhetoric of the rule of law, as Justices Curtis, Douglas and Scalia have pointed out.

Legal rights are better than natural rights. No matter how much people may agree on natural rights, unless natural rights are combined with the power of the enforcing authority, and thus become legal rights, they are mere statements of will. Blacks' may have had a "natural right" to attend the University of Alabama, but not the legal right before *Brown v. Board of Education*. John Locke argued that this defect in the state of nature was one of the prime reasons for the social contract and the purpose of government. Without the power to enforce the law of nature of natural rights, of the morality of equality, that "law" is "in vain."

Despite Samuel Livermore and others' denigration of a written Bill of Rights in the Constitution, history has proven Richard Henry Lee right.[2] A written specification of rights is better than the unenumerated "natural" rights "retained by the people" in the Ninth Amendment of the Bill of Rights. Likewise, a written constitution is superior to an unwritten one for the same reasons a written contract is better than an unwritten or implied one. Chief Justice Marshall quite rightly called a written constitution "the greatest improvement on political institutions," in order that "[t]he powers of the legislature are defined and limited; and that those limits may not be mistaken or forgotten, the constitution is written." An explicit social contract may also improve the political institutions necessary to create and maintain an individualistic society.

Avoiding mistakes and forgetfulness are sufficient reasons alone for a written Social Contract, but there are other reasons. Only a written Social Contract can also definitively resolve the issues of who is a citizen of Society, of identifying who within Society is a morally capable individual, and who is not, of establishing the specific limits of majority rule and the use of coercive force, of creating the power of alliance necessary to create and maintain Society, and of creating an institutional power capable of effectively preventing any majority from using destructive power to take an individual's possessions other than to maintain Society.

Choice not Consent

Who is a citizen of the society? From time to time, most often in the context or as a consequence of revolution, whether one is a member of the society has become a crucial legal question upon which both life and property have depended.³ Locke states that accepting an inheritance or entering the territory of a government, is sufficient tacit consent to the government's authority. But owning a house surely is not consent to legally authorized slavery, or involuntary conscription to fight a war one opposes, or the extermination of a minority the government considers undesirable? In Rousseau's theory, the extermination of a minority would not be the general will of society but the "will of all" or a dominant faction so there could be no consent to it and a right to resist. Under Locke's theory, this is not one of the legitimate purposes of government, is therefore not consented to, and the people have a right of revolution against such a government. These distinctions are surely internally consistent with the political theory of each, but of no comfort to those interned and interred in Nazi concentration camps, the killing fields of Cambodia, or the ethnically clean villages of Bosnia.

If tacit consent is not unlimited, then it is consent only to what one approves. If the government is a democratic one, does tacit consent mean consent to everything a majority may choose to do? Does it matter whether there are constitutional limits on the power a majority may exercise? What if a majority decides that feebleminded people are a menace to society and must be sterilized or the preacher needs a house?

If tacit consent is unconditional consent to a government as Locke describes it, limited to protecting the natural rights to life, liberty and property, it is merely a matter of semantics: unlimited consent to limited government or limited consent to unlimited government. The whole purpose of consent is to legitimate the use of coercive force, that is, force against a person's will and without his consent, express or implied.

Tacit consent is like assuming everyone knows the law. It is a necessary but entirely fictitious assumption. Even in present society, some legal rights are so important that they cannot be waived without express consent. Every police officer knows that when he makes an arrest, he must read the suspect his *Miranda* rights, without which no confession may be used as evidence.

As a written contract, the New Social Contract requires each party to choose whether to agree with all other parties to it that the morality of equality is the *ought* of Society. The choice to become a member of Society is the choice to be a moral person, to act according to the morality of equality, the moral basis of Society, and the limits of coercive force in Society, whether used by an individual or any majority. The choice of the *ought* of the artificial rights and duties of Society is certainly as important as one's *Miranda* rights, and deserve an explicit, provable choice. The execution of the New Social Contract is more than tacit consent or acquiescence, it is an unequivocal choice to become a party to the Social Contract and a citizen of Society.

Many primitive and civilized societies have rituals to mark the transition from childhood to adulthood. Many religions require courses of study and tests before one may become a full member of the church. The Jewish religion has the Bar and Bat Mitzvah. Many Christian denominations have similar requirements.

In secular society, reaching the age of majority is a sign of becoming an adult, subject to the adult criminal law and responsible for one's actions. Before that, a child cannot enter into a legally binding contract or vote or buy alcohol or cigarettes. At eighteen, males must register with the Selective Service Administration. Every person must register with the Social Security Administration to get a job. To operate a motor vehicle, one must pass an examination demonstrating knowledge and proficiency with operating an automobile and of the traffic laws and obtain a license.

These secular transitions to adulthood are, however, extremely weak indicators of or preparation for becoming a full member of society. There is no secular equivalent to choosing to become a moral individual. Society does already require an express choice for some people. To become a lawyer, one must go to law school, demonstrate a knowledge of the law and the rules of ethical practice by passing the bar exam, and swear to uphold the state and federal constitutions and conduct himself according to the lawyers' ethical code. To become a doctor, one must go to medical school, pass the medical exam and get a license from the state. Doctors, dentists and most professionals must subscribe to a code of ethics, some voluntary, some mandatory, that govern how they must act in their profession. In the last fifty years, many other organizations have adopted a code of ethics for their members. Some are legally enforceable; others are not.

No one is compelled to become a lawyer or doctor, and no one is compelled to sign the Social Contract and become a citizen of Society. One must choose to enter the profession and choose to act in accordance with its ethical rules. Even plumbers and electricians must pass a test and get an occupational license. Naturalized citizens must pass a test and expressly choose to become a citizen.

Moral Capacity and Education

As discussed earlier, humans are not born with moral capacity. Those without moral capacity cannot be expected, and perhaps not trusted, to choose to use only constructive power to satisfy their desires. Thus, one basic problem of an individualistic society is to differentiate clearly between those individuals with and without moral capacity. Under current practice, moral capacity is never considered. It is assumed except in criminal cases when the defendant pleads insanity. After reaching the age of majority, society never considers a person's capacity to conform to the law until he commits a crime or becomes so psychotic he is a danger to himself or others. If an adult criminal serves his time, he can walk out of prison and say, "I'm going to rape another child," but until he is caught committing another crime, he is as free as all law-abiding citizens. Rehabilitation of criminals is largely a failure because some people are unable or unwilling to choose to conform to the law. Is the only sufficient proof of moral incapacity the commission of a crime? I think not.

Humans who cannot understand the difference between constructive and destructive power or make choices not to use destructive power are not morally capable. Such people are, regardless of chronological age, like children who require supervision commensurate with their immaturity. This does not mean that every eighteen-year-old without moral capacity must be locked away in a cell, quite the contrary. Children under eighteen are not locked in cells, but their freedom of action and their ability to participate fully in society is restricted. The degree of immaturity determines the restraint. A young child may not cross the street alone, play with matches, or view adult movies without a parent. Older children may not drive a car, become a bartender, or make a binding contract, to name only a few. Children also must have a parent or legally appointed guardian who is responsible for making choices for them that are beyond their maturity. A person who is not morally capable, but has reached the age of majority, should not need to commit a crime, and get caught, before Society can take steps commensurate with the risks to protect its citizens. Rather than assuming moral capacity from age alone, every person should be required to demonstrate his moral capacity and expressly choose to use only constructive power as a condition of becoming a full citizen. And, until they do, they must have a guardian responsible for restraining them commensurate with their limited moral capacity.

Other-conscious is like other innate human abilities. Without being taught, a child can learn to speak but will never learn to read, write or acquire the subtleties of language. A child may learn to whistle or sing a tune, but without training will never learn to play the violin or piano or be a member of an orchestra. Children will learn how to use their power to try to satisfy their desires, but they will not learn to make moral choices to use only constructive power. Other-consciousness must be nurtured and reinforced if children are to acquire their full potential to make moral choices. Every elementary and secondary school should have a curriculum to develop the emotional, psychological and intellectual systems necessary for other-consciousness and to educate children on how to choose to use only constructive power. Before any child is allowed to leave school, with or without graduating, she should be required to demonstrate an understanding of and the ability to make moral choices. Upon demonstrating this ability, she should be given the opportunity to choose to sign the Social Contract and thereby agree with all other citizens to use only constructive power.

By nurturing other-consciousness and teaching constructive power, Society will give every child the greatest possible opportunity to acquire moral capacity and an understanding sufficient to act morally toward all other people. The infant human may not be a perfectible creature, but it, more than any other animal, is the product of its history. It may have nascent tendencies toward moral choices, but that capacity needs nurturing and encouraging for the full moral capacity of the individual to emerge. An individualistic society must be in the classic sense the "teacher of virtue."[4]

Until a person can demonstrate the ability to choose to use only constructive power, Society must be able to effectively prevent him or her from using destructive power. The means used to accomplish this range from a mentally retarded person remaining in the care of a parent, family member, friend or spouse, to the death penalty for those who actually commit the most heinous crimes. Everything in between would be available, including further education to enable the person to acquire eventually moral capacity. The current method of the criminal justice system is deterrence and punishment. The purpose of the identification of moral capacity is prevention and protection.

If a morally capable person chooses not to sign the Social Contract, by that choice he declares to Society his rejection of the morality of equality and his willingness to choose to use destructive power whenever he believes the benefits outweigh the risks. This person is as dangerous to Society as any bank robber or murderer. Possible punishments will never deter this person. He will never believe that he will get caught and punished or that the risk of punishment outweighs the benefit. Punishment and compensation can never make the victim whole. Prevention and protection must be Society's first line of defense, not punishment and deterrence. Society must take whatever steps are necessary to prevent uses of destructive power and protect its members.

At a minimum, morally capable noncitizen–those who understand but refuse to become a party to the Social Contract–must be clearly identified so that citizens can protect themselves. Deporting or isolating them in an area with other noncitizens or incarcerating them in traditional prisons are all options. Choosing not to sign the Social Contract is a declaration that a state of might makes right exits between the person and the power of alliance that maintains society. Thus, the noncitizen has no artificial rights that require the power of alliance of Society to enforce.

Nothing can prevent a person intent on a career of crime from demonstrating their understanding of constructive and destructive power and their ability to choose to use only constructive power. Becoming a priest does not prevent pedophilia. Signing the Social Contract will not eliminate crime, but after signing it, no childhood deprivation or abuse will excuse or mitigate a choice to use destructive power because the choice to become a citizen is not only a choice to be a moral person, but also a representation to all members of Society that one can and always will choose to use only constructive power. After a person chooses to become a citizen, there are no excuses for choosing to use destructive power, except as allowed in the Social Contract.

Signing the Social Contract will not eliminate a plea of reduced capacity, but a plea of insanity or diminished capacity would be an admission of a lack of moral capacity, not a denial of the use of destructive power. Since a person must have moral capacity to be a citizen, a plea of lack of moral capacity is a renunciation of citizenship and a reversion to the status of a ward. Society must then take all steps necessary to prevent and protect all citizens and wards from future uses of destructive power by the defendant. The artificial rights of wards are discussed in detail in Chapter X.

Power of Alliance

When each representative of the American Colonies signed the Declaration of Independence, he declared to the world his agreement with its statements of will, and he pledged his life, his fortune and his sacred honor to make its statements of will a reality. By signing the Social Contract, each individual chooses to join the power of alliance of all other parties, and he commits all his power to make and maintain an individualistic society based on the Social Contract an existing state.

The Limits of Majority Rule

Hobbes offers no limits on majority power because he states the sovereign's power must be absolute. Rousseau also claims that the general will of the sovereign, the majority of the people, not only has absolute power, but it cannot err. Locke's limits on the power of a political majority derive from his limited purpose of government to protect the natural rights as enforced by the law of nature. Realizing the law of nature might not be adequate, Locke identified four checks on the abuse of government power: (1) the purpose of the social contract--to interpret not to limit natural rights, (2) periodic elections, (3) the legislator's sense of community and shared interest in the purpose of the contract, and (4) the right of revolution.

The first is no limit at all. It merely repeats how government *ought* to operate. The second is no limit on a majority because elections are decided by majorities and Locke claims a "majority have a right to act and conclude the rest." The third is nothing but a road to certain defeat in the next election if the legislator ignores the will of the majority. The last is the worst of all. It is a complete failure of organized society, a reversion to might makes right and a license for the strongest to use their power of alliance against all who disagree.

As discussed in the previous chapter, constitutional procedures and super-majorities offer no protection at all for a minority that disapproves of the Constitution. Alexander Hamilton was right when he advocated the necessity of an independent judiciary:

> By a limited constitution I understand one which contains certain specified exceptions to the legislative authority, such, for instance, as that it shall pass no bills of attainder, no ex post facto laws, and the like. Limitations of this kind can be preserved in practice in no other way than through the medium of the courts of justice, whose duty it must be to declare all acts, contrary to the manifest tenor of the Constitution, void. Without this, all the reservations of particular rights or privileges would amount to nothing.[5]

The Social Contract unites the morality of equality with the law because the only effective limit on the power of a majority is for a court to look to the fundamental law of Society, not divine it from noble sentiments,[6] whether in the Constitution or not, and to declare the majority's acts invalid. And, with a written Social Contract, judges will have less freedom or need to resort to their own intuition or ambiguous noble sentiments in order to decide cases. In this way a single individual can invoke the power of alliance of all Society against any majority and, if right, prevail.

Under the Constitution, the Supreme Court is responsible for protecting a single individual from the will of a great political majority when the majority violates the Constitution. *Ex Parte Milligan* (1866),[7] is an example. Milligan, a civilian and twenty year resident of Indiana, was arrested by the Union Army for inciting insurrection. A military court-martial rejected his objection to its jurisdiction over him as a civilian and tried, convicted and sentenced to him to hang. The military chain of command, all the way up to President Andrew Johnson, approved the conviction and sentence. Milligan sued in federal court for a writ of *habeas corpus* challenging the jurisdiction of the military court-martial to try and sentence him. The Supreme Court held that the military authorities had no jurisdiction and ordered Milligan freed.

Ironically, as in *Marbury v. Madison*, before the Supreme Court could free Milligan, it had to decide whether the statute that authorized it to hear Milligan's case was constitutional. Had the Court concluded the statute was unconstitutional, and therefore it could not hear Milligan's case, Milligan would have been entirely right, but dead. The Court's decision also turned on a statute authorizing the President to suspend the writ of *habeas corpus* anytime he determined the public safety required it. Four justices concurred in Milligan's release not because Congress did not have the constitutional authority to allow Milligan to be tried by military court-martial instead of a civilian court, but because Congress simply had not done so. In other words, four justices would have allowed the Army to hang Milligan without a trial by jury in a civil court of law if a majority of Congress had authorized it.

As suggested in Chapter VIII, the United States Constitution is not the basic charter of an individualistic society, although it grew out of social contract theory. It creates the political institutions and processes through which people may use their power to try to impose their version of the "right thing" on others by enacting laws or amending the Constitution. Despite its natural rights and social contract theoretical underpinnings, the Constitution does not include the law of nature, natural rights, natural justice or any other coherent, absolute limit on a majority. It does not answer the most basic question of political society: when may coercive force be used. This omission left unresolved, and unresolvable, the conflict between the fundamental law–the *ought* of society–and the governmental use of coercive force that Justices Chase and Iredell first addressed in 1798. It is the leitmotif of the history of the Supreme Court, and it will continue as long as no answer is provided. Until the moral basis of Society and the limits of government's authority to use coercive force against a minority are explicitly made the fundamental law, this conflict within the Supreme Court and society at large cannot end. Only a written Social Contract can provide that answer.

The Necessary Uses of Destructive Power and Their Priority

If all humans were morally capable and always chose to use only constructive power, there would be no need for government. But as Madison observed, humans are not angels, and the physical world does not always allow them to choose to use only constructive power. Thus, destructive power is necessary to make human political society as close to the condition requiring no government as possible, to make biological society an individualistic society.

The purpose of government is to make the morality of equality a reality by eliminating all uses of destructive power. It is an unfortunate fact that destructive power is necessary to effectively oppose destructive power. Therefore, government must use destructive power in response to all threats or actual uses of destructive power. Government's first obligation is to protect its citizens and wards from all uses of destructive power by defending against all external threats to Society's existence. Government must provide for the national defense.

Not all uses of destructive power come from outside Society. As discussed above, there will always be people within Society who are not morally capable, i.e., children and others who have not acquired moral capacity and those who have chosen not to be bound by the Social Contract. There will also be citizens who for various reasons do not always choose to use constructive power. Therefore, government's second obligation is to use destructive power to protect each and every citizen and ward from internal uses of destructive power. This requires an internal police force to prevent conscious uses of destructive power or to apprehend and punish those who use it. This is the criminal law and its enforcement.

And, because some citizens may find themselves unable to provide their necessities of life without using destructive power, as a last resort government must provide the necessities of life so that no citizen or ward must ever have to choose between using destructive power or surviving. Because the government cannot provide the necessities without using destructive power, this is the third obligation of government which requires destructive power.

When the people who are government provide the necessities, they use destructive power for the person who cannot provide her own necessities with constructive power. The government must provide the necessities as a last resort for two separate, but equally important, reasons. First, this is the only way to maintain the moral foundation of Society and prevent any citizen from ever having to choose to use destructive power or die. Second, government spreads equally among all of Society the consequences of the destructive power used against any one citizen to provide the necessities, and therefore minimizes it.

For all members of Society who are not citizens, i.e., who have not yet demonstrated moral capacity and chosen to sign the Social Contract, destructive power is authorized when and as necessary to prevent noncitizens from using destructive power against a member of Society. This authorization extends beyond government to include private individuals who are the guardians of noncitizens. Every noncitizen must have a guardian who is responsible for preventing his ward from using destructive power. The guardian may be a parent or family member or spouse or a government agent whose job is that of guardian, e.g., a prison warden or probation officer.

When the use of destructive power cannot be prevented, there must be a means to enforce each citizen's agreement to use only constructive power and to restrain noncitizens to prevent or punish uses of destructive power. This is both the civil law of unconscious uses of destructive power, and the police power. Constructive power requires everyone to use his best foresight of the consequences of his acts on others. If an act lessens another's possessions, that use of power is destructive. Unconscious use of destructive power is now subsumed by the civil law of damages. Conscious uses of destructive power would, like now, be subject to both civil damages and criminal punishment. The means of establishing another's use of destructive power and the criminal sanction and measure of compensation required is the judiciary. Therefore, the Social Contract must require as the fourth obligation of government the creation of a judiciary.

At times the purposes of the government under the Social Contract will conflict. No Society can completely remove all of these conflicts. Therefore, the Social Contract must set priorities for resolving these conflicts when they arise. These priorities are in the order presented above.

The Police Power

The police power in an individualistic society is used to prevent uses of destructive power. No matter how honestly and diligently an individual tries to anticipate all the destructive consequences of his acts, he cannot anticipate them all. The collective experience of human society always exceeds that of any one person and can better anticipate destructive consequences. Thus, the government may pass laws that prohibit acts the collective experience of Society demonstrates involves an unreasonable risk of destructive consequences to others. Drunk driving laws, fire codes, building codes, quarantine orders, mandatory vaccination laws, regulations on the use of hazardous substances, gasoline storage tank integrity regulations, all define acts in specific circumstances that the collective experience of Society shows involve an unreasonable risk of destructive consequences. Also, some kinds of information are always necessary to prevent certain exchanges from being the result of the destructive power of involuntary persuasion. All the current disclosure laws fall into this category, e.g., odometer disclosure, business disclosures in connection with selling securities, sexually transmissible disease status when persuading another to engage in sex, product labeling laws, etc. All of these are uses of involuntary persuasion and thus destructive power and violate the Social Contract. To enforce the Social Contract agreement not to use destructive power in relations with private individuals, the government may make specific acts presumptively a use of destructive power because if a morally capable person had the collective experience of Society at her disposal when choosing how to act, she would know that those acts would be a use of destructive power, and she would choose not to do so because of her other-consciousness, not because of the fear of punishment or adverse consequences.

Another facet of the police power involves situations for which the collective experience of Society is insufficient to have a reasonable belief that one's acts will not create an unreasonable risk of injury to the person or possessions of another member of Society. Constructive power requires that one choose only acts with a reasonable belief that no such injury will result. Therefore, if no such belief can be formed, the act must not be done. The government may regulate acts for which there is insufficient collective experience or specify what experience must be obtained to form a reasonable belief that they will not be a use of destructive power, e.g., testing a drug or genetically altered food, plant, or other organism before putting it on the market or releasing it into the environment, nuclear power plant operation or radioactive materials disposal, or cloning of humans.

All exercises of the police power merely apply to specific situations the principle of constructive power. By enforcing the rule of constructive power between individuals, government protects the health and safety of members of society, and because the morality of equality is the morality of Society, it also protects the morals of Society. This protection of morals is, however, limited to preventing uses of destructive power. It does not include what has historically passed for protection of the morals, such as prohibiting prostitution or gambling or dancing.

Prostitution and other "victimless crimes" may not be outlawed, but these exchanges must always result from voluntary persuasion. Government may require the disclosure of all alternatives and information necessary for each participant to choose what will be more valuable to them. For instance, like the used car odometer disclosure law, the government could pass a sexual odometer law that requires prostitutes to disclose the number of persons he or she has had sex with since the last government required medical checkup, and their transmissible disease status. The Florida Statute quoted in Chapter IV that requires the disclosure of one's sexually transmissible disease status to a sex partner is just such a law. The government could also require the seller of a non-theraputic drug to disclosure information similar to that required for prescription drugs. And, like drunk driving is outlawed as a destructive use of power, other activities under the influence of drugs could also be prohibited, but not the choice to use the drug to satisfy one's volitional will without using destructive power.

Since the purpose of government is to prevent uses of destructive power, the sale of drugs or other substances or other acts with persons not morally capable, e.g., minors, must be restricted to prevent destructive uses of power against them because they cannot make choices for themselves. But, universal equality and the principle of constructive power are based on the belief that all morally capable individuals can and are entitled to choose what possessions including experiences are most valuable to them in the pursuit of their volitional will. No one can make that decision for another without using destructive power. Thus, whenever government prohibits any act that is not a use of destructive power, it exceeds its police power to enforce the Social Contract's rule of constructive power as between morally capable individuals.

The police power is not limited to individual acts which alone would be destructive power. The government may prevent individual acts from cumulatively amounting to destructive power. Such laws include the environmental laws regulating clean air or greenhouse gases from auto and industrial emissions into the atmosphere, or discharges into the water supply, or the use of toxic substances such as pesticides or poisons that may accumulate in the environment. If the cumulative effect of individuals acting independently would constitute destructive power if done by the employees of a corporation, then the government may prevent these uses of destructive power.

The government has also made laws that establish artificial rights and establish presumptive rules for the interaction of members of society. These artificial rights often give preferences or advantages to some people over others. If such legal preferences are enforced with penalties or the transfer of one person's possessions to another, by taxing or otherwise, they use destructive power. By making constructive power the fundamental law of Society, the Social Contract addresses these kinds of laws as well.

This category includes, among others, both legal segregation and affirmative action, and laws regulating businesses "affected with a public interest," such as in *Munn v. Illinois*, and tax breaks for preferred businesses. These laws, and especially legal discrimination based on race, religion, etc., are never anything more than the use of destructive power by a majority against a minority. All such laws under the Social Contract would be void, because they are not necessary to fulfill a governmental purpose under the Social Contract to maintain an individualistic society. An exception might be a subsidy or tax break for a ship builder necessary to build ships for the Navy for national defense.

In the United States the effects of the use of destructive power against some minorities, once justified, and in some instances still justifies, affirmative action as a remedy for the past use of destructive power. But, for an individualistic society to exist, at some point the political competition for preferences ceases to be a remedy for past uses of destructive power and becomes just another political majority using destructive power against a minority. That the group given the legal preference may be a minority in Society is irrelevant. The preference can only be made a law by a political majority, and anyone against whom the majority uses the destructive power of government, is the minority.

To prevent individual uses of destructive power, the Social Contract requires government to provide the physical or civil necessities to any citizen or ward who without them must choose to use destructive power to survive. After a generation has grown up under the Social Contract, there can never again be a claim that the destructive power of segregation or legal discrimination used against past generations of women or religious or ethnic groups can authorize destructive power. The political competition for legal preferences must end. Once every member of Society has an equal *opportunity* to achieve their volitional will with constructive power, the advantages or disadvantages of parentage can no longer justify legal preferences. The child born to a wealthy, well-educated family or with greater innate intelligence or athletic ability is no more responsible for the circumstances of his birth than is the less naturally blessed child born to a poor, uneducated family. The unfortunate child may not use destructive power against the fortunate one any more than the fortunate one may use it against the unfortunate without reverting to might makes right.

Increasing the Opportunity for Individual Happiness

The government has no license to improve the general welfare or increase the prosperity of Society. Such laws always involve using destructive power to increase some people's possessions by lessening another's possessions and are nothing but a majority's use of the coercive power of alliance of Society against some minority. These uses of destructive power are a denial of universal equality as surely as if the government took a Muslim's house and gave it to a Baptist minister. Maybe "society" will be better off from a utilitarian point of view, but that calculation is a reversion to biological society and the mathematics of population genetics, not the actions of an individualistic society.

Government may, however, make laws that increase the opportunity for *each and every* citizen to achieve his volitional will with the use of constructive power. These laws are similar to Rousseau's description of the general will. They must benefit everyone. And most important, they do not involve a use of destructive power; rather, they facilitate the individual's use of constructive power. Examples of these laws are the Uniform Commercial Code which establishes the default rules for negotiating and contracting to buy and sell all goods; the traffic laws for driving on the streets; the laws establishing various legal forms of doing business, such as partnerships, corporations, trusts etc.

If a law purports to rest only on government's authority to increase the opportunity for individual happiness, it must increase the opportunity for *everyone* without exception, or it is an invalid preference. Opportunity must not be equated with a result, however. The government could start a national university and set the entrance qualifications for all applicants. Rejecting those who do not meet those qualifications is not a denial of opportunity. The opportunity is the freedom to try to meet the entrance requirements, not to be admitted. And if admitted, opportunity is the freedom to try to meet the graduation requirements, not to graduate. The traffic laws allow everyone who can pass the driver's test to drive safely on the streets at the same time. The inability to pass the driving test does not mean the traffic laws do not increase every person's opportunity to drive, at least if the driving test is uniformly administered and a failing score is a valid measure of an unreasonable risk the person presents to others on the road–like a licensed driver under the influence is prohibited from driving. The traffic laws are authorized both to increase the opportunity for individual happiness, which does not involve a use of destructive power, and a use of the police power to prevent uses of destructive power in the operation of a motor vehicle. Opportunity means that every person can compete to meet the qualifications for the possession desired and that whether the person achieves her desired objective depends on all persons competing for the same possession doing so with their constructive power.

Affirmative Obligations of Government

A written constitution is the means of establishing a government to function within a society, not the charter of Society itself. The United States Constitution does not impose a single affirmative obligation on the federal government to act for any individual. That role is left entirely to the will of a political majority in the legislatures of the states and the federal government. The Constitution does not prohibit a political majority from repealing Social Security, Medicare or all the clean air and water laws. If retired people died of hunger or lack of medical care or if an entire town's drinking water were contaminated and all the residents developed leukemia and died, no court could now compel the government to provide for the destitute or stop the pollution of ground water without a law passed by that very government. Without a law passed by the legislature, the police may not prevent the commission of a crime. They can only arrest one upon probable cause that he has actually committed a crime. In fact, since common law crimes were abolished, no act that injures another is a crime unless it is specifically and clearly declared to be a crime by the legislature.

By contrast, the Social Contract I propose imposes an affirmative, legally enforceable obligation on the government to do whatever is necessary to create and maintain an individualistic society. (How the judiciary would decide cases to enforce this obligation is discussed in more detail in Chapter X.) Government has an affirmative obligation to protect its citizens from all external and internal threats and uses of destructive power. It may not avoid this obligation to every citizen and ward by claiming inadequate manpower or resources.[8] The resources must be obtained or there is no individualistic society, only biological society.

The Social Contract imposes a legally enforceable obligation to provide the necessities to any citizen or ward who cannot provide his own with constructive power. Without the guarantee that one will never have to choose to use destructive power, there can be no individualistic society, only biological society in which some people receive the benefits of human society and others do not. An individualistic society exists only if it allows every single morally capable person to always choose to use constructive power.

Now let us turn to the Social Contract I propose and how it would be interpreted as the founding legal document of an individualistic society.

Chapter X

Interpreting
The New Social Contract

The Social Contract has four basic subjects: the relationship of the individual to other individuals, of government to the individual, of the individual to government, and the termination and modification of the contract. The New Social Contract I propose is as follows:

THE SOCIAL CONTRACT

I,_____, having successfully completed the prescribed course of study preliminary to entering into this contract, hereby agree with every other person who has already executed or hereafter executes this contract as follows:

I. INDIVIDUAL TO INDIVIDUAL

   A. I agree to use my power only constructively, and never destructively, except in self-defense after another has used destructive power against my or another party or ward's life, or as an agent of the government in conformity with this contract or as necessary to fulfill my obligations for my wards.
   B. I agree to conduct all relations with other parties to this contract with good faith and honesty in fact.
   C. I agree to act only upon a reasonable belief that the act will not create an unreasonable risk of injury to the person or possessions of another party to this contract or a ward.
   D. I agree to act toward all wards commensurately with their mental and physical capacities.

II. GOVERNMENT TO INDIVIDUAL

A. The government shall be so constituted as a majority of the parties to this contract shall from time to time specify, but shall, regardless of form, always be subordinate to this contract and the judiciary required by this contract.

B. The government shall make all laws and take all actions necessary to implement and enforce this contract.

C. The government shall provide for the protection of all parties to this contract and wards from all external and internal uses of destructive power.

D. Upon request, the government shall provide the physical or civil necessities to each party to this contract or his or her ward who is unable to supply his own physical or civil necessities through the use of constructive power.

E. The government shall establish an independent judiciary that shall openly, timely and uniformly adjudicate all claims arising from this contract. No adjudication of an individual's rights shall be made without reasonable notice and the ability to confront and compel witnesses and evidence for and against each party, nor shall an adjudication of an individual's rights be re-opened once final, except upon proof that it was obtained with destructive power or proof beyond any doubt that it was based upon facts that are untrue. Before assuming office, all judges shall take the following oath: Upon my honor, I will interpret and enforce the Social Contract for every citizen and ward free of any interest other than to establish and maintain a society devoted to the greatest opportunity for each and every member to achieve happiness.

F. All persons claiming to act with the authority of the government shall do so only after taking an oath to strictly abide by this contract and all decisions of the judiciary.

G. The government shall make no law or regulation whose objective or effect hinders the opportunity to achieve a citizen's will, except as is necessary to perform its duties under paragraphs A through F of this Article.

H. The government shall use destructive power only as a last resort and only for the purposes set forth in this contract.

III. INDIVIDUAL TO GOVERNMENT

A. I agree to obey all laws and regulations made by any government established according to this contract unless and until such law or regulation is declared by the judiciary to violate any term of this contract.

B. I agree to submit to any reasonable sanction imposed upon me for my own violation of this contract.

IV. MODIFICATION AND TERMINATION

A. No party's rights under this contract may be terminated by the government without the party's express, written agreement except upon an adjudication of a conscious use of destructive power in breach of this contract involving physical power against another party or ward creating a substantial risk of serious injury or death or upon an adjudication of repeated breaches involving the conscious use of destructive power.

B. This contract may not be modified without the written agreement of all living parties to it.

Entered into this ____ day of _____ .

Government of _____
BY:_____

Individual
BY:_____

Entering Into the Contract

Whether to become a party to the Social Contract, and thus a citizen of Society, is purely an individual choice that must result from voluntary persuasion because the Social Contract cannot begin by violating its founding principle. But, can a Hobbesian egoist, a Lockean believer in natural rights, natural justice and the law of nature, a libertarian, a utilitarian, a Christian, a Kantian, a devout theist, an atheist and a Rawlsian all sign the Social Contract?

Hobbes and the egoists can sign the Social Contract because a rational calculation of self-interest leads to the conclusion that one's self-interest will be best served if everyone abandons the use of destructive power and because self-preservation is one of the systems of lesser complexity

Society guarantees, as much as life allows, to each party to the Social Contract and his wards. Therefore, not only from a purely self-interested perspective, but also from a biological perspective, by becoming a party to the Social Contract, the egoist assures his maximal, conscious self-interest and his biological interest in perpetuating his genes since the wards of all parties are also guaranteed their necessities of life, unless they choose not to become a party once they become morally capable individuals.

The psychological egoist can sign the Social Contract for the same reasons as the pure egoists, but for the additional reason that choosing to use constructive power will also make her feel better because it resolves the internal conflicts between self-interest and other-consciousness.

Locke and other natural rights adherents can sign because the natural right to life, liberty and property are possessions. The agreement not to use destructive power is the individual recognition of those "natural rights." Government is limited to using destructive power to enforce each individual's agreement not to use destructive power and as necessary to maintain the moral basis of Society.

If the libertarian objects that coercive force should not be used against him to provide the necessities to those members of Society who cannot provide their own with constructive power, the answer is simple: people who must use destructive power to survive will do so. Thus, the issue is not whether destructive power or coercive force will be used, but by whom and how will the consequences of that destructive power be distributed among members of Society? By government providing the necessities, the potential for violence and greater destructive consequences than necessary and their being visited on only a few victim are instead distributed uniformly across Society. Thus, every citizen suffers the smallest possible consequences of the use of destructive power.

The utilitarian can sign the Social Contract because the guarantee of the necessities to every member of Society is, as far as the necessities are concerned, the greatest good for the greatest number–everyone. And, the distribution of the non-necessities will necessarily produce the greatest good for the greatest number because all non-necessities will be either the possession of the person who created it with his own constructive power or have been acquired through an exchange resulting from voluntary persuasion. The distribution of goods through such exchanges always results in all participants having more valuable possessions than before, and thus a greatest good because more individuals' desires are satisfied. Furthermore, by distinguishing between necessities and non-necessities, the Social Contract eliminates the problem of measuring the good of one person or group resulting from one distribution of possessions versus an alternative distribution. So long as constructive power is used, and everyone has the necessities, the greatest good for the greatest number is an autonomous process.

The Christian and the Kantian can sign because the morality of equality is a more specific statement of the Golden Rule and categorical imperative that allows for the charity of caring for the less fortunate, the freedom to seek one's own personal ends whether secular or religious, and protects personal autonomy from any interference. Constructive power in the context of adequate complexity, i.e., the guarantee of the necessities, is how everyone wants others to do unto them. It is a principle that everyone can wish to be a universal axiom for human behavior and society. In fact, the most devout followers of any religion and the ardent atheist can both sign the Social Contract as long as he or she is willing to renounce destructive power in obtaining converts or in practicing his religion.

The Rawlsian[1] can also sign the Social Contract because in an "original position" with a "veil of ignorance" about what one's actual position will be in Society, the Social Contract is a "conception of justice" based on "principles of justice" that people would agree to an original position "that embodies widely accepted and reasonable constraints on choice of principles."[2] Even better than the veil of ignorance required by Rawls' original position, the Social Contract does not require the elitist, highly abstract and hypothetical assumptions and reasoning that Rawls employs. One need not be a Harvard philosophy professor to be able to understand the basis of Society and its basic principle of constructive power. Nor does the Social Contract produce intuitive rules of justice such as, no one can have more possessions than anyone else unless everyone and "especially the least advantaged members of society" are also benefitted by it.[3] This concept makes no allowance for one who works longer, harder and smarter than anyone else. And, by providing a first principle of morality, constructive power, the Social Contract answers Rawls' condition for refuting intuitionism as the source of justice.[4] Intuitionism is merely an incomplete understanding of other-consciousness and the complexity necessary for an individualistic society to emerge.

I believe the only person who would not be satisfied with the Social Contract is one who claims that the satisfaction of his desires are more important than anyone else's and that he should be able to do whatever he wants whenever he thinks he can get away with it. In other words, such a person must deny the equal value of all person's satisfaction of their desires. Of course such a person will object to a Society that gives equal value to everyone, but that is precisely why such individuals must be identified by Society. Any theist, Marxist or disciple of an "ism" who thinks it is his lot to save or prey upon the world by forcing those who are too stupid to realize they need saving or too weak to resist are the only ones who will reject the Social Contract.

By entering the Social Contract, all members of Society are bound by it and entitled to all of its protections. Before children acquire the moral capacity to choose to sign the Social Contract they are wards. Other persons within Society who are not citizens are also wards and members of Society, except for all morally capable persons who refuse to sign the Social Contract. By refusing to sign, the latter declare their choice and intent to use destructive power whenever it suits them. They are not members of Society. Thus, a citizen may use any power, destructive or otherwise, against non-members of Society who have by refusing to sign the Social Contract declared that they will do the same. Citizens will not necessarily use destructive power against non-members for the same reason other-conscious people do not beat their dogs, but the government, as the enforcer of the Social Contract possessed with the power of alliance of all parties, is neither required nor authorized to aid any non-members. To do otherwise would be like requiring General Motors to pay dividends to people who do not own GM stock, or requiring NATO to defend Russia from an invasion by China.

The possibility of being injured or killed by a member of Society who is not subject to legal prohibition or apprehension and punishment by the government would surely be a powerful reason to choose to become a party to the Social Contract. Now, even a terrorist intent on destroying the United States can invoke the protections of the collective power of the United States. Only members of Society are entitled to the protection of Society's power of alliance. Non-members have no artificial or legal rights, because all rights require a power to enforce them. Since Society has no obligation to protect a declared enemy, non-members have only the natural right to try to do anything.

Hierarchy of Law

The Social Contract is the fundamental law of Society, both for the relations between private individuals and for government. When the judiciary decides disputes, it must apply the proper hierarchy of legal authority, which is (1) the Social Contract, (2) the constitution establishing the government (3) the legislated laws created by the government, (4) any non-legislated laws e.g., administrative rules or regulations, and (5) private contracts, the most basic of which is the Social Contract. When any law is inconsistent with a superior law, and once it is so declared by the judiciary, it is invalid and the people of government may not enforce it no matter how great the majority that passed it.

Individual Sections of the Social Contract

Preamble

I,_____, having successfully completed the prescribed course of study preliminary to entering into this contract, hereby agree with every other person who has already executed or hereafter executes this contract as follows:

To choose to become a citizen, a person must have moral capacity. Society prescribes a course of study to create the moral capacity necessary to choose whether to be a moral individual for all of the reasons discussed in Chapter IX. When a person signs the Social Contract he must also understand its terms and his rights and obligations as a party. Furthermore, each citizen should be familiar with the history preceding the Social Contract in order to understand why there is a Social Contract and its role and importance in Society. This will be more important in the early history of the Social Contract before constructive power and individualism become "self-evident." The course should also touch on the goal of life and how others have viewed it throughout history, not to proselytize a particular religion or social philosophy as the best, but to show the nature of volitional will versus unconsciously accepting others' goals. Complete agreement about the goal of life is impossible and unnecessary. What is important is that each individual pursue his goal of life without using destructive power.

The only societal goal of liberal democracy, except proselytizing liberal democracy, is economic growth, which assumes that more possessions equals greater happiness. Human society almost certainly cannot pursue unlimited economic growth indefinitely in a world of exploding population and finite natural resources. As a goal of life, economic growth seems misguided anyway. As most people who have stared down their own mortality realize, the most valuable possessions are not cars or houses, but the relationships with the people in our lives.

In an individualistic society, the individual is the source of his own happiness. This does not mean that religious or philosophical teachings are wrong or discouraged or that selfishness is a virtue, quite the contrary. An individualistic society will have as many St. Francises, Clara Bartons and Mother Theresas as any in history, and probably more. But, only an individual can choose to be a St. Francis by his own volitional will. Each of us is, by necessity and default, whether an individualistic society ever emerges or not, responsible for our own happiness. Part of becoming a morally capable individual is understanding one's personal responsibility for both his actions and his happiness.

Some people will complete the course of study with ease while others may have difficulty. The course is not intended to exclude people from becoming citizens or to create a subclass of members of Society who cannot "pass" the course. Since the consequence of signing the Social Contract is to choose to become a moral individual, each new citizen must demonstrate that she understands her responsibilities under the Social Contract, the necessity of obeying it, and her ability to choose to use constructive not destructive power. The only failing grade is if the person cannot demonstrate the mental capacity to understand and choose to act in conformity with the Social Contract.

Psychologists have identified several stages of development in the sophistication of moral thought. The first is the pre-conventional stage in which pre-adolescent children label objects or actions as good or bad. The next is conventional moral thinking when the child sees good behavior as pleasing to or evoking approval of others, especially authority figures. Behaviors are often judged by whether the actor "meant well." More important, however, it includes "an 'orientation toward authority, fixed rules, and the maintenance of the social order. Right behavior consists of doing one's duty, showing respect for authority, and maintaining the given social order for its own sake.' . . . [T]here is concern not only with conforming to one's social order, but also with maintaining, supporting, and justifying this order."[5] In adolescence, the post-conventional stage emphasizes abstract moral principles with universal application. Social, political and moral beliefs of parents or other authority figures are no longer accepted without question. Rather rights and standards based on consent are emphasized. Finally, with further cognitive development, a small number of people develop what Kholberg called the highest stage of moral reasoning when the individual attempts to "formulate 'abstract ethical principles appealing to logical comprehensiveness, universality, and consistency.' . . . [and] not on social approbation."[6]

Citizens need not be moral philosophers. They need only reach the conventional level of moral thinking to understand and accept the Social Contract as the authority and fixed rules necessary to maintain the social order of an individualistic society. Higher level moral thinking may be valuable, even necessary, for certain positions in Society, such as to be a judge, but not to become a citizen.

Research has also shown that thinking on a certain moral level does not necessarily translate into acting on that same level. Each new citizen must demonstrate his understanding not only of the moral principle of constructive power, but also his ability always to choose to act in conformity with it. Signing the Social Contract is a promise, a warranty, always to choose to use constructive power.

The government, and ultimately the judiciary, will decide how moral capacity is successfully demonstrated. At a minimum, the person must be able to demonstrate that she understands (1) the difference between constructive and destructive power, (2) the obligation to refrain from using destructive power, (3) the obligation to obey the laws, (4) the right to challenge any law as violating the Social Contract, and (5) the right to demand government provide the necessities, including protection from destructive power, if she is unable to do so with her own constructive power.

A person may choose to become a party to the Social Contract whenever he can demonstrate his moral capacity. The government may set a maximum age by which each person would be required, if mentally capable, to choose whether to execute the Social Contract. For people with limited mental ability who are never able to demonstrate moral capacity, they will remain wards of their parents or Society. How wards without moral capacity will be treated is discussed below.

The Social Contract is executed by an individual for himself, and by a representative for the government. Since only citizens can be government agents, government is a party to the Social Contract. It binds all persons who have or will execute it. It gives perpetual existence to Society, like the articles of incorporation do a corporation. It remains in effect and Society continues as long as the government fulfills its obligations to each and every members of Society.

I. Individual to Individual:

The relationship between individuals creates the greatest opportunities for happiness. Article I establishes how individuals must act toward each other, and is therefore the source of all individual legal rights. A breach of this article gives an injured person a right to compensation in a civil action. Acts of conscious destructive power may also be punished as a crime because they are a choice to use destructive power.

A. *I agree to use my power only constructively, and never destructively except in self-defense after another has used destructive power against my or another party or ward's life, or as an agent of the government in conformity with this contract, or as necessary to fulfill my obligations for my wards.*

This section is every party's choice to abandon destructive power. It is the ultimate objective of the Social Contract. All human interactions with constructive power are just and produce greater happiness. Destructive power will never be completely eliminated, however, so government must use destructive power when necessary to enforce this section.

A party may use destructive power against another party or ward only in self-defense, and only after another party has used destructive power against the person of another member of Society. Shots need not be fired nor a blow struck because a threat to shoot is as much a use of physical destructive power as is the actual shot. Destructive power may only be used to defend life, not property or personal dignity. "Fighting words," taunts, insults defamation and all other possible uses of destructive power must be remedied through the judiciary.

Only destructive power can eliminate destructive power. As government agents, citizens may use destructive power, but only for the purposes and with the limits imposed by the Social Contract. As government agents, these citizens act in self-defense of Society.

B. *I agree to conduct all relations with other parties to this contract with good faith and honesty in fact.*

Good faith and honesty in fact are separate but related elements of voluntary persuasion. Good faith means to act so that each participant in an exchange has the opportunity to exercise his best judgment about what is most valuable to him. Honesty in fact means to disclose all relevant information without prevarication.

An affirmative misrepresentation is a use of destructive power, involuntary persuasion, and a breach of the duty to act with good faith and honesty in fact. To use a half-truth hoping another will miss the half lie, is also a use of destructive power and a violation of good faith and honesty in fact. It is a conscious attempt to get another to do what he would not do if he were conscious of all the relevant information.

Good faith and honesty in fact are broader than the current law on fraud and material omissions. Good faith and honesty in fact require a person to divulge all information he has reason to believe is material to another party's choice to make an exchange. There would be no *caveat emptor*, no holding back material information simply because the other person failed to ask.

The legal test for whether one has failed to act with good faith and honesty in fact is whether the person disclosed all information (a) that he would have considered material if he were on the other side of the exchange, and (b) that he has reason to believe the other person considers material to the other person's choice to make the exchange, even if the information is not material to his own decision. A few examples will help explain what is required:

> A. A person has a used car for sale with a leaking master cylinder that causes the brakes to fail every 50 miles from fill-up with brake fluid. If the seller knows about the master cylinder and tells the buyer the car is in good condition, that would be an affirmative misrepresentation, fraud, a use of destructive power, and a violation of good faith and honesty in fact.

> B. If the buyer asks the seller about the brakes and the seller says they work fine *now*, without disclosing the master cylinder problem, that would be a half-truth, a fraudulent omission, a use of destructive power, and a violation of good faith and honesty in fact. By the buyer asking about the brakes, the seller knows the brakes' condition is material to the buyer's decision, and the seller must tell all he knows, or say what information he is withholding.

> C. If the seller responds truthfully and completely to the buyer's questions about the tires, transmission, engine and lights, but the buyer does not ask about the brakes, under the principle of *caveat emptor* this would not be fraud if the seller did nothing to actively induce a wrong conclusion by the buyer. It would, however, still violate good faith and honesty in fact. The seller would know from the buyer's questions that the mechanical condition of the car is material to the buyer. The master cylinder leak would be material to the seller's choice whether to buy or to any other person intending to use the car for transportation over 50 miles. Good faith and honesty in fact require a seller to disclose all information material to what the item is ordinarily used for, e.g., a car for transportation, a house for living in, food for eating, a lawnmower for cutting grass.

D. If the car is an antique but has some new parts and the seller uses the car for transportation without knowing its value as an antique and the buyer indicates his interest in it as an antique and that with original parts it would be very valuable, the seller must disclose the new parts because he knows that is material to the buyer although irrelevant to the seller. If one party knows information that he has reason to believe is material to the other's choice, even if it is irrelevant to his own choice, he must either reveal the information fully or say he has material information but is withholding it.

E. If the buyer recognizes the car as an antique, but the seller thinks it is only a junker, good faith and honesty in fact would require the buyer to tell the seller all the information the buyer considers material to buying the car. If the buyer considers his knowledge of the value of the car to be a possession he does not want to give up, he may tell the seller that he is withholding information about the value of the car in negotiating the price. But, in withholding the information, good faith and honesty in fact require the seller not to minimize the significance of the information withheld, but rather to convey to the seller the importance of the information withheld. This might be accomplished by the buyer saying that he is an antique car dealer, that he intends to take the car and resell it to someone he knows who wants one, and that he expects to make a substantial profit as a result. The seller can then choose whether he is better off selling or not. Good faith and honesty in fact applies to all parties in every exchange.

Good faith and honesty in fact are similar to the law of fiduciary duty.[7] A fiduciary duty exists when one person undertakes to act for another with complete loyalty, trust, utmost good faith and candor. An agent owes his principal a fiduciary duty regarding everything within the scope of his agency. Employees owe their employer a fiduciary duty, as do attorneys to their clients, trustees to their beneficiaries, a partner to his partners, corporate officers to their corporations. A fiduciary must with fairness, promptness, and completeness, disclose all facts within his knowledge that are material to his responsibilities to the other person. A material fact is generally one to which a reasonable person would attach importance in choosing a course of action.

By signing the Social Contract, each party creates a relationship of trust and confidence with all other parties not to use destructive power. A fiduciary duty differs from good faith and honesty in fact because information can be a possession that one may not be compelled to give up in an exchange. A fiduciary may not withhold any material information from the one he owes his duty. In "arms length" transactions under the Social Contract, there is a fiduciary duty to disclose all material information or to disclose that specific material information is being withheld.

Ideally, whenever citizens exchange possessions, each citizen should know as much as the other when choosing to make the exchange. Voluntary persuasion is not a game of wits. An exchange by constructive power is never a zero sum game. Voluntary persuasion always results in each person believing he has more valuable possessions as a result of an exchange. As other-conscious individuals, citizens do not desire to profit at the expense of other citizens or wards.

Good faith also requires every citizen not to aid or assist another in using destructive power against another citizen or ward. This obligation is measured by the same objective standard, of reasonable foresight as any use of destructive power. All citizens must refrain from aiding or assisting any use of destructive power. If a real estate developer hires a contractor to build an office building and instructs him to use inferior materials that could result in the building collapsing, the contractor must refuse. If the contractor instructs an employee to use the inferior materials, the employee must refuse.

Good faith and honesty in fact in the Social Contract are necessary to eliminate completely destructive power and to guarantee that only constructive power is used. The economy under the Social Contract will not come to a halt if people cannot use their superior information sources to buy low and sell high from trusting people ignorant of important information. If some information is a possession, it need not be disclosed if the fact that withholding that information is disclosed. Without honesty in fact and good faith, exchanges will be just another way to satisfy one's desires by taking another's possessions.

> C. *I agree to act only upon a reasonable belief that the act will not create an unreasonable risk of injury to the person or possessions of another party to this contract or a ward.*

To use constructive power requires one have a reasonable belief that an act will not create an unreasonable risk of injury to the person or possessions of another member of Society. Unconscious uses of destructive power endanger others as much as conscious ones. If a person is run over in a cross walk and rendered a quadriplegic, whether the driver of the car consciously intended to do it or he was changing the radio station, the victim is still a quadriplegic. The destructive consequence of the act is identical.

Anglo-American law uses the concepts of negligence and strict liability to require compensation for unintended injury. An in-depth discussion of the law of negligence or non-intentional torts is unnecessary. Suffice it to say that negligence is under all the circumstances doing of something that a reasonable person would not have done or failing to do something a reasonable person would have done which results in injury or damage to another. Negligence measures all conduct by what a mythical reasonable person would have done under the same circumstances. If this mythical reasonable person would have acted differently and injury would not have occurred, the law imposes liability on the person who caused the injury. Strict liability is imposed on a manufacturer or seller of a product that is defective when it is sold and that defect causes injury, regardless whether the manufacturer or seller knew of the defect or took all reasonable steps to prevent it.

This section of the Social Contract includes negligence, but it also requires that if there is insufficient information available to conclude that no unreasonable risk of injury will be created, then the act must not be done. Reasonableness applies to two separate considerations. The first is whether the act will lessen another's possessions, and is solely a matter of the foresight of the destructive consequences. Some possible injury is foreseeable from most acts. Thus, the second consideration of reasonableness is of the probability and severity of the damage created by the act. When an electric company places power poles near the side of a street, it creates a risk that a vehicle might collide with it and cause injury. Many factors affect the probability of a collision and the severity of any resulting injury. All these factors must be considered when deciding whether the risk created is "unreasonable."

As discussed earlier, the government may pass laws governing specific acts that violate this section, which are commonly referred to as an exercise of the police power. An example is the Florida statute that provides:

> It is not lawful for any company or individual to leave open any pit or other hole outside of an enclosure of a greater depth and breadth than 2 feet; provided, however, such pit or hole may be left open by enclosing the same with a fence or other enclosure that would be a safeguard against horses, cattle or other domestic animals falling into the same; . . .[8]

This statute establishes that it is foreseeable that people or animals will fall into an open pit and be injured. It also determines that the probability of the loss occurring and its severity are unreasonable without fencing the open pit. Other examples of such laws include elevator safety codes, electrical codes, building codes, etc. Although the government may enact such laws, they are presumptive only. Any citizen may challenge them as not a proper implementation of this term of the Social Contract.

Suppose a city enacts an ordinance prohibiting running a red light because it creates an unreasonable risk of injury and makes the offense punishable by a fine. The city then sets its traffic lights on a short cycle making it virtually impossible to avoid running a red light so the city can raise revenue by giving out tickets. This law when applied with the light timing would be struck down as a violation of the Social Contract. By setting the lights to increase revenue from tickets rather than to reduce the unreasonableness of the risk of injury from running a red light, the city uses destructive power not to reduce the risk of injury but to increase its revenue. In fact, by making running a red light more probable, not less, the city itself uses conscious destructive power.

In ordinary daily life, driving a car, mowing the lawn, or cleaning the pool, the negligence concept is adequate. For these kinds of acts, common experience is sufficient to foresee the risks posed and the reasonableness of the consequences. The problem with the present negligence standard is that science and technology have progressed so rapidly and will no doubt continue to do so, that the consequences of some acts may be unforeseeable. An example is the introduction of large quantities of man-made chemicals, such as DDT, chloro-fluorocarbons, or greenhouse gases or genetically altered organisms into the environment. When these acts were done, there may well have been no information sufficient to indicate any unreasonable risk associated with them. There was, however, an insufficient fund of human knowledge for anyone to have a reasonable belief that the widespread release of these chemicals would not create an unreasonable risk of injury. The Social Contract requires all citizens to have a sufficient fund of knowledge and experience to reasonably believe that their acts will not create an unreasonable risk of injury to another member of Society, or they must not act.

Today, the reasonableness of the risks is determined in several ways. Legislatures may use the collective experience of society as when they pass a statute like the open pit statute. Or, they may establish a government agency to assess the risks of proposed actions, such as the Food and Drug Administration that is charged with determining that any drug sold is both "safe and effective." Courts also make these decisions when they impose or deny liability for injuries. Statistical methods of risk management are used to predict the probability and severity of an injury with the reasonableness of an insured risk reflected in the cost of insurance. Many professions, trades and industries have organizations that establish rules about the risk of injury. The Society of Automotive Engineers, The Joint Commission on the Accreditation of Hospitals, the American National Standards Institute, Underwriter's Laboratories and many others promulgate standards on how to avoid injury. All of these methods would be available under the Social Contract, but the final decision rests with the judiciary as the final interpreter of the Social Contract.

There is a difficult issue that will always exist in a technological society. When a manufacturer designs a product for mass distribution. it must consider how the product may cause physical injury to people or property. No design is perfectly safe. The question is, what is safe enough? The Ford Pinto exploding gas tank case illustrates this problem.

In the early 1970's, Ford Motor Company designed the Pinto with a gas tank near the rear axle. When Ford tested the Pinto, it learned that in rear end accidents, the gas tank would rupture and result in a fuel fed fire that could burn the occupants to death. Ford analyzed the likelihood of these accidents and the cost of defending lawsuits and paying the burn victims versus the cost of fixing the gas tank design, and found that fixing the design would cost more than paying the claims. When the jury in one of these cases heard of Ford's deliberate calculation to pay burn victims instead of fixing the design, it awarded punitive damages of $125 million.[9] Not coincidently, this amount was what Ford estimated it would save by not fixing the design.

Every product design has advantages and disadvantages, risks and benefits. The Pinto was designed to be basic transportation for under $2000. Correcting the gas tank design would have cost Ford a substantial amount of money, and increased the price of the car. The number of accidents in which the gas tank would rupture and cause a fire was small compared to the number of Pintos sold and the miles driven. The decision not to change the gas tank design was an entirely rational one that furthered the self-interest of Ford and its shareholders. But every conscious use of destructive power is a rational calculation of self-interest, and without the possibility of punitive damages, would be made every day by businessmen. Even if the design had been changed, all fuel-fed fires would not have been prevented. So how safe would Ford have to make the Pinto if the Social Contract were the standard? Would Ford have used destructive power by selling the Pinto without fixing the gas tank?

Ford knew that without fixing the gas tank some people would be burned alive. Ford was like the person with a rifle shooting in the air. The chances of someone being struck and killed by the bullet is very small, perhaps one in 10,000. But, Ford expected to sell hundreds of thousands, if not millions, of Pintos, thus guaranteeing that some people would be burned to death. The risk was small for any one person, but it was a certainty that some people would be burned to death.

Ford did not fully and completely disclose the risk of fire in rear end collisions when it sold the Pinto. No Pinto purchaser had an opportunity to choose whether he would be better off with a Pinto with the poorly designed gas tank versus a different car. The gas tank information was certainly relevant to the choice whether to buy a Pinto. Without disclosing this information, Ford would have used the destructive power of involuntarily persuasion. Had Ford disclosed all relevant information and customers chose to accept those risks, all other things being equal, Ford would not have used destructive power *as to its purchasers*.

Manufacturers must make choices about the risks and benefits of the design of their products, but purchasers must be able to choose whether to accept the choice of risks and benefits a manufacturer makes. When a manufacturer uses voluntary persuasion, a purchaser cannot later complain that his decision to accept those risks was wrong. That is the personal responsibility of a morally capable individual. This choice is no different than buying a stock knowing the price can go down but hoping it will go up. If the risk of loss becomes a reality, one cannot complain that his judgment of the value proved wrong.

If a seller provides written information about the risks of its product and the purchaser fails to read it, the purchaser cannot later blame the manufacturer. A manufacturer may not, however, simply provide a boiler plate disclaimer or disclosure of risks in fine print that would take a determined effort to find, read and understand.[10] Voluntary persuasion requires a disclosure of relevant information that will bring to the other's attention with the same degree of emphasis and importance that the person disclosing those facts would place on them if they were purchasing the product themselves. Anything less is a half-truth.

The government has a role in determining the risks and benefits of various products as it does with other uses of destructive power. The government may set standards to prevent unreasonable risks. For instance, the government could adopt gas tank design regulations based on a determination that the mass production and sale of gas tanks with a noncomplying design would constitute an unreasonable risk of injury. If Ford used a noncomplying gas tank, Ford would have to disclose to any customer that its gas tank did not comply with the government standards and the risk of the noncomplying design. If a person knowing all this chose to purchase a Pinto anyway, as between Ford and the purchaser, Ford would not be responsibility for any injury resulting from that design. The acceptance of the risk is a part of the determination of value necessary for every exchange to result from voluntary persuasion, and is not subject to second guessing.

For all other members of Society who do not choose to accept the risks of the gas tank design and are injured by it, Ford would be liable for using destructive power. For the latter parties, the government standard would be the equivalent of what is now strict liability. Not only would the manufacturer of the non-compliant product be responsible for the consequences, the person who chose to buy the product would also be equally responsible. The absence of or compliance with a government regulation would not foreclose a determination that a design presented an unreasonable risk of injury to the person or property of a member of Society, because the government is not required to adopt regulations and the judiciary has the ultimate decision on that question as the final interpreter of the Social Contract.

The most probable result of destructive power as the standard for in the design of products would be that manufacturers would likely not sell products the government concluded presented unreasonable risks of injury, and if they did, purchasers would probably not buy them. The Pinto probably would not have been a successful car had Ford fully disclosed that the gas tank would rupture and catch fire. If Ford knew that it would have to disclose its decision to allow a certain number of people to burn to death rather than spend five dollars per car to fix the design, it probably would have fixed the design. Had Ford chosen to sell the Pinto without fully disclosing the information about the gas tank, that would have been a conscious use of destructive power, which would justify criminal prosecution of all Ford officers and employees who made that choice or consciously carried it out.

If every manufacturer must disclose its decisions about the risks and benefits of its designs to avoid the conscious use of destructive power, the competitive advantage of making cheaper, less safe products, will surely disappear. The argument that manufacturers cannot afford to make safer products because their customers will purchase their competitors' cheaper less safe ones, will cease to have validity.

Voluntary persuasion is also the standard for determining cases involving informed consent. Before a doctor may treat a patient, she must obtain the patient's informed consent. It is called informed consent because the doctor is required to disclose to the patient the risks and benefits of the treatment. The patient must then choose or consent for himself whether to undergo the procedure. An case involving a lack of informed consent turns on whether the patient would have consented if the necessary information had been provided. This is the question in every case involving a claim of involuntary persuasion. What would the person have done if all the relevant information had been disclosed?

In most jurisdictions if the mythical "reasonable person" given the necessary information would have undergone the treatment, the doctor is not liable. Many courts use the "reasonable person" test because they fear that patients who have suffered an adverse result will with hindsight say they would not have consented just to win a case against the doctor. In some instances, however, courts have allowed the personal beliefs of the patient to prevail. While most reasonable people consent to blood transfusions, a follower of Jehovah's Witness is not deprived of the choice to refuse on religious grounds.

The common element in all the above legal decisions is the concept of voluntary persuasion. In all exchanges, each participant must choose whether he will have more valuable possession as a result of the exchange. As long as exchanges result from full disclosure of relevant information, choices cannot be later questioned because that requires the substitution of one person's value for another's. When full information is not disclosed, the person's value judgment is distorted. Every person who makes an exchange has the power to insulate himself from any claim of destructive power by simply disclosing *all* the information relevant to the other's judgment of value of the possessions exchanged. If in doubt, disclose. Whoever fails to disclose the full information must bear the consequences, including any risks of litigation being decided against him and the impossibility of predicting precisely what would have happened if full disclosure had been made. In legal terminology, the one who fails to fully disclose must always bear the burden of proof and persuasion on how events would have occurred if he had fully disclosed all relevant information.

D. *I agree to act toward all wards commensurately with their mental and physical capacities.*

Society will have many people within its boundaries who are not citizens. Some will be minor children of citizens who have not yet acquired moral capacity. Some of these will never acquire the moral capacity to become a citizen. Some people will choose not to become a citizen, and some will be former citizens who have withdrawn or whose citizenship has been revoked for lacking moral capacity. And, there will be temporary visitors or immigrants who have entered Society either legally or illegally.

How will Society deal with noncitizens?

Wards

Wards are all those persons, and animals, who have not acquired the moral capacity to become a citizen of Society.

Children Before Reaching the Age of Maturity

Before children acquire moral capacity, they are wards of their parents or Society. Parents are responsible for their children's well-being and for supplying them with the physical and civil necessities because if a child demands the necessities, Society must use destructive power to provide them. Therefore, the foreseeable consequence of having a child and failing to provide it with the necessities is a use of destructive power against all citizens who must share the burden of providing the necessities.

For quite a long time, the law has required parents to provide their children with the necessities.[11] The Letters of Guardianship of the Person and Property of a Minor in Georgia instruct the guardian as follows:

> It is your duty to see that the ward is adequately fed, clothed, sheltered, educated, and cared for, and that the ward receives all necessary medical attention.[12]

Parents who abuse or neglect their duties to their children can have them taken away and their parental rights terminated. Parents who consciously use destructive power against their children can be charged with a crime. The legal obligation of parents to support their children does not depend on government imposing it, but is inherent in the Social Contract obligation not to use destructive power.

Minor children of citizens are members of Society and are entitled to protection from destructive power the same as any citizen, except that parents may use the destructive power necessary to discipline, train and educate their children to acquire moral capacity and to prevent them from using destructive power against others before they acquire moral capacity and choose whether to sign the Social Contract. A parent's use of destructive power against a child must be commensurate with its mental and physical capacities, in the same way a government agent's use of destructive power to achieve a government purpose must be necessary and not excessive. Only the least destructive power necessary may be used. Government may thus regulate the destructive power parents use to discipline and train their children, keeping in mind Society's objective to nurture children to become morally capable of choosing whether to become a citizen, and to prevent children from using destructive power against others before they become citizens. The government only establishes the curriculum to educate children to acquire moral capacity. Parents may choose whatever additional education their children will receive.[13]

Once a child acquires moral capacity and chooses whether to execute the Social Contract, its parents' responsibility to provide the child's necessities ends. Parents will surely continue to help their children further their education or find a job or buy a house or any of the thousands of other ways parents have always helped their children. Like current law, however, a parent's obligation to provide any of the necessities ends once their children become morally capable.

Children Who Never Reach Maturity and Citizens Who Become Incapacitated

Unfortunately, some people will never acquire the moral capacity to choose to become a citizen. They will remain wards of their parents or, if orphaned, the government. They may be given a job compatible with their mental and physical capacities. Many mentally retarded people seem to enjoy jobs that others find intolerably boring. To be commensurate with the ward's mental and physical condition, a job must be dignified and humane given the ward's capabilities. Society's obligation to provide for permanent wards is another inducement for morally capable people to become a party to the Social Contract. This obligation reflects a substantial advance over the ancient practice of infanticide.

Some citizens will lose moral capacity due to a brain tumor, stroke, injury, disease[14] or aging. A person need not commit a crime for his incapacity to become known. Today adjudications of incompetency are common. When a person is found to be incompetent, the court appoints a guardian for the person's physical needs or to manage his financial affairs or both. Under the Social Contract, the standard of competency is moral capacity.

If a citizen pleads insanity or diminished capacity to a crime, he admits a lack of moral capacity and a breach of his agreement always to act in accordance with the Social Contract. The person thus automatically reverts to being a ward. For the person charged with a crime, the court might well consider the circumstances that led to the crime and the claim of incapacity in determining whether punishment or treatment or both is appropriate, but once a person pleads lack of moral capacity he would almost certainly be a ward for life. Only the most unusual circumstance would allow a former citizen to be restored to citizenship.

Non-Human Animals

We cannot be certain of the mental capacity of other animals. The more they are studied, the more like us they seem to become. For animals that can be shown to have mental capacities approaching or equal to those of human children or mentally retarded humans who are wards of the state, these animals should be treated the same as human wards, at least by those humans responsible for bringing them into the world, like bringing children into the world.

For instance, animal breeders, especially of great apes such as chimpanzees, orangutans and gorillas, should be responsible for them the same as children. This is not to say that such animals cannot be considered property while children are not.[15] It does mean that a person who breeds any animal is responsible for its well-being the same as he would be for a child of equal mental and physical capacities. If the breeder sells the animal to another person, the buyer would become its guardian with all the same responsibilities of the original breeder.

Medical research is not necessarily prohibited with great apes or other animals, but the government may legislate about how animals may be treated commensurate with their mental capacities, i.e., a chimpanzee must be treated more humanely than a mouse or a gold fish.

All citizens need not become vegetarians, but other-consciousness as the foundation of morality does not end at the tip of the human nose. Animal cruelty laws are an extension of other-consciousness to non-humans, and they may extend to the conditions in which animals raised for food are bred, raised and slaughtered. The infliction of unnecessary pain and suffering on animals often creates as much internal conflict as the similar treatment of humans.

Temporary Wards: Visitors and Immigrants

Society cannot be isolated from the rest of the world. Foreigners will visit, and some will want to become citizens. Government will determine who may immigrate and set the conditions of their entry. Before entering Society, an immigrant or tourist must agree to comply with the Social Contract and Society's laws like any citizen or citizen's ward, and thereby becomes a temporary ward. Temporary wards, whether legal or illegal, may not demand Society provide them any of the necessities. They are not parties to the Social Contract, and citizens only agree to use Society's power of alliance to provide the necessities to citizens and their wards. Otherwise, by illegally entering the territory of Society, a person could use the power of alliance against the very people who created it. This would be like allowing a burglar to break into a house and then go to court to require the owner to feed, clothe and educate him. Only citizens and their wards may invoke that power. If a temporary ward cannot provide his or his ward's necessities, he and his wards should be deported. Nothing, however, would prohibit citizens from using their constructive power to provide temporary wards who legally enter Society with any of the necessities, but temporary wards may not demand that Society use its destructive power to provide them.

Noncitizens by Choice

While it is difficult to imagine any sane person with moral capacity choosing not to become a party to the Social Contract, there will certainly be some. Non-members have no artificial rights protected by Society's power of alliance. They cannot require the government to provide them with the necessities. They have only the natural right to try to do anything as does every citizen and ward.

If a non-member contracts with a citizen, the non-member may not sue to enforce the agreement, but a citizen may invoke the power of Society to enforce his side of the contract. If a citizen runs over a non-member in the street with a car, either negligently, drunkenly or intentionally, the non-member has no artificial right to compel the government to make the citizen pay compensation or to punish the citizen. If a non-member has a house, and someone moves in while the non-member is away, the non-member has no artificial right to have government remove a citizen or anyone else from his house. He does not own a house, because ownership is an artificial right enforced by the power of alliance of Society.

The full power of Society should be no match for any internal use of destructive power by one or more non-members within Society. If some non-members run a protection racket, government may treat them like lions escaped from a zoo or a pack of wild wolves.

Former Citizens

Finally, there will be people who have renounced their citizenship or had the Social Contract revoked pursuant to Article IV. The latter will usually be in government custody when the revocation occurs. If the person's acts are severe enough to revoke his citizenship, he will certainly be a sufficient threat to Society that government will either keep the person in custody, expel him from Society or execute him to protect members of Society.

Like non-members by choice, former citizens have no artificial rights regarding their conditions of confinement, exile or execution. Society, for the peace of mind of its citizens' other-consciousness for those who do not have it themselves, may make the conditions of confinement or execution humane, but a non-member has no artificial right to demand such treatment.

II. GOVERNMENT TO INDIVIDUAL

Government Power

Government must always be thought of as individuals using destructive power toward other individuals. The methods employed may be as direct as a police officer shooting a fleeing bank robber or as indirect as requiring an employer to send part of every employee's wages to the government. Government is nothing more than one group of people, with gun in hand, telling another group what they can and cannot do. The people of government do not always directly point the gun, but they always have it. If one disobeys, the gun is always government's last resort, and the gun is always destructive power.

Government programs, such as Welfare, Aid to Families with Dependent Children, Social Security, education and research grants, and funding for the National Endowment for the Arts or National Public Radio use the gun as surely as do the police. Government cannot spend without first receiving. The association between the people of government taking with destructive power and giving to others has been weakened because the two have been separated. If Social Security taxes were collected by a soldier with an M16 knocking on our door demanding money and then handing it to a retired executive standing next to him on our doorstep, we would connect the two. We may "voluntarily" have part of our wages deducted from our paycheck and "voluntarily" file a tax return, but the payment is no less compelled by destructive power. Without the compelled payment, government could spend nothing. The very nature of government is the use of destructive power by some individuals against others.

 A. *The government shall be so constituted as a majority of the parties to this contract shall from time to time specify, but shall, regardless of form, always be subordinate to this contract and the judiciary required by this contract.*

The specific form of government to enforce the Social Contract may be determined from time to time by a majority of society. The Social Contract does not establish the form of government because the form of government is relatively unimportant compared to government being subject to the Social Contract whatever its form. It can be a monarchy, hereditary or otherwise, democracy or oligarchy. The citizens may prefer democracy because it provides a feeling of having some influence, no matter how small, in how government is run and what laws are made. After several generations under the Social Contract, however, this feeling will likely diminish because the individual will have more real power. The critical, indispensable element for any government under the Social Contract is a judiciary that owes its allegiance only to the Social Contract and Society, not any person or group within Society. Its decisions about whether the Social Contract has been violated, especially by government agents using destructive power, must be enforced unfailingly against any majority that opposes it.

A written Social Contract enforceable by the judiciary is the real protection from destructive power, from might makes right, that every citizen and ward of Society must have. As the enforceable fundamental law of Society, the judiciary is the ultimate power of a single individual against any majority, like the Supreme Court freeing Milligan in spite of the whole U.S. Army and executive branch wanting to hang him. But unlike in *Milligan,* no act of Congress, not even a constitutional amendment approved by ninety-nine percent of Society, can override a person's legally enforceable artificial rights created by the Social Contract. Every citizen and ward can invoke this power against all of Society. Might does make right, and the judiciary under the Social

Contract is like a magnifying glass through which every citizen and ward can focus the might of all Society to enforce his artificial rights in the Social Contract.

If a hereditary monarch may act only to achieve the purposes of the Social Contract and is subject to the judiciary's decisions about her proper use of destructive power, then the absence of a specific, though minutely small voice at the ballot box, likely will eventually not be missed. Democratic or republican institutions are not critical to an individualistic society, though they may be preferred. To vote and be in the minority means nothing. To stop any majority from violating one's artificial rights under the Social Contract against any odds is true individual political power. As long as every citizen and ward of society has this power, the form and procedures of the legislature or executive branches of government is important primarily as a matter of efficiency, and other forms of government may well prove preferable. Thus, liberal democracy or liberal republicanism is not the end of history.

As discussed in Chapter XII, the Social Contract almost certainly will be adopted by an existing government and its citizens. Thus the existing government will most likely continue, perhaps with some modifications. As long as the Social Contract is the ultimate source of all artificial rights and thus the law within Society, the form of the government can be changed from time to time so long as the judiciary is not disturbed and the new government remains subordinate to the Social Contract and the judiciary's interpretation of it.

Any government constitution is inferior legal authority to the Social Contract so a change in the constitutional form of government would be more like the repeal of a statute by Congress or a state legislature, or the change of a state constitution today in the United States. Such changes are regularly made without fear of social unrest because of the power and stability provided by the federal government. The judiciary and the Social Contract would provide a similar power and stability for changes in the national government. The Social Contract's limitations on government's power and the imposition of affirmative governmental duties will give Society its legitimacy and stability, not the constitution of the government.

> B. *The government shall make all laws and take all actions necessary to implement and enforce this contract.*

After the form of government is selected, or continued, the government must implement the Social Contract. Government's first responsibility is to defend Society against all external threats to its continued existence. Next, government must protect each member of Society from uses of destructive power by others within Society. Next, the government must establish the independent judiciary required by the Social Contract. Next, the government must provide the physical or civil necessities for those unable to provide their own. Finally, the government may take any other actions that are consistent with the Social Contract it deems necessary and appropriate to accomplish its objective.

While the functions of government have priorities, an individualistic society cannot emerge without each function being fully accomplished. Each of these functions is necessary to maintain the systems of complexity for an individualistic society to emerge from biological society. A failure on any level prevents an individualistic society from emerging.

C. *The government shall provide for the protection of all parties to this contract and wards from all external and internal uses of destructive power.*

Protection from an external use of destructive power is the basic defense of Society from invasion or attack. The people who are government are responsible for defending Society from all such destructive power by all necessary means. So long as there are nations or societies not founded on the Social Contract, Society will need a military.

Although any citizen may bring an action in the judiciary to enforce the Social Contract, the executive and legislative must have almost exclusive discretion in the conduct of the defense of Society from external threats. For instance, whether to maintain a standing army, navy or air force, the strength and weapon systems available, and whether to provide foreign aid to other countries; whether to enter into treaties or agreements with other nations for defense and many more "national security" issues, must be left to the discretion of the citizens given the responsibility for that job and who have taken an oath to act in conformance with the Social Contract.

The judiciary would not be entirely impotent in this area, but its role would be extremely limited. Only if the government proposed to surrender to an external threat, and thus abdicate its duty to protect Society, could a citizen sue the government to require it to defend Society. The judiciary could then order a defense or replace the government with those who will defend Society.

In the end, however, the vitality and survival of Society will come from its citizens' commitment to the Social Contract and Society, not from coerced obedience to a judicial or government order. If the citizens are not willing to use the entire power of alliance of Society to defend it, it will surely perish, and no judicial decree will impede its demise. In forming the government, input by citizens to the decisions on defense and national security may well be the best means of assuring that an adequate defense is maintained. For this reason a republican form of government may be desirable, as long as every nation is not governed by the Social Contract.

To enforce the Social Contract's ban on internal destructive power, government must create and maintain a police force and correctional system to protect Society from and *prevent* uses of destructive power. If the best efforts at prevention fail, then the police must apprehend, try and punish violators of the Social Contract. The following example from a Florida case will illustrate the difference between the present system and the Social Contract.

Since 1979, Florida has had a Domestic Violence statute that allowed a court to issue an injunction against physical abuse by a spouse or former spouse. Originally the complaining spouse had to identify abuse that had already occurred and that had been made the subject of a police report. By 1994, the statute had been amended to require a spouse to prove only a "reasonable cause to believe he or she is about to be the victim of any act of domestic violence." In *Rey v. Perez-Gurri*,[16] Rey testified:

> On September 14, 1994, [her former husband] told [her] to the (sic) read the article in the Miami Herald. [He] was making reference to the article of the murder-suicide that took place in Hialeah on September 13, 1994. [She] states that [he] told her "Read it, because that is what is going to happen to you." Metro-Dade Police case # 479259-P. [She] states that in the past, while they were married [he] would physically abuse her by pulling her hair, slamming her head against the wall and locking her in the closet for hours. [She] states that [her former husband], on three occasions pointed a gun at her and threatened to kill her. Also, in 1992, [he] attempted to run her over with his car. [She] states that at this time she is in fear for her safety because [his] behavior is erratic and she truly feels he will fulfill his threat to kill her.

Perez-Gurri denied everything, and the trial court denied a permanent injunction because Rey "failed to prove [Perez-Gurri] had the apparent ability to carry out the threats he allegedly made." The court of appeal reversed, holding that all Rey needed to show is that she "has a reasonable cause to believe that she is *about to become* a victim of domestic violence," and she had adequately shown that.

Without the Domestic Violence statute, which existed only by the grace of the legislature, the police and courts can do nothing to *prevent* abuse or murder. Under the Social Contract, no enabling statute is required. The Social Contract imposes an affirmative obligation on government to protect members of Society from all uses of destructive power. If the police fail to protect a person, she can sue for adequate protection as long as the threat exists. If the government does not have enough police to provide the protection, it must hire them or arrest the person making the threat. A lack of resources is no excuse. The nature of the threat of physical destructive power or the relationship of the parties is irrelevant. The Social Contract creates a legal right in every citizen and ward to be protected from destructive power by the government.

As in the *Rey* case, only a reasonable cause to believe that destructive power will be used is sufficient to require government protection. Unlike the Florida statute, however, an injunction is not sufficient protection as shown by the reference in the *Rey* case to a murder suicide that had occurred in spite of an injunction.

Article I of the Social Contract *is* an injunction against destructive power. Anyone who threatens another with destructive power violates their promise never to use destructive power. If the threat of future destructive power is real, the government *must* respond in a way sufficient to prevent the threat from being carried out. If the only way to prevent the physical destructive power is to arrest and lock up indefinitely the person who made the threat, then that must be done. If a police officer must be posted around the clock at the person's house, that must be done. If a neighborhood is being terrorized by street gangs, and it takes a battalion of soldiers to protect the residents, then that must be done. Physical destructive power must be eliminated from Society no matter how much it costs. The power of alliance of the Social Contract is created for that purpose, and whenever it fails, Society fails.

Domestic disputes can produce great emotional distress and impaired judgment, but by executing the Social Contract every citizen warrants that he can and will choose always to act in all situations without using destructive power. Choosing to use destructive power against a spouse or child borders on renouncing the Social Contract, which would authorize its termination for that person with all the consequences that entails.

> D. *Upon request, the government, shall provide the physical and civil necessities to each party to this contract or his or her ward*

> who is unable to supply his own physical or civil necessities through the use of constructive power.

"Upon request" means that the government has no affirmative obligation to seek out citizens, as opposed to their wards, without the necessities and force them to take the necessities from the government. Each citizen learns before entering the Social Contract, that if she is unable to provide her or her ward's necessities with constructive power, she can demand and receive them from the government. But, there are consequences for using the destructive power of government to obtain the necessities, and each citizen is entitled to choose for herself whether to accept those consequences, which include complying with all reasonable conditions the government imposes upon providing the necessities.

Each ward of a citizen is entitled to his necessities from his parents, but if the parents cannot provide them, then government must provide them. While a ward has an artificial right to require government to provide the necessities, she may not be mentally or physically capable of exercising that right. When a parent fails to provide the necessities to his ward and fails to request the government to provide them, the parent uses destructive power against his ward, and of course, that destructive power is not necessary to educate and train the ward to acquire moral capacity or prevent the ward from using destructive power. Government must protect wards, like citizens, from destructive uses of power such as physical abuse and neglect by parents or guardians failing to provide the necessities, especially for wards too young to be able to notify the government of the destructive power used against them. Therefore, the government must identify wards without the necessities as part of its obligation to protect all citizens and their wards from destructive power and to provide them with the necessities.

A number of circumstances can result in a citizen requesting government to supply the necessities. There may be high unemployment as in the Great Depression, so that all those who want to work cannot find a job. There would be voluntary unemployment insurance through private entities and savings and help from family, friends, church or other charitable organizations. Any use of constructive power to provide a person's necessities is permissible, as constructive power always is. It would be rare for a person to lose his job today and need the necessities from government tomorrow. But, if a citizen's resources run out, the government must provide the necessities, if requested, in order to maintain the moral foundation of Society.

Some people will never be able to provide their necessities with constructive power due to physical handicaps. These people may be citizens if they lack only physical capacity, not moral capacity. Government must provide these citizens' their necessities, if requested.

Due to mental deficiency, a person may never acquire moral capacity to choose to become a citizen. The parents of such wards are responsible for the wards' necessities, but if the parents die or cannot provide them, government must. A lack of moral capacity, does not necessarily mean that a ward cannot be self-sufficient with constructive power. Several people with Down's syndrome have become successful actors. Without passing judgment on whether they have moral capacity or not, assuming that they do not, they apparently can supply their own necessities. And, there may be other means for wards to supply their necessities with constructive power. While these wards will always require a guardian, the government may not need to provide their necessities. For those who cannot supply their own necessities, the government must supply them.

In providing the civil necessities, Society guarantees no one that she will be a doctor, lawyer, physicist or tool and die maker. If, however, one has the ability to meet the standards for a job or profession, then no lack of economic means can prevent her from getting the necessary education. No child can ever be allowed to think that any educational goal is beyond her reach because the economic means are not available to achieve it.

> E. *The government shall establish an independent judiciary that shall openly, timely and uniformly adjudicate all claims arising from this contract. No adjudication of an individual's rights shall be made without reasonable notice and the opportunity to confront and compel witnesses and evidence for and against each party, nor shall an adjudication of an individual's rights be re-opened once final, except upon proof that it was obtained with destructive power or proof beyond a reasonable certainty that it was based upon facts that are untrue. Before assuming office, all judges shall take the following oath: Upon my honor, I will interpret and enforce the Social Contract for every citizen and ward free of any interest other than to establish and maintain a society devoted to the greatest opportunity for each and every member to achieve his or her happiness.*

No single individual can enforce the Social Contract for himself or for others. Any attempt to do so is a reversion to a pre-Social Contract condition of the natural right to try to do anything. Society must have an institutional means for each individual member of Society to invoke the full power of alliance of Society to enforce the Social Contract against any opposing power within Society, whether that opposing power is the government or a private citizen or the Social Contract is "in vain."

Every individual must be able peacefully to invoke and command the full power of alliance of Society against anyone who violates the Social Contract. The institutional means for that is an independent judiciary whose function is to determine whether the Social Contract and every artificial rights that derive from it have been violated. If anyone uses destructive power contrary to the Social Contract, the judiciary must order the government to use the power of alliance to stop and remedy that use.

When Society is initially established, if an existing government is not continued, including its judiciary, one of the first duties of the new government will be to establish an independent judiciary. Independence is essential to the judiciary because of its unique role as the guardian of the individual and the Social Contract. The judiciary must be entirely above suspicion. No judge can have any loyalty or interest other than to the Social Contract. Otherwise, no one can be certain the judiciary will protect him against any violation of the Social Contract.

The government may initially decide how the judiciary will be organized and its judges selected. Because the judiciary has the final word on the Social Contract, once the judges are selected, they must decide whether the initial organization and method of selection complies with the Social Contract, and if not, they may change it. As with the form of government, the specific form of the judiciary is not fundamental, but the judges' independence and unquestionable loyalty to the Social Contract is.

Independence means that no judge can have any possible divided loyalty, either from past circumstances, present conditions, or future ambitions. Past circumstances are the person's life before selection as a judge. Present conditions means the time during which the judge holds office. Future ambitions refers to any possible future benefit not already fixed upon assuming office as a judge.

Judges may not be removed from office for any reason associated with the faithful performance of his official duties, and removal must be by the judiciary itself. The government may specify grounds it considers sufficient to remove a judge, and may bring before the judiciary, as may any citizen, information questioning the independence of a judge, but the judiciary must determine whether the judge has violated his independence. A measure of paranoia by judges about maintaining their independence will be healthy. Any disloyalty to the Social Contract or conscious breach of the Social Contract would require removal from office, and termination of the judge's citizenship because a breach of loyalty by a judge is the worst possible breach of the Social Contract and treason against Society. Another present condition is sufficient compensation. The government may set the compensation, but if over time it proves inadequate, the judiciary may amend it.

Independence from future ambition means a judge might not derive any benefit or advancement in the future that could in any way call his independence into question. If judges do not have life tenure, they could hold no judicial or government office beyond the initial term. If a judge's continued or future service is determined by anyone other than the judiciary, the judge will necessarily appear to be, if not actually be, beholding to that person. Tenure need not be for life, but if it is for less than 10 years, those who could serve would be severely limited. If the term is long enough, it may as well be for life.

The method of selecting judges is also left to the majority of Society in establishing the government or to the government. The government might use examinations, similar to civil service. Another alternative is a national judicial college to prepare lawyers to be judges. Graduates would become clerks to judges, after a time they would be eligible to become judges. New judges would start in small claims court, and after proving their ability move up to the trial courts with general jurisdiction, and then the appellate courts. A person who has completed law school, passed the bar exam, and practiced law for a number of years does not necessarily have the breadth of life experience, the intellect or the higher order moral reasoning necessary to be a judge.

All determinations of artificial rights, whether called trials or not, must be open to any citizen to attend. This is one of the essential safeguards against the abuse of power by the judiciary. All appellate court decisions should be explained in sufficient detailed that the losing party's lawyer can adequately explain the result to his client. Decisions without stated reasons would not be allowed. Perhaps even judges' deliberations, their conferences when deciding cases, should be open to the public for the same reasons the deliberations of legislative bodies are subject to sunshine laws.

Cases must be decided timely. There must be a sufficient number of judges and staff to decide all cases within a time to provide a meaningful, complete remedy. Timeliness varies depending upon the nature of the claim. A claim that the government has failed to provide the physical necessities to a party who has requested them must be very quickly determined. Any person who files a sworn statement that he has requested the government provide the physical necessities and he has not received them should be immediately issued a "Writ of Physical Necessity" that orders the government to provide these necessities until the person chooses not to accept further assistance or the government proves the person can provide his own physical necessities with constructive power.

The same would be true for the civil necessities. For instance, if a citizen or ward needs a lawyer to protect his artificial rights, a "Writ of Civil Necessity" would be immediately issued requiring the government to provide legal counsel. If a citizen or ward needs the means to obtain some education, but the course does not start for three months, a "Writ of Civil Necessity" may not issue until after an adjudication of the facts of inability to obtain the necessity with only constructive power.

If the violation is the use of destructive power in an exchange, and an award of damages with interest would adequately and completely remedy the violation, then a somewhat longer time would be sufficient. A reasonable time is one that in itself will not result in further damages. For instance, if the person will be put out of business if he must wait two years for the money, that loss cannot be completely remedied by a damage award with interest. What Ford or General Motors could ignore for years might put a small businessman out of business in a matter of months.

If a woman is misdiagnosed and will die of cancer in six months, her claim must be resolved within a time that would make the relief granted meaningful to her. Too often people cannot bring their case because no lawyer will take it because the client will not live long enough to see its end. This should never happen.

Timeliness also means to the final decision not just the initial decision in a trial court. There must be a final interpreter of the Social Contract, i.e., a Supreme Court. This finality and uniformity must also be timely given the nature of the case. This does not mean every litigant must be able to get a final decision by the equivalent of the U.S. Supreme Court within 6 months or even a year, but a litigant should not have to wait an unreasonable time from initiating an appeal until receiving a decision. A citizen incarcerated for a crime, even one who has had his citizenship revoked as a result of his conviction and who challenges his conviction or revocation of citizenship, is entitled to a decision within a time that will not require the citizen to remain incarcerated for an unreasonable time. Of course, the conditions of the confinement, e.g., house arrest versus solitary confinement, would affect the reasonableness of the time.

Maybe judges will grow lazy and expand their numbers and compensation beyond all reason. But, the budget for the entire Federal Judiciary of the United States for fiscal year 2001 is only $4.8 billion dollars. In a budget that exceeds $2 trillion, if the cost of the judiciary doubled or quadrupled, it would still be insignificant.

As a trial lawyer, I have a bias in favor of trial by jury; however, many other developed nations do not use juries in civil cases. I do not believe the Social Contract should forever enshrine this institution because better ways to determine the truth may evolve and there is no definitive evidence that jury trial is in fact the most reliable method. The Social Contract neither requires nor prohibits a majority of Society in establishing a constitution or the legislature in adopting a statute to make trial by jury the means of adjudication.

Many of the rules of criminal procedure and liberties in the Bill of Rights are inherent in the Social Contract while others, like the right to jury trial, may be adopted in forming the government. The guarantees in the Social Contract are as follows:

The First Amendment guarantee of freedom of religion, speech, assembly and petition (Social Contract, Article II, B, G and H.)

The Second Amendment guarantee of the right to bear arms. (Social Contract, Article II, B, G and H.)

The Third Amendment guarantee against the quartering of troops. (Social Contract, Article II, B, G and H.)

The Fourth Amendment guarantee against unreasonable searches and seizures. (Social Contract, Article II, B, G and H.)

The Fifth Amendment guarantee against double jeopardy, due process of law, or taking of private property without just compensation. (Social Contract, Article II, B, E, G and H.)

The Sixth Amendment guarantee of speedy, public trial, information about the charges, confrontation and compelled attendance of witnesses, and right to counsel. (Social Contract, Article II, D, E.)

The Eighth Amendment guarantee against excessive fines and cruel and unusual punishment. (Social Contract, Article II, B, G and H, III, B.)

Because the government may not use destructive power except as a last resort and only for the purposes set forth in the Social Contract, there are few conceivable circumstance in which the First Amendment freedoms could be abridged without using destructive power. For government to limit these rights, it would have to be for one of the purposes in the Social Contract, and would also have to be the last resort for accomplishing that purpose. It is most unlikely that such a situation would ever arise. Even under the First Amendment, speech may be regulated, but that regulation is subject to a legitimate purpose and must use the least restrictive means.

Words, like other acts, can have destructive consequences, however. Defamation, words that incite violence, and words that induce children to use destructive power, against themselves or others, could be regulated and give rise to a civil action for damages caused by them. Words communicated to citizens would be less subject to regulation because citizens have moral capacity and the ability to choose not to use destructive power. Citizens know the difference between words and actions and destructive consequences and their obligation not to use destructive power. Children often do not.

Words are the same as any other act. Government may regulate acts to prevent uses of destructive power. Thus, government may censor NAMBLA (North American Man Boy Love Association) because it advocates and instructs people how to use destructive power against children. It aids others to use destructive power, which is a violation of good faith and honesty in fact. Society does not have to tolerate white supremacists or anyone else who advocates or instructs others how to use destructive power against any members of Society any more than it must tolerate an invading army.

A clear distinction must be maintained between execrating another and advocating or inciting using destructive power against them. Only words that advocate or can cause the use of destructive power may be regulated or prohibited. Government must always use the least destructive power, and must show a valid causal relationship between the regulation and the prevention of destructive power, but if these two criteria are met, government may regulate speech like any other act. And even when the government does not regulate it, speech which causes destructive consequences is a destructive use of power for which those whose possessions have been taken are entitled to a judicial remedy.

Searches and seizures for criminal prosecutions are subject to the same limitations on legitimate purpose and least restrictive means. There is, however, no inherent guarantee against self-incrimination.[17]

The role of the judiciary under the Social Contract is perhaps more powerful than any judiciary ever before, but no judiciary has ever been explicitly responsible for protecting every individual against the collective power of Society. Even with its expansive role and responsibilities, it is still a weak branch of government. Its only power is to decide. It does not use physical power other than to decide whether the Social Contract has been breached. Because of the stringent requirement of independence, neither the judiciary as an institution and nor an individual judge can benefit from any of his decisions, except regarding compensation. Under the Social Contract, and indeed any society in which government derives limited powers from and whose objects are limited by the people it governs, someone must enforce those limitations or like any artificial right without the power to enforce it, they are meaningless.

Judges do not command armies or have police forces. They cannot decide what cases they will decide, unlike a legislative body that sets its own agenda, or the Supreme Court. Their decisions are public. The process of decision is open to public scrutiny during a trial. In short, there is great power in deciding that all Society may not do an act because it violates the rights of only one person who objects, but that is exactly what the Social Contract is established to allow because only then is every citizen free to seek happiness with the least possible interference by others. Someone must have this power, and an independent judiciary is the least dangerous to have it.

The obligation to use constructive power does not end when litigation begins. The constructive use of the power of persuasion requires each individual to disclose all information that could influence a judge or jury's decision. While information may be withheld in individual exchanges if it is a possession that could be lost if disclosed, there is no possession in the information necessary to a judicial decision. Any judgment obtained with destructive power, including involuntary persuasion, could be voided at any time by any interested person showing that it was obtained with destructive power. The government must also use constructive power in all judicial proceedings, and when it does not, the judgment may be reopened or reversed. Present law is similar when the government prosecutes a person for a crime.[18]

The Social Contract would also change various privileges. When each party must on his own, disclose all information relevant to a case, the information disclosed to or the advice received from one's attorney, if it is relevant to the determination, must be disclosed like all other relevant information. Because the lawyer's client must disclose all relevant information, the lawyer, as merely his client's agent, has the same obligation. This is not quite as radical a departure from current American law as it might first seem. In some states, if a litigant deliberately withholds or lies about relevant information, his case can be dismissed or judgment entered against him.[19] Similarly, when a lawyer knows that his client has not disclosed all required information, the lawyer is required to call upon his client to disclose the information, and if the client refuses, to take steps to prevent harm from the nondisclosure, or to disclose it himself.[20]

Each party in both criminal and civil cases today, except in criminal cases in the Federal Courts and some states, has the right to obtain discovery of relevant information from the other party and from persons and entities not parties to the action. This process is cumbersome, costly, archaic and rife with cunning and deceit. The trial lawyer's main function under the Social Contract will be to assist his client in disclosing all relevant information to the court, whether or not it is helpful to the client's case. Since all parties must make this disclosure, and any judgment can be reopened if it is not made, the process will become more efficient, fair, and more likely to produce a correct decision.

Under the current adversarial system, the trial lawyer has an inherent conflict between putting forward the strongest case for his client on the facts and the law, and the disclosure of all relevant information. Lawyers can face enormous pressure to parse a request for information as narrowly and legalistically as possible to avoid disclosing harmful information. The case books are full of cases where these legalistic, and sometimes deceitful and dishonest practices have been discovered. An effort to be "literally truthful but not helpful," as President Clinton described his testimony in the Paula Jones case, epitomizes the present practice that the Social Contract would prohibit.

The adversary system of justice is based on the assumption that the most reliable judicial decisions are made when each party has the right and obligation to present to the court all of the facts and legal arguments that support his claims. Unfortunately, theory and practice are substantially different. Instant replay for NFL football games proves that we can never be absolutely certain about past events. Despite three different camera angles, it is often impossible to determine whether there was pass interference. Technology has improved the reliability of some factual determinations. Juries once decided paternity cases based on the parties' testimony about sexual relations and whether a child resembles the putative father. Now, DNA testing makes paternity more certain than pass interference. Rape cases were, and sometime still are, decided by how convincingly the victim can identify the defendant as her rapist. When DNA is left behind, the rapist's identity is as certain as a parent's. No innocent person accused of rape, or any other serious crime, can have any confidence in the outcome of a trial where the victim has identified them, but there is no DNA. Fingerprinting, ballistics, and other technologies offer more reliability to judicial determinations, but too many innocent people get convicted, too many undeserving plaintiffs win large recoveries, and too many culpable defendants get away scot-free.

The failure of the judicial system to make correct decisions, is sometimes because of, not in spite of, the adversary system. It is a fact of life that some lawyers, like some race car drivers, are better than others. People with adequate resources usually hire the best lawyers. The advantages that wealth, intelligence, or skill provide to one party over another cannot be eliminated; however, the judicial system should not promote those disparities. Nor should the legal system be a crap shoot. It is most unlikely that either Klaus Von Bulow or O. J. Simpson would have been acquitted had they been represented by a public defender. The Spaziano case[21] in Florida shows how thin a thread of evidence can send someone to the electric chair.

In 1976, Spaziano was convicted of murder solely on the testimony of a 16 year-old boy whose father beat him regularly, and told him that Spaziano would "acquaint himself with girls and then injure them by cutting them up." The victim was allegedly cut up and her body thrown into a dump. At first the 16 year-old did not remember anything to link Spaziano to the murder. Only after the police and prosecutors "hypnotically refreshed" his memory, did the boy testify that Spaziano had taken him to the dump and shown him the body and bragged that he had killed her. Spaziano's public defender knew the boy's testimony had been "hypnotically refreshed," but he prevented the jury from hearing about it. Although the jury recommended life in prison, the trial judge sentenced Spaziano to death.

Numerous unsuccessful appeals followed. In one, the Florida Supreme Court rejected a claim that Spaziano had received ineffective assistance of counsel because his public defender had failed to reveal to the jury the suggestive hypnotically "refreshed" testimony, even though it had previously decided that *all* hypnotically refreshed testimony was inherently unreliable and inadmissible. In 1996, after five death warrants had been signed, Spaziano finally won a new trial after the boy recanted his hypnotically refreshed testimony. Throughout this time Spaziano was represented either by a public defender or a volunteer lawyer without pay. One can only imagine how Spaziano's case might have been different with either Simpson or Von Bulow's resources and lawyers.

Some businesses litigate to promote laws to protect their interests. Casualty insurance companies frequently pick cases with facts most sympathetic to the rule of law they want adopted and with the least vigorous or competent opposing lawyer to try to get a court to make the law favorable to the insurance company. In 1982, a Florida statute required the use of seat belts, but a jury could not consider the failure to wear a seat belt in setting the amount of damages for injuries sustained in a motor vehicle accident. Allstate Insurance Company thought it could save substantially on claims if the courts recognized a "seat-belt defense," so it set about trying to get a Florida Appellate Court to create it.

Allstate raised the defense in a case in which the plaintiff had been rendered a quadriplegic, but if he had worn a seat belt, he would not have been injured. The jury awarded $16.5 million. The plaintiff's lawyer was one of the best in the country and would have vigorously opposed Allstate's appeal to have the seat-belt defense adopted. Allstate refused to appeal this case, but Allstate did appeal another case[22] involving an award of $3,700. In the latter case, the Florida Supreme Court adopted the seat-belt defense.[23]

While the adversary system would not be abandoned entirely, judges and lawyers would have a more concerted role under the Social Contract. Cases would be initiated by the filing a notice of action briefly describing who allegedly violated the plaintiff's artificial rights and how. A judge and the lawyer for each party, if they have one, would then meet to review the claim. The judge and lawyers would discuss the law and the relevant information necessary to decide the claim with the parties present. The judge would then issue an order outlining the law of the case, and detailing the information each party must disclose for the final determination of the case. After sufficient time for full disclosure, a trial would be held to decide the case.

While these changes might be difficult under the present system, because of the many different legal theories and statutes that apply to specific situations, under the Social Contract there is really only one legal theory of artificial rights between citizens, constructive versus destructive power. The breach of a private contracts is a variant of destructive power. Each contract is a more or less involved exchange that must result from voluntary persuasion. If one obtains another's possessions in an exchange by promising to provide a possession in the future and he fails to deliver it, that is a destructive use of power. While there may be laws that apply to specific situations, i.e. safety laws, the UCC, traffic laws, etc., those laws are all an explication of either the law of destructive power or presumptions established about the terms of exchange between parties to the Social Contract.

Judicial decisions applying the rule of constructive and destructive power in specific situations will develop a body of precedents for aiding and deciding new cases. Still, the essential legal issue in any civil case between citizens turns on whether one party used destructive power and thereby lessened another's possessions. Was the destructive power a use of physical power or by the power of persuasion. Was the persuasion voluntary or involuntary? If it is claimed that the persuasion was involuntary, what information was disclosed and what information was available or known to each of the parties at the time of the exchange. If any relevant information was withheld, was the withholding of that information specifically disclosed? If there was an agreement, did each party perform his agreement when and as required? These would be the basic questions of every lawsuit between individuals under the Social Contract. If the government's action is challenged, then the issue is still whether destructive power was used, but it also depends on the clause of the Social Contract the government is claimed to have breached. With the issues limited and essentially the same in every case, the complexity of litigation would be substantially reduced, and the court could more efficiently, quickly and consistently decide cases.

The adversary system would be preserved to the extent that each party or his lawyer would be allowed to question his opponent to assure that he had fully disclosed all relevant information, to test the completeness, accuracy, and significance of any evidence, and to present legal authorities and arguments to support his position.

There will be great resistance to a new judicial system by lawyers. They will see such a system as threatening their importance and very existence, but these fears are ill-founded. As long as there are artificial rights, there will be lawyers.

The above is a basic description of how the judicial system under the Social Contract would operate. A detailed discussion of how existing rules of law and procedure would be used or changed will have to wait another day.

> F. *All persons claiming to act with the authority of the government shall do so only after taking an oath to strictly abide by all decisions of the judiciary.*

This section is self-explanatory. It establishes the supremacy of the judiciary and emphasizes to all government agents that they are responsible to act according to the Social Contract. All acts of government agents are subject to review by the judiciary for violation of the Social Contract. Thus, the primacy of the Social Contract will constantly be in the minds of all government agents.

If a person claims to act as a government agent and is not one he would be subject to punishment for consciously using destructive power in misrepresenting his status. To fail to abide by the judiciary's decisions is also a violation of the Social Contract subject to criminal punishment and even termination of citizenship.

> G. *The government shall make no law or regulation whose objective or effect hinders the opportunity to achieve a citizen's will, except as is necessary to perform its duties under paragraphs A through F above.*

This section empowers government to act beyond just what is necessary to establish and maintain Society, but only for the express purpose of increasing the opportunity for individual happiness for *all* parties to the Social Contract. This power is not, however, a license to "do good." Too often one person's good is another's injury. Even the best intentions usually produce gains for some at the expense of others, sometimes unintentionally, and sometimes quite intentionally either under the belief that the others can best afford it, e.g., the progressive income tax, or as an abuse of power to benefit those in power. Whether a conscious objective or an incidental effect, when some benefit at the expense of others, destructive power is always the source of the benefit. The Social Contract does not allow government to use destructive power to take from one person and give to another[24] except as necessary to fulfill its affirmative obligations under sections A through F, which are necessary for the existence of an individualistic society.

Government's only purpose beyond maintaining an individualistic society is to increase each and every citizen's opportunity to achieve his will. This must never be confused with the current pandemic of utilitarianism. The Social Contract does not allow government to act on a utilitarian calculus. The greatest good for the greatest number is anathema to an individualistic society. The morality of equality of the Social Contract requires every single individual have an equal opportunity to achieve his will with constructive power. All concerns about community well-being are subsumed by government's affirmative duties to establish and maintain the complexity necessary for an individualistic society to emerge.[25]

Individual happiness can only be achieved by the individual. An opportunity for individual happiness is the chance to use one's power, destructive and constructive, to try to achieve one's will. Since one can become a party to the Social Contract only by choice, no party is compelled to forego any use of power to achieve his will. Rather, every party to the Social Contract chooses to use only constructive power because she believes this exchange with all other parties will create the greatest opportunity to achieve her volitional will, which she values more than the freedom to use destructive power whenever she thinks she can get away with it.

In Society, an opportunity for individual happiness is the opportunity to use constructive power. Laws authorized by this section, e.g., Uniform Commercial Code, traffic laws, partnership and corporation laws, are designed to facilitate exchange through constructive power. These laws do not put people into classes and treat them differently based on their government assigned class; rather, they create classes that any citizen may choose to become a member. For instance, the UCC distinguishes between sellers and buyers. Anyone can choose to be a seller or a buyer. Partnership law allows people to choose to be a partner with another or not. Corporation laws allow people to choose to be a shareholder of a corporation or not. The traffic laws allow people to choose whether to be drivers or not. And, by establishing common expectations, these laws facilitate each and every individual's opportunity to achieve her will with constructive power.

Opportunity also means that government may not impose criteria for a school, job or licenses that do not validly serve the governmental purpose for which they are imposed. The government could conclude, for example, that a doctor needs a certain minimum knowledge of medicine and that practicing medicine without that minimum creates an unreasonable risk of injury to patients. Thus, government may require a medical degree and passing an examination to demonstrate the minimum knowledge of medicine in order to become a doctor. The same is true of any other occupation. The entrance qualifications for an educational program or occupation must be consistent with preventing uses of destructive power and must be rigorously applied without allowance for a person's background, race, or other characteristics unrelated to preventing uses of destructive power.

If a citizen challenges the qualifications government sets, the government would be required to demonstrate that the criteria used and the test for those criteria actually reduces unreasonable risks of injury. The government cannot, for instance, decide that there are too many brain surgeons and that the examination or test scores to get into medical school should be so difficult that only the desired number of people can pass the test. This would deny the opportunity to be a brain surgeon based on reasons other than protecting citizens from unreasonable risks of injury.

In other words, the government may not manage the supply of people qualified for certain occupations by restricting access to the education necessary to qualify for the occupation or imposing licensing requirements. The government may only regulate job qualifications to avoid foreseeable uses of destructive power or to avoid unreasonable risks of injury to citizens or their property. Not everyone would be able to become a brain surgeon, but no one with the ability, motivation, discipline and determination could be denied the opportunity to become one because she lacks the economic resources to get the necessary education.

Section G prohibits any law that hinders a use of constructive power by any individual except as necessary for government to accomplish its other mandatory obligations. One example of a law prohibited by this section is the Anti-Trust laws. These laws use the utilitarian calculus that the greatest number of people will be better off if competition is promoted even if some people may not use their constructive economic power. The Social Contract forbids the government to use destructive power to benefit the many by harming the few. Such laws are nothing more than a political majority using destructive power against a minority, and, of course, that is what the Social Contract is intended to prevent. Either a law creates greater opportunity for *all* or it is invalid. The Social Contract will eliminate the constant competition of political factions for special treatment by the government. If any law uses destructive power to favor one group over another, the judiciary must strike it down.

Section G is stated in the negative to contrast it with the affirmative obligations of government because (1) government is not required to do anything beyond enforcing the Social Contract, (2) government may do more than establish and enforce the Social Contract, but only with the conscious objective and actual effect, of increasing every individual's opportunity for happiness, and (3) the negative statement emphasizes the restriction on government in using this discretionary power.

Unlike the affirmative obligation of government, the judiciary may not compel government to use this discretionary power. The judiciary, relying solely upon this section, may not order government to do anything. This power remains exclusively within the political sphere of government and Society.

> H. *The government shall not use destructive power except as a last resort and only for the purposes set forth in this contract.*

The basic forms of destructive power are involuntary persuasion, physical force and threats of physical force. Although all destructive power is outlawed between parties to the Social Contract. This section mandates that government use constructive power to perform its duties if possible. If not, then government may use destructive power. Therefore, any government action or law may be challenged for using unnecessary or excessive destructive power.

Absent exigent circumstances, the police must knock, announce their presence and request entry to a citizen's house before searching it rather than simply breaking in the door. In general, government agents would be required to request compliance from members before threatening or using physical force, again absent exigent circumstances. If the government regulates prostitution, or any other acts, to prevent destructive uses of power, it must do so with the least amount of destructive power.

If a government act or law is challenged, government must prove that it could not or cannot perform an affirmative duty without using destructive power. If destructive power is necessary, government must prove that the destructive power used has or will cause the least reduction of opportunity for individual happiness necessary to accomplish the government's objective. This requires distinguishing between greater and lesser uses of destructive power.

The degrees of destructive power may be measured in the following ways. Destructive power used to counter or prevent an actual or imminent use of destructive power, or to apprehend one who has used destructive power, may be of the same kind and extent as the destructive power sought to be countered or prevented since the destructive power already threatened or used is equal to that used to prevent it. There is equal or less harm in using the same destructive power to apprehend one known[26] to have used destructive power because such destructive power is to remedy the loss already caused and to prevent future similar uses of destructive power.

Destructive power causing death is greater than that causing serious bodily injury. Causing less physical injury is less than causing more severe physical injury. Causing temporary physical injury is less than causing permanent physical injury. Causing no physical injury is less than causing any physical injury. Intentional involuntary persuasion or threats of physical force to counter or prevent an actual use of physical destructive power is less than causing death or physical injury or using physical destructive power. To deceive someone holding a hostage into believing that by releasing the hostage and surrendering he will be set free without any consequences is less destructive power than luring the person into a position where he can be shot and killed. These rules apply mainly to police or military operations to counter or prevent future uses of physical destructive power or to apprehend and punish those who have already used physical destructive power. Government is not limited to destructive power equal to that used by members of Society. It may use whatever destructive power is necessary, but no more. The limitation on the use of destructive poer does not apply to war since destructive power is used against non-members of Society.

When dealing with members who have not threatened to use or actually used destructive power, the degrees of destructive power are slightly different. In this case, government does not act to prevent destructive power or to apprehend those who have already used destructive power. Rather, government uses destructive power against members of Society to fulfill government's affirmative duties. In this context, the following rules apply. Intentional deception may never be used, and every government agent is bound to act with good faith and honesty in fact. The rules measuring the harm done by physical force are the same. In addition, destructive power used against a member's person is greater than that used against his property. Destructive power used against physical property is greater the closer the physical property is to the person. In other words, physical force against or within a person's house is greater than if in his yard, because the house is closer to the person than the yard. And, the yard is closer than an office, which is closer than a bank account or other nonphysical property. Thus an intrusion into the person's privacy and security in his body and dignity is more harmful than taking his money. A threat of physical force is less than the actual use of physical force. So for each of the actual uses of physical force, to threaten to use physical force is less harmful than to actually use it.

The more uniform the destructive power is used against all citizens, the less it is used against each individual. For instance, if a tax is imposed on mink coats to raise $1 million, the number of parties who will bear the tax will be substantially less than if the tax is imposed as a percentage of the sale of all goods or all parties' incomes. Uniformity refers not only to the number of people affected but also to the extent each is affected. If an income tax is imposed, a tax of 15% on all incomes is more uniform and therefore less a destructive use of power than a progressive income tax that exempts some and taxes others at a higher rate. Finally, destructive power against the dead or unborn is less than destructive power against the living, and against the dead is less than against the unborn.

None of these uses of destructive power are forbidden to government if necessary to accomplish any of its affirmative duties, but government must use constructive power before resorting to destructive power, and when using destructive power, government must use the least destructive power necessary to accomplish its purposes. In other words, the lesser destructive power must be inadequate to accomplish government's obligations in order to justify the greater destructive power.

How will the judiciary decide whether the government's use of destructive power is the least necessary? Both the quality of the result produced and the timeliness of it must be considered. If two uses of destructive power will produce the same result within the same time, then the lesser must be used. If the same result can be reached with either, but the lesser one will produce it in a meaningfully longer time, then the greater is authorized. If an equal result cannot be achieved with lesser destructive power, then the greater must be used.

The determination of whether a past act of government violated this section will necessarily be different than whether a law with future application uses the least destructive power necessary. When past acts are at issue, the determination will be the same as when a court now decides a claim of self-defense or a police use of excessive force. Given all the circumstances, did the government agents reasonably believe the destructive power used was necessary according to the hierarchy discussed above? The issue is not whether the destructive power used was actually reasonable, but whether the government agents reasonably believed the destructive power used was necessary.

When laws are challenged, the determination is less certain because the consequences have not yet occurred. The court must examine whether the law has been in force for a long time and will continue? If the law has a history, have past uses of less destructive power been sufficient to achieve the government purpose? If the lesser has been sufficient, then virtually overwhelming evidence would be required to authorize greater destructive power. If less has been insufficient, greater is authorized.

If no attempt has been made to accomplish the purpose with less destructive power, then the objective of the law and degree of destructive power chosen must be examined. If the objective is one of government's affirmative duties and reasonable people can disagree about the destructive power necessary to achieve it, the judiciary must initially defer to government's choice and uphold the law. As experience with the law grows, however, it could be re-examined in light of its accumulated history.

These examples are not meant to be exhaustive of the questions that might be presented to the judiciary. They are only a basic guide to show that these determinations are neither esoteric nor impossible.

Government discrimination against members in using destructive power is not prohibited, but there must be overwhelming reason to overcome the basic premise of the Social Contract that destructive power can only be used in a way that has uniform effects on all parties. Thus discrimination against persons on the basis of race, creed, sex, etc, are virtually inconceivable. What possible reason could there be to use greater destructive power against a black, a catholic or a woman than against any other person? There is no possibility of discrimination in government's obligation to protect all members of Society from private uses of destructive power and to provide the necessities if requested because these artificial rights are guaranteed by the Social Contract itself.

The Social Contract does not outlaw private discrimination. One person may choose not to exchange any of his possessions with another person for whatever reason he may choose. Again, to force one person to give up his possessions to another is a use of destructive power, whether it is to promote racial, religious, or ethnic harmony or not.

I believe once the Social Contract has been in place and vigorously enforced for a time, perhaps as long as a few generations, private discrimination will disappear. I believe this will happen when every citizen has moral capacity and a belief that his opportunity to become and do what he wants will be truly limited only by his own desire, ability and discipline. When this self-conception of other-conscious people becomes self-evident, then personal prejudice will virtually disappear. It may never disappear entirely, for some people will always envy other's possessions, natural abilities and accomplishments. Destructive power should not be used to compel people to live or work or socialize with anyone they do not choose to, any more than people should be compelled to marry someone they do not choose to marry, or to adopt a child they do not choose to adopt. All relationships between people should be a choice through constructive power. Otherwise, one person's desires will be satisfied by taking another's possession.

III. INDIVIDUAL TO GOVERNMENT

Individual to Government

Obedience to the commands of government may be either the individual's choice or coerced. When a person chooses to become a party to the Social Contract, he chooses to obey the people who are government only for the purposes specified in the Social Contract. Since government exists only to enforce the Social Contract, which all citizens choose to be a party to, the government is enforcing each citizen's statement of will for an individualistic society, one without destructive power. Government has no authority to use destructive power to take away the citizen's freedom to pursue his volitional will with constructive power unless necessary to fulfill its obligations under the Social Contract. A corollary to obedience is the acceptance of reasonable sanctions or punishments for the breach of the Social Contract and laws made in conformity with it.

> A. *I agree to obey all laws and regulations made by any government established according to this contract unless and until such law or regulation is declared to violate any other term of this contract.*

All rights within Society derive from the Social Contract. There are no "natural" rights other than to try to do anything. Any debate about whether a person has a "right" to do or have something other than as provided in or derived from the Social Contract, is meaningless. In Society, there are *only* legal rights and legal remedies.

Each party agrees to obey all laws of any government validly established under the Social Contract. Government, whatever the form, will undoubtedly make laws from time to time that violate the Social Contract. Until a law is declared void, every member must obey the law. No individual may judge for himself what laws do or do not violate the Social Contract. Only the judiciary may decide these issues, and each citizen agrees to use the judiciary to challenge any law and to obey its decisions. To violate a valid law that is, later declared void is as serious as violating a valid law. Citizens and wards must obey the law, regardless of good intentions or probable success in challenging it. Since any party may challenge any law that affects him and have it declared void, civil disobedience will be obsolete.

> B. *I agree to submit to any reasonable sanction imposed upon me for my own violation of this contract.*

Society will no doubt incarcerate some people for offenses involving the use of destructive power that does not result in revocation of the citizenship in Society. For instance, intentionally using involuntary persuasion now known as fraud or a failure to disclose material information, might not result in termination of citizenship, but would have some serious punishment. Also there will be uses of physical destructive power that do not result in physical injury to citizens, wards or their property. Prisoners, as citizens, would have artificial rights regarding the conditions of their confinement because the citizen's obligation is to submit to all "reasonable" punishments for his violation of the Social Contract.

This may not always be the means by which government operates, but until Society operates otherwise, citizens must comply with all orders for compensation or punishment as a condition for remaining a party to the Social Contract.[27] The ultimate sanction is expulsion from Society by revoking a party's citizenship.

This section requires any sanction to be reasonable, that is, the punishment must be proportionate to the violation. Obviously, the death penalty for stealing a loaf of bread would be an unreasonable sanction. The government will determine what punishments to impose, and may make them as lenient or strict as it deems appropriate. Ultimately what is reasonable will be determined by the judiciary.

IV. MODIFICATION AND TERMINATION

> A. *No party's rights under this contract may be terminated by the government without the party's express, written agreement except upon an adjudication of a conscious use of destructive power in breach of this contract involving physical power against another party or ward creating a substantial risk of serious injury or death or upon an adjudication of repeated intentional breaches involving the use of destructive power.*

Any citizen may choose to withdraw as a party to the Social Contract the same way he became a party, by express, written agreement. By withdrawing, however, the person will become as any morally capable person who originally chose not to sign the Social Contract. He will have no artificial rights under the Social Contract, and by withdrawing he declares himself a danger to Society.

Any express withdrawal should be viewed with skepticism and should only be accepted under circumstances at least as formal and as skeptical as a plea of guilty to a capital crime in order to be confident the person is as mentally capable of choosing to withdraw as she was to join Society. Citizens who become mentally ill and lose moral capacity may attempt to withdraw when they should actually be determined to lack moral capacity and be a ward rather than a morally capable noncitizen.

Wards, like citizens, are entitled to medical care as a necessity if they or their guardians are unable to provide it with constructive power. The citizen who loses moral capacity because of mental deficiency, injury or disease is also entitled to adequate medical care even if he does not know he needs it. This is not a license to commit unpopular individuals to mental institutions. When a person has violated the Social Contract and the issue is whether his citizenship should be terminated, it must be determined that he had moral capacity when the breach occurred and when the punishment is imposed.

Humans make mistakes, even serious, criminal mistakes. Not every crime should be sufficient to terminate a citizen as a party to the Social Contract. Some breaches of the Social Contract are, however, sufficient in themselves to evidence a choice to withdraw as a party. The Social Contract may be terminated without a citizen's express, written agreement only for a conscious use of physical destructive power against another party or ward creating a substantial risk of serious injury or death. The use of destructive power must be conscious, that is, the person must be proven to have understood that the consequences of his action involved a substantial risk of serious injury or death to a party or ward. This would certainly include murder, attempted murder, conspiracy to commit murder, rape, mayhem, sexual assault & battery, assault with a deadly weapon, robbery with a deadly weapon, and other crimes of violence that currently require intent or reckless indifference as an element. It would also include the use of clearly unauthorized or excessive destructive power by a government agent, such as the New York police officer convicted of ramming a broom handle into the rectum of a person in custody. The essential character of these acts is that they are an unequivocal repudiation of, and thus a choice to renounce, the Social Contract.

Only citizens and wards have artificial rights and are entitled to require the power of alliance of Society to protect their artificial rights under the Social Contract. Therefore, a citizen's use of destructive physical power must be against a citizen or ward of Society to justify termination. Intentionally killing or maiming a person who is not a party to the Social Contract or a ward would not qualify for termination, although it would not necessarily be without consequence.

Acts of destructive power not involving physical violence may also be sufficient to terminate a party to the Social Contract. Repeated uses of involuntary persuasion or other conscious uses of destructive power against another citizen or ward, would be sufficient if they indicated a clear and unequivocal repudiation and renunciation of the Social Contract. The number of times and the severity necessary to allow termination would be left up to the government to establish.

Termination without a citizen's express written agreement should be rarely used, or it could become a means of inquisition against unpopular individuals who vigorously assert their artificial rights under the Social

Contract. Termination should only be used when a use of destructive power is so clearly proven that it is an unequivocal choice to terminate the Social Contract. When the proof of the conscious use of destructive power does not clearly and unequivocally show a choice to renounce the Social Contract, it may nevertheless clearly and unequivocally show that the person lacks moral capacity, and if so, he may be made a ward instead of a full citizen. Society must then protect itself from future uses of destructive power by the person.

What would not qualify for either termination or reversion to ward status, are unconscious uses of destructive power, what would in the common law be called negligent acts that create a substantial risk of or actually result in death or serious bodily injury. Also in the latter category, are acts that the person should have foreseen a significant risk, but did not actually foresee the risk. Without proof of actual foresight of the consequences, these acts would not be an unequivocal repudiation of the Social Contract or lack of moral capacity. The person would be liable to compensate all persons damaged by his acts and he could be punished for his act and required to again demonstrate his moral capacity, but the Social Contract could not be terminated.

The judiciary must be ever vigilant to prevent termination or reversion from becoming the tool of a political majority to persecute or eliminate a minority. Ultimately, the judiciary will decide whether the laws specifying how and when a citizen's status is terminated comply with the Social Contract. While the government would have the power to establish the circumstances justifying termination, which would be entitled to great deference, the judiciary would always have the final decision of the circumstances sufficient to authorize termination. The judiciary could never make the conditions for termination less restrictive than the Social Contract, but it could make them more restrictive to prevent such proceedings from being used to persecute an unpopular minority.

B. *This contract may not be modified without the written agreement of all living parties to it.*

Once an individualistic society is established, the Social Contract cannot be modified by any governmental action. The government is subordinate to the Social Contract, so it can never have the power to modify it. Nevertheless, changes could be made, but they could never alter the original Social Contract without the agreement of all parties. For instance, like any contract between several parties, no one person can change the contract without the agreement of all other parties to the contract. But, one or more parties could make a supplemental agreement that does not alter the original contract for everyone, but adds to or clarifies it as to less than all parties. Every contract between less than all parties is a supplement to the Social Contract.

If the government were to propose a modification, amendment or addition to the Social Contract, citizens could choose to execute it or not. If they did, as among all citizens executing it and the government, the new version would govern. For citizens who choose not to execute the new version, the old version would still govern. While this sounds like a totally unworkable situation, it should not be as long as any modifications or amendments do not create inconsistent obligations or artificial rights. Since legislatures have been enacting and amending statutes, courts have been deciding which version of a statute applies in a specific case. There is a well-developed body of law on how to make these decisions, which would be the beginning point for resolving any conflicts between versions of the Social Contract.

It is difficult to imagine how the obligation to use only constructive power could be amended without effectively destroying the Social Contract. Most changes or amendments would be clarifications that would be within the power of government to make as laws, always subject to review by the judiciary.

The Need for Knowledge of the Law

No legal system can function by allowing a person to avoid responsibility for his acts by simply pleading ignorance. The complexity of the current legal system, however, produces some absurd results. In *Hall v. Humana Hospital Daytona Beach*,[28] the hospital required patients before being admitted to guarantee payment at the hospital's "then prevailing rates," which included $11.50 for a single Zantac tablet and $52 for a single Tylenol with codeine tablet. Hall paid her bill, but then sued the hospital claiming the charges were excessive and unreasonable. The court never decided whether $11.50 or $52 was excessive or unreasonable because it said that by paying the bill after getting out of the hospital, Hall had agreed the charges were reasonable:

> Every man is supposed to know the law, and if he voluntarily makes a payment which the law would not compel him to make, he cannot afterwards assign his ignorance of the law as a reason why the state should furnish him with legal remedies to recover it.[29]

Thus, if money is all that is at stake, ignorance of the law is no excuse, but if a serial killer is fully aware of his *Miranda* rights, he must be set free if the police do not read those rights to him before he confesses.

A person cannot become a citizen without first demonstrating an understanding of and an ability to make choices to use only constructive power. Thus, no citizen charged with a crime could ever claim not to know that the conscious use of destructive power against another is wrong. Destructive power is always wrong, except in self-defense, as a government agent or to care for wards. The same principle governs all of the civil law. Even if one does not know every law addressing specific acts that constitute a use of destructive power, every citizen knows and has chosen to follow the basic law that destructive power is prohibited.

In the *Hall* case, voluntary persuasion would have required the hospital to tell Hall that it charged $52 for a Tylenol with codeine tablet. Hall probably would not have agreed, but if she had, the exchange would not be due to ignorance and she could not complain later. Since medical care is a physical necessity, no one must choose between dying or paying $52 for a Tylenol with codeine tablet.

Ignorance of the law will not be entirely eliminated, but to become a citizen one must demonstrate she understands the fundamental law of Society.

Chapter XI

Life in an Individualistic Society

An individualistic society would have many similarities to life in a liberal democracy, but there would be some significant differences. Some would be due to the adoption of the moral principle of constructive power while others are due to the affirmative obligations of government under the Social Contract, and others are due to the clear distinction between morally capable citizens, wards and noncitizens.

Unlike any government before, the Social Contract establishes enforceable obligations of government to individual citizens and wards. The United States government has obligations to its citizens such as Social Security, Medicare and other "entitlement" programs, but all these programs exist at the grace of government adopting or repealing the program. As we have seen, the American Constitution imposes no obligation on government to do anything for any single individual citizen. While the obligation to establish the government and defend against all external threats is mostly within the discretion of the citizens who are government, the obligation to protect members of Society against internal threats of destructive power and to provide the necessities upon request are affirmative, legally enforceable obligations imposed on government and owed to all citizens and their wards who can to enforce them.

Another significant difference is the prohibition of laws "whose objective or effect hinders the opportunity to achieve a citizen's will." No longer may a political majority use the destructive power of government to further its interests at the expense of even a single citizen. A number of examples have already been given, e.g., victimless crimes and the anti-trust laws.

Another significant difference would be the government's obligation to provide the necessities upon request of any citizen or ward who cannot provide his own with constructive power. The social systems to guarantee to all citizens and their wards food, clothing, shelter, medical care, education, legal representation, and protection from destructive power are the systems of lesser complexity necessary for an individualistic society to emerge from biological society. Without these systems in place, the moral foundation of Society cannot exist.

The Social Contract does not specify how the necessities must be provided. That will be up to Society, but given the extreme adaptability of humans, any Society that unconditionally guarantees all citizens and their wards the physical necessities of life risks creating a large class of people content to exist upon the largess of Society. They will find no need to work for what they can simply demand and receive.

Demanding that Society provide the necessities is a destructive use of power. It is equivalent to saying, "If the government does not provide me with the necessities, I will use my destructive power against anyone I can to survive." When the government provides the necessities, every citizen accepts that threat as real and surrenders to it by giving up some of his possessions to provide another's necessities. It is like the robber saying, "your money or your life." The victim turns over his wallet to preserve his life. The government, on behalf of all citizens, provides the necessities to preserve Society. Society should not tolerate anyone who chooses to use destructive power for his necessities when he can provide his own with constructive power. Because humans can adapt to and even thrive in most any condition with sufficient nourishment to survive and reproduce, Society must provide the physical and civil necessities in a way that discourages any person from *choosing* to live with the government providing only the necessities.

The following is one way, and certainly not the only way, to provide the necessities without creating a subsistence class. There is, of course, nothing magic or immutable about my own suggestions on how to provide the necessities. What is immutable, however, is the reason why government must provide the necessities for those who cannot provide their own without using destructive power, and the fact of human nature that some people, if given the opportunity, will choose to live with nothing but the necessities provided by the government, especially if they are provided in a way that makes life comfortable and pleasant. The long-term success of an individualistic society may well depend on providing the necessities without destroying the desire of every able citizen to be self-sufficient.

I cannot emphasize too much or too often that the suggested way of providing the necessities to citizens is not to punish or demean or shame citizens who cannot provide their own necessities. It is only to prevent citizens, as opposed to wards, who will be treated somewhat differently, from becoming comfortable and complacent and choosing to live by the destructive power of demanding the necessities from Society when the citizen is capable of self-sufficiency with constructive power.

Every community with more than 10,000 people would have a necessities camp that would be a combination apartments complex, army barracks and halfway house. Each necessities camp would have a staff to oversee residents and their efforts to become self-sufficient in order to leave necessities camp, such as looking for a job or attending school or training for another job. Residents would receive a credit for any work performed in necessities camp equal to a wage outside necessities camp toward the expense of being provided any of the necessities. Each citizen would have an open account to be repaid over time after becoming self-supporting and leaving necessities camp, similar to a student loan.

Before anyone would need to go to necessities camp, there would be numerous alternatives such as unemployment or disability insurance, personal savings, family assistance or charitable organizations. These programs would provide a buffer between citizens being on the job one day and in necessities camp the next. Unlike similar programs today, however, they would be entirely voluntary, otherwise they require taking from some people to benefit others. One could choose to have no unemployment or disability insurance and go directly to necessities camp if he loses his job or becomes disabled. Most citizens would likely opt for some type of safety net insurance rather than risk immediately going to necessities camp. That decision would, however, be entirely the citizen's choice.

Necessities camp would be a last resort. Citizens would not receive any money. All necessities would be provided in kind. Freedom of choice and selection would be narrowly restricted so that life in necessities camp is undesirable. Again, the goal is always to provide the physical necessities promised by the Social Contract, but to also provide every possible incentive to each citizen to leave necessities camp and live by the use of constructive power rather than the destructive power of demanding the necessities. Ever effort must be made to prevent complacency. Life in necessities camp should not be pleasant or comfortable, but it should not be cruel, abusive, or necessarily demeaning. Everything about necessities camp should be designed to encourage and assist every citizen to prefer self-sufficiency over necessities camp.

By executing the Social Contract, each party agrees not to use destructive power. Of course, requesting the necessities is an exception to this rule, but if one cannot provide his own and his ward's necessities, *a fortiori* he cannot provide the necessities for any new child he or she might have while in necessities camp. Having a child without being able to provide for its necessities is an enormous use of destructive power because Society must use destructive power to provide any child with it necessities, and perhaps for its lifetime. To prevent this destructive power until the residents of necessities camp discharge their debt for necessities, they should be required to use the safest, most effective birth control available to prevent them from adding any new child for whom Society must provide the necessities. Whatever birth control is used, it must be safe and fully reversible. Abortion, while available, would never be required, but multiple births to citizens or wards in necessities camps should not be allowed. If a family goes to necessities camp, parents should be required to pursue some means of getting out of necessities camp, and children below school age should be cared for during the day while school age children should be in school.

Experience might show that citizens' freedom and choice can be allowed without encouraging dependency. The longer a citizen or his family stays in necessities camp, however, their freedom and choice might be progressively restricted to encourage self-sufficiency. If a massive economic disruption such as the Great Depression occurred, the restrictions might be further relaxed until economic conditions change for the better. What must always be avoided is allowing the artificial right to the necessities on request to create an underclass of citizens who choose to live a subsistence existence with destructive power against Society.

For physically disabled citizens, orphaned wards, and mentally deficient wards who cannot supply their own necessities with constructive power and therefore who do not choose to be there, life in necessities camps should be comfortable and pleasant. These wards do not choose to be in necessities camp so there is no need to provide the necessities in a way to encourage them to leave necessities camp.

Selfishness

Some will argue that a Society founded upon a moral principle that elevates individualism to its primary objective, will be selfish and uncaring. This cannot be true for two reasons. First, while only individuals can decide what is in their self-interest, no individual may pursue his self-interest with acts that lessen another citizen's possessions without using destructive power. Second, the human animal is a social being. For most humans, the greatest joys of life come from the love, affection and deserved respect of their family, neighbors, colleagues and fellow citizens.

Most people who live selfish lives eventually realize, often too late, the value of other people when they come close to or actually lose some or all of them. The process of creating one's volitional will is the search for what gives meaning and enjoyment to life. Much of life is the pursuit of desires that cannot be satisfied through the exchange of physical objects, but they are nevertheless the most powerful and basic desires: to find a mate and raise a family, to find and keep friends, to learn new ideas and explore the horizons of human knowledge, to serve one's fellow man through new discoveries in science, medicine or philosophy, or to obtain spiritual or religious enlightenment and peace and help others find it too.

When this process is consciously chosen, I am confident that the same other-consciousness that is the source of morality will identify our happiness with a respect, kinship and affection for other people. While the desire to acquire property, to establish one's place in a social hierarchy and to distinguish oneself from others in various ways will probably never be erased from the human genome, I firmly believe that individuals will, over time, learn that there is more joy in a healthy, caring marriage and family than in a new luxury car or a second, or third house, or any other non-necessity. I believe individuals will come to believe that the well-deserved respect and admiration of one's family and fellow citizens is far more desirable and satisfying than simply the power to control them with one's might. When individuals realize that they and they alone are responsible for choosing and pursuing their own volitional will, their happiness, they will, of necessity, ask themselves what is most valuable to them, and most will conclude that their relationships with other people are much more valuable than any other possession.

Whether this prediction is right or wrong, there will certainly be selfish people in Society, but probably no more than now. And, if these selfish people must use only constructive power, whether they are selfish or not, is of little concern to the rest of Society.

Economic Growth

The object of Society is not economic growth, but economic growth is not evil. On the contrary, if economic activity is viewed as the cumulative effort of all citizens to satisfy their will with constructive power, then economic growth is one indicator of the overall increase in satisfaction of the individual will of all citizens. We must not, however, mistake economic activity–exchange of possessions through voluntary persuasion–as the goal of Society, for, as mentioned, the volitional will is not satisfied by bread alone.

Taxation

One of the least popular effects of the Social Contract will be a heavy inheritance tax, which is required for several reasons. First, taxes are an exercise of destructive power, which the government must use only as a last resort and the least amount necessary. It is less destructive power to take from the dead than from the living. Because Society guarantees all its members that they will have the greatest possible opportunity for education to develop their skills to acquire possessions, and they will never go without the physical or civil necessities, no person need fear that they must leave a sufficient legacy to assure their children will be able to achieve their full potential.

Second, history teaches that the chief cause of class strife and social decline is the transmission of large sums of unearned and undeserved wealth from one generation to the next. The ancient Greeks and Romans demonstrated this with their constant class warfare between those with great accumulated wealth, especially land, and those with nothing but their labor. I believe we are in the beginning of the same stages. Generation X is one of material plenty provided by parents and wholly unearned. A life of unearned ease often, but not always, leads to an indolence and loss of the very character that created the wealth and strength of social organization that is taken for granted.

Wealth will be transmitted from one generation to the next in Society, but it will be as a result of merit and effort, not by birth and parentage. Whenever a citizen dies, except for some modest exempt amount which would be within the government's power to decide, all the deceased member's possessions would pass to the government. If there were a surviving spouse, the property would pass to the government when the surviving spouse died on the theory that the possessions were accumulated from the joint effort of both spouses. The government would then sell everything and keep the proceeds. The government might give family members preferred terms to purchase property from their parent's estate, such as a family farm or business. Usually, estates are converted into cash before they are distributed to the heirs, rather than specific property being distributed. Government would thus have the entire wealth of each generation to use for government purposes without ever taxing a living person. This should be sufficient revenue for the government of Society, absent war or other great national emergency. It would also transmit from one generation to the next the wealth created by each generation, and do so to the living who have themselves created wealth.

Third, this will prevent the inherited power in Society. There may be families that contribute more than others over the generations due to the value each generation places on economic achievement or public service, but the legacy of each generation of such families will be in their example of an admirable life, not in their accumulated wealth.

Eugenics

Citizens and wards in necessities camp will not be allowed to have more children. Some will attack this as a form of eugenics. It is not. Eugenics programs limit human reproduction with an intent to influence the genetic makeup or characteristics of future generations, and thereby "improve" the human race. Eugenics is essentially selective breeding of humans like the selective breeding of horses or any other domesticated animal to produce a more desirable individual animal. Reproduction is restricted in Society to self-sufficient citizens not to produce a more desirable human but to prevent those who cannot or, more important, will not, supply their or their children's necessities from using even greater destructive power by begetting more children. Mandatory birth control is not intended to affect the human gene pool. It would be applied totally without regard to the race, gender, national origin, religion or *any* other criterion. The sole criterion is whether the citizen or ward can supply his or her necessities and that of any child without resorting to destructive power.

Mandatory birth control would only last as long as a citizen or ward cannot supply his own necessities with constructive power. Thus, no one would be permanently prevented from having children except those citizens or wards who never become self-sufficient during their reproductive years.

Whatever method of mandatory birth control is used, it *must* always be safe and completely reversible to the person's reproductive potential at the time of reversal. If a woman enters necessities camp at age twenty-five without any children, and does not become self-sufficient until after her child-bearing years, the reversal will return her to an essentially non-reproductive condition. If the same woman became self-sufficient by age thirty, she would have to be returned to her reproductive condition as a thirty-year-old. While the same would be true for men, the biological difference between the reproductive ability of men and women is obvious.

Self-sufficiency for reversal of mandatory birth control means that the person (1) is able to provide his or her current necessities without resort to destructive power, (2) has repaid any balance due Society for necessities already provided, and (3) has the means to provide the necessities for any child he or she already has and may have so that the person after having one or more children will not have to go back to necessities camp in order to provide his or her children with the necessities. If a person had one or more children before entering necessities camp, he or she would be given mandatory birth control, and after becoming self-sufficient again for both himself and all his wards, he or she would be removed from mandatory birth control.

Citizens would not lose or quit a job one day and the next go to necessities camp and be put on mandatory birth control. As with entering necessities camp generally, they could use all available means to avoid requesting government to provide the necessities. So long as a person does not enter necessities camp and provides his wards with the necessities, he will not be required to use birth control. If a parent fails to provide his ward's necessities, the child may be taken into the custody of Society for abuse or neglect, and the parent will be required to use birth control the same as if he had voluntarily entered necessities camp. Whenever and for as long as Society must provide a child's necessities, both parents will be required to use birth control.

Mandatory birth control is *not* a punishment. It is a recognition that the biological urge to reproduce is a powerful drive that many people may consciously or unconsciously fail and produce a child that Society must support, which is probably the greatest use of destructive power possible. When children have children, almost by definition they will not be able to support themselves or their children with constructive power and will require Society to provide the necessities. These children would also be required to use birth control until they become citizens or can provide their own and their children's necessities with their constructive power.

Wards incapable of becoming a citizen, may never get out of necessities camp, and thus may always be on birth control. They may not reproduce because they cannot provide their necessities with constructive power, not because of their mental deficiency. Some of these wards may be able to supply their necessities or they may find a spouse who will support them without Society having to provide the necessities. These wards would not have birth control because they do not use destructive power. If a person can provide their necessities even without being a citizen, birth control is not required.

A citizen capable of a self-sufficient life, may choose to live in necessities camp in spite of all the disincentives. But that citizen may not use the additional destructive power of having a child.

People may be in necessities camp because of economic conditions that result in many people being out of work for a sufficient time to exhaust their savings or unemployment insurance. They would not choose to live in necessities camp because they prefer it to a self-sufficient life. Rather, they would have no other choice except to abandon the Social Contract and resort to their natural right to try to do anything to survive. Such people may well be admirable individuals forced into necessities camp by circumstances beyond their control. In fact, they may have very socially or genetically desirable traits. Nevertheless, when they require the government to furnish their necessities, they use destructive power, and until they again become self-sufficient, they must use birth control.

There are any number of other situations that might result in a person going to necessities camp. The one exception to keeping account and requiring all deficits to be paid before one may stop using birth control is when a child is orphaned before reaching the age of majority. Such a child would be cared for by the state in necessities camp and educated as would the child of a citizen. Ideally, when the child reaches the age of maturity, assuming it chooses to become a citizen, he or she can then leave necessities camp. It may be, however, that the child has not finished its education and cannot pay to complete it. Then the new citizen is like any other citizen who desires an education that he cannot supply with his own constructive power. The government must provide it upon request.

It is entirely possible that mandatory birth control in necessities camp will limit population growth thereby benefitting Society and the human species. While technology may enable 10 billion people to live on earth, it will surely be a different place than it is now, and possibly not a very desirable one. I personally believe that uncontrolled population growth is *the* most dangerous problem facing mankind. If mandatory birth control helps control human population, then that is an unintended, but altogether salutary effect.

Religion

The philosophy behind the Social Contract is entirely secular. A resort to religion is unnecessary to establish or maintain Society. All religiously based moral principles with which I am familiar are essentially incomplete efforts to express the morality of equality and the moral principle of constructive power. This is true at least for those religious moral principles that addresses the relations between individuals within Society as opposed as to those that address the relationship between individuals and the God or Gods of the religion. Certainly the Golden Rule and the Ten Commandments that proscribe lying, stealing and killing are but facets of the moral principle of constructive power.

While I have scrupulously avoided religious justifications for the morality of equality, the moral principle of constructive power and the Social Contract, that avoidance is not out of a fear or condemnation of religious faith. On the contrary, it is out of the deepest respect for the many different religious faiths that serve basic human needs.

The moral principle of constructive power and government's obligation to prevent destructive power guarantee freedom of religious belief and expression as much as it does any secular or nonreligious or anti-religious belief. The Social Contract, and accordingly the government, has no role in the debate between creationism and evolution except to prevent either side from obtaining adherents by using destructive power.

In the search for one's volitional will, some people, perhaps the vast majority, will find it in religious faith. They may choose to devote their lives to their religious faith and to act as they believe their God or Gods wish or command them to act. Others may find their volitional will in an unending quest to acquire as much wealth and power as they can. Neither of these volitional wills is right or wrong or even preferable. Rather the purpose of the Social Contract is to give every individual the greatest possible opportunity to find and pursue his own volitional will.

History is overrun with examples of wars fought and atrocities committed in the holy name of religion. The Crusades and Spanish Inquisition are examples enough of religious justification for torture, murder and confiscation of property. Under the Social Contract, the practice of religion would be protected by the prohibition against destructive power, and limited by the same rule. With both this protection and limitation, quite likely religion will flourish among a large segment of Society, much as religion does today in the United States. Any effort by one group to impose with destructive powers its beliefs, religious or otherwise, upon those who do not agree with them, will be met with the same response from government that any other threat or actual use of destructive power requires. The religious faithful, organized religion, and atheists have nothing to fear in a Society under the Social Contract so long as each uses constructive power to acquires new converts and practice his beliefs.

Likewise, the citizens who are government may not make religious or secular beliefs a part of the law. All secular or religious beliefs outside of the Social Contract belong in the sphere of voluntary persuasion.

Limitations of the Moral Code of the Social Contract

The moral code of the Social Contract will not satisfy all people as the rule for judging others' actions or for guiding *all* of their choices for several reasons. First, the Social Contract provides the rules of social behavior necessary to establish an individualistic society. The Social Contract provides a structure of Society for each individual's pursuit of his volitional will. Self-interest is the primary interest of individuals, but some people may find self-interest an insufficient guide for all choices.

Second, there are many beliefs and ideas about how people ought to act toward one another, which for lack of a better description are to the Social Contract what the superstructure of a ship is to its hull. A ship can float with only its hull, but with nothing else, it is not a complete ship. Life lived by the rote of the morality of equality of the Social Contact can survive and perhaps even materially prosper, but it may be hollow and unsatisfying, like Beethoven's Fifth in C major.

Possessions are never permanent. Even a car or a house wears out and must be repaired or replaced. A marriage, a business partnership, a job, are all possessions that can be acquired or lost by destructive power. The choices spouses make create a marriage and expectations of future performance. These choices, although they may be made as forever, often are not. The same is true of a business partnership or a job. Religions and moral philosophies different about whether one spouse *ought* to continue in a marriage. The Social Contract establishes the moral rule for pursuing one's self-interest, it says nothing about what is actually in one's self-interest. How one decides what is in his self-interest can be the loneliest, most difficult of choices. Every religion, philosophy and pop guru will be free to proselytize his own version of what is in one's self-interest. If man has a soul capable of salvation, then surely it is in every man's self-interest to act to obtain salvation. Salvation will be the aim of the individual's volitional will.

This is a very important point. The Social Contract is not intended to replace religion or end moral philosophy in the sense that they tell us what happiness is or what our volitional will *ought* to be. Society founded on the Social Contract will, however, offer the greatest possible opportunity for each and every person to find his own answers to those questions. The Social Contract does not help us decide what our volitional will is or how to pursue it, only how *not* to pursue it. Creating or finding one's volitional will is about choosing what makes life worth living. The government created by the Social Contract may not enter the debate over whether man has a soul, is a spiritual animal, should be loyal, kind, generous, magnanimous, charitable, loving, supportive, altruistic, virtuous, courageous or any other personal identity and value choices.

In the final analysis, once the physical needs of life are satisfied, the rest of life is a search for meaning. That meaning may be found in family, religion, mysticism, asceticism, romance, sex, music, art, work or any number of pursuits, but if history teaches anything, it is that no religion or idea, and certainly no political system, yet holds the final answer. The greatest tragedies and atrocities in man's history are found when one man or group has tried to force his religion or ideas about the meaning of life on others who are "to blind to see the truth." In my judgment, Truth, with a capital "T", needs no might to make it right. Executing the Social Contract must always be an act of voluntary persuasion because forcing someone to join would violate the first premise of the Social Contract and destroy it in the process. A resort to might is a confession that Truth has not yet been found, for when it is, if it is, it will be plain for all to see. So long as there are diverse views about the meaning of life, there must be the opportunity to explore the diversity and search for the "Truth." The Social Contract is the framework for that search, not the answer. No more. No less.

Chapter XII

Revolution or Evolution

Can an individualistic society emerge by the evolution of an existing society or does it require a popular revolution? If revolution is scrapping all social institutions and starting from scratch, that seems an unlikely and undesirable way for an individualistic society to emerge. Revolution is likely to destroy the systems of lesser complexity necessary for an individualistic society to emerge. Evolutionary is far more likely and desirable, although power is the basis of even an individualistic society. The evolution to an individualistic society founded on the Social Contract would likely go through several stages.

If the morality of equality appeals to a sufficient number of people, then they could execute the Social Contract without the government being a party. Individuals, corporations, churches and business entities could sign the Social Contract and agree that Article I will govern their actions and those of their agents whenever they acted for the entity. As a private contract, everyone who has executed the Social Contract agrees to act toward all other parties according to Article I, i.e., with only constructive power. If any party breaches Article I in his relations with another party, he could be sued in the existing courts for breach of contract the same as any other breach of a private contract. For those who execute the Social Contract, it would become a substitute civil law. If the existing civil law and the Social Contract conflict, the courts would resolve such conflicts the same way they resolve conflicts between private contracts and a statute. If the statute cannot be waived, it would control. Except for those differences discussed earlier, the Social Contract does not conflict with existing law. Rather, the Social Contract is more comprehensive than the present law. In parties' relations with all non–parties, the existing law would still govern.

With advances in the Internet and information technology, it should be relatively easy to keep up who has executed the Social Contract. Each party could register with a website, like registering a new piece of software, and receive a copy of the Social Contract they signed to carry with them like they would a Social Security Card or driver's license. A database would be created so one's status could be found like looking up someone's address and phone number on the Internet.

Once the number of parties reaches a sufficient number, either a Social Contract political party would be organized or an existing political party might adopt the Social Contract as one of its objectives. In the United States, Congress or the states could propose a Constitutional amendment calling for the President to execute the Social Contract on behalf of the federal government. The Social Contract would then become the fundamental law of the land superior to the Constitution. The federal courts would become the judiciary, loyal to the Social Contract before the Constitution. The method of selecting judges would remain the same unless the judiciary found the required independence was not achieved.

In the initial phase after the Social Contract is executed by the government, there will likely be a significant number of people who have for any number of reasons, not executed the Social Contract. It will take a considerable time for everyone to learn about the Social Contract and choose whether to become a party. There would be a transition period, perhaps as long as an entire generation, but certainly long enough for all people to learn about the Social Contract and choose whether to become a party.

During the transition, everyone in Society is bound by the Social Contract whether they sign it or not because even an individualistic society operates on might makes right. Parties to the Social Contract will use their power of alliance through the existing political system to make the Social Contract the fundamental law. This is no different than everyone in the United States being subject to and entitled to the protections of the U.S. Constitution whether they expressly agree to it or not. All adults would be treated as parties who had executed the Social Contract. Article I would be the law governing all relations between adults the same as the civil law now made through the political process binds everyone whether they agree with it or not. All citizens under the existing law when the Social Contract is adopted would have all the artificial rights granted by the Social Contract unless and until their rights are terminated in accordance with Article IV. Then they would either become wards of Society if they lack moral capacity or non-members of Society with no artificial rights.

There would not be an immediate, wholesale repeal of existing laws. Rather, all existing laws would be presumed valid. Everyone must obey the prior law unless the judiciary declares it to violate the Social Contract.

Children will immediately begin their study of the Social Contract and other-consciousness to develop moral capacity. Upon reaching the age of maturity during the transitional phase, they will choose whether to become a party to the Social Contract. Over a generation, everyone will have the opportunity to be educated about the Social Contract and the obligation to choose whether to become a party. Children who reach maturity after being educated about the Social Contract must choose whether to become a party. Eventually only people who have chosen to become parties will have the artificial rights of the Social Contract. Society will then be firmly established, and all citizens will have consciously chosen the Social Contract as the human society that provides the greatest opportunity for them to achieve their happiness.

The first generation of children raised under the Social Contract will almost certainly not see it as self-evident. Only when the Social Contract, and the moral principle of constructive power, become self-evident will Society be securely established. This is an evolutionary process not just politically, but also in the way in which humans, as inherently philosophical creatures, see the world, themselves and their society.

Notes

Preface

1. Edward O. Wilson, *Consilience, The Unity of Knowledge*, paperback edition (New York: Vintage Books, 1999); Edward O. Wilson, "Back from Chaos," *The Atlantic Monthly*, 281, no. 3, (March 1998), 41-62.

Introduction

2. Magna Charta, Chapter 40, required judges "doe equall right, to the poore and to the rich." A.E. Dick Howard, "Rights in Passage: English Liberties in Early America," in *The Bill of Rights and the States,* ed. Patrick T. Conley and John P. Kaminski, (Madison, Wis.: Madison House, 1992), 3.
3. John Locke, *Two Treatises of Government,* ed. Thomas I. Cook, (New York: Hafner Press, 1973).
4. Ibid.
5. Philip B. Kurland and Ralph Lerner, ed., *The Founder's Constitution,* (Chicago: Univ. of Chicago Press, 1987), 1:499-500. See also the referenced contemporary documents.
6. *McCulloch v. Maryland,* 17 U.S. 316, 431 (1824).
7. 60 U.S. 393 (1856).
8. 163 U.S. 537 (1896).
9. *Zamora v. State,* 371 So.2d 776 (Fla. 3d DCA 1978). For the decision rejecting the claim of ineffective assistance by Zamora's counsel, see *Zamora v. State,* 422 So.2d 325 (Fla. 3d DCA 1982).

Chapter I

1. Francois Jacob, "Evolution and Tinkering," in *Biological Foundations and Human Nature,* ed. Miriam Balaban (New York, London: Academic Press; Philadelphia, Rehovot: Balaban Publishers, 1983), 15-42.
2. Ilya Prigogine and Isabelle Stengers, *The End of Certainty: Time, Chaos and the New Laws of Nature* (New York: Free Press, 1997).
3. Edward O. Wilson, "The Biological Basis of Morality," *The Atlantic Monthly,* 281, no. 4, (April 1998), 53-70; Leonard D. Katz , ed., *The Evolutionary Origins of Morality: Cross Disciplinary Perspectives,* (Devon: Imprint Academic, 2000).
4. For a similar discussion in the context of neuro-biology, see Antonio R. Damasio, *Descartes' Error: Emotion, Reason, and the Human Brain* (New York: Putnam, 1994), and, *The Feeling of What Happens: Body and Emotion in the Making of Consciousness* (New York: Harcourt Brace & Co., 1999).
5. The literature on cognitive science has grown exponentially. Some easily accessible sources of such literature can be found on the internet at sites maintained by reputable scholars. See e.g., Center for Consciousness Studies at the University of Arizona, http://www.consciousness.arizona.edu; Emergent

Mind.Org, http://www.emergentmind.org.

6. It should come as no surprise that there are as many purposes as there are causes and effects. In other words, one can engage in a *reductio ad absurdum* in postulating the purposes of the will to cause effects. Indeed, if the definition of life is accurate, for every effect cause by a living organism as opposed to those due solely to the orderly movement of matter, there must be a corresponding purpose supplied by the will of the living system. Engaging in any sort of reductionary analysis of purposes and causes and effects has nothing to offer for present purposes toward understanding the will of living systems and how it operates in humans or human society. Consequently, I shall leave to others this aspect of the question.

7. Gelber, B. 1958, "Retention in Paramecium Aurelia." *J. Comp. Physiol. Psych.* 51:110-115.

8. Reasoned behavior is to be distinguished from abstract reasoning, which is a consciously employed system of rules and linguistic concepts to reach conclusions, which humans generally believe is exclusively their own province.

9. Alison Jolly, *The Evolution of Primate Behavior,* 2d ed. (New York: Macmillan, 1985), 448.

10. Rousseau makes the same observation of a great prince who has only to follow the model that a good legislator must create, and the inventor of a machine versus the person who winds it up and turns it on. Jean-Jacques Rousseau, *The Social Contract,* The Hafner Library of Classics (New York: Hafner Publishing. Co., 1947), 36.

11. Robert Ardrey, *The Territorial Imperative,* (Kingsport, Tennessee: Kingsport Press, 1966), 23-24.

12. I use the word "may" because there are other mechanisms of adaptation which could explain the rat's behavior. It could be simply conditioned behavior based on the repetitive trips through the maze. Then again, it may be due to the rat acquiring a consciousness of the course of the maze and the consequence of turning one direction versus the other and thus consciously choosing one course over the other. The instances of rats escaping from the maze and going directly to the food suggest a more complex mental operation than solely autonomic learning. Regardless whether the rat consciously chooses or not, clearly other animals besides humans, such as the dog, do consciously choose between alternatives based on their understanding of the alternatives.

13. Prigogine has offered an explanation of both the arrow of time and for indeterminism as fundamental properties of all systems. Prigogine, *The End of Certainty.*

14. "If a man has the power and the wish to do a thing, then he has done it; for every one does do whatever he intends to do whenever he can do it, there being nothing to stop him." Aristotle *Rhetoric* 2.19.1392b.16-20.

Chapter II

1. Craig Packer and Anne E. Pusey, "Divided We Fall: Cooperation among Lions," *Scientific American* (May 1997), 52-59.

2. Wilson, "Morality," 53-70; Edward O. Wilson, "Sociobiology and the Idea of Progress," in *Bological Foundations and Human Nature,* ed. Miriam Balaban (New York, London: Academic Press; Philadelphia, Rehovot: Balaban Publishers, 1983), 201-216.

3. The discovery of DNA and the manipulation of it through recombination and splicing of genes, cloning and other techniques may well be the next mechanism of evolution of biological organisms. First there was self-replication and random gene mutation. Then there was sex and then selective breeding. Now there is the consciously directed and designed manipulation of DNA. Maybe there will be computational life–not computer viruses, but the complete representation of biological organisms in computer or machine memory. Maybe in the end "life" will escape the mathematics of population genetics. Frank J. Tipler, *The Physics of Immortality: Modern Cosmology, God and the Resurrection of the Dead,* (New York, London: Doubleday; Anchor Books, 1994), 18-65.

Chapter III

1. Oliver Wendell Holmes, Jr., *The Common Law,* (1881; Birmingham, Ala.: Legal Classics Edition, 1982), 1-33.

2. Dan P. McAdams, *The Person,* 2d. ed. (Ft. Worth, Tex.: Harcourt Brace College Pub., 1994), 549; Gordon Gallup, Jr., Daniel J. Povinelli, "Can Animals Empathize," *Scientific American Quarterly* (November/Winter 1998).

3. Ibid. Gallup argues that self-awareness is sufficient, while Povinelli argues that self-awareness is not sufficient.

4. Tex A. Sordahl, "Evolutionary Aspects of Avian Distraction Display: Variation in American Avocet and Black-necked Stilt Anti-predator Behavior," in *Deception, Perspectives on Human and Nonhuman Deceit,* ed. Robert W. Mitchell and Nicholas S. Thompson (Albany, N.Y.: State Univ. of New York Press, 1986).(hereinafter *Deception*)

5. James E. Lloyd, "Firefly Communication and Deception: 'Oh, What a Tangled Web'," in *Deception.*

6. H. Lyn Miles, "How Can I Tell a Lie? Apes, Language, and the Problem of Deception," in *Deception.*

7. Ibid.

8. Ibid.

9. Ibid.

10. McAdams, *The Person,* 549-50.

11. Jerome Kagan, *The Nature of the Child,* 2d ed. (New York: Basic Books Harper Collins, 1994), 112-152.

12. Mark H. Davis, *Empathy, a Social Psychological Approach,* (Madison, Wis.: Brown & Benchmark Publishing, 1994).

13. Compare Kant's description of conscience. Immanuel Kant, *Contents, Preface and Introduction to the Metaphysical Elements of Ethics,* Encyclopedia Britannica, Great Books Edition, v. 42:378.

14. Locke, *Two Treatises.*

15. Ibid., 147-150.

16. Ibid., 122-123.

17. The Roman juris consults held that a theft required an intention to steal. Victor Duruy, *History of Rome and the Roman People, from its Origins to the Establishment of the Christian Empire*, J.P. Mahaffy ed., comp. Kelly & Co., 5 vols. (London: Kegan, Paul, Trench & Co. 1886), 5:639.

18. Rita J. Simon and David E. Aaronson, *The Insanity Defense, A Critical Assessment of Law and Policy in the Post-Hinckley Era*, (New York: Praeger, 1988).

19. Duruy, *History of Rome*, 5:639-640.

20. *Piccott v. State*, 116 So.2d 626 (Fla. 1959)(Hobson, J., dissenting).

21. *Rex v. Arnold*, 16 Howell State Trials, 695, 764 (1724).

22. *United States v. Freeman*, 357 F.2d 606, 617 (2d Cir. 1966).

23. *M'Naghten Case*, 10 Cl. & Fin. 200, 8 Eng.Rep. 718 (1843).

24. Model Penal Code § 4.01 (Tent. Draft No. 4, 1955).

25. For a similar formulation of the role of empathy in morality, see Martin L. Hoffman, "The Contribution of Empathy to Justice and Moral Judgment," in *Empathy and its Development*, ed. Nancey Eisenberg and Janet Strayer (Cambridge, New York: Cambridge Univ. Press, 1987), 47-80.

26. The story was based on a true account of the Scottish sailor, Alexander Selkirk, 1676-1721, who was put ashore at his own request in the Juan Fernández Islands, where he remained for over four years before his rescue in 1709. R.L. Megroz, *The Real Robinson Crusoe*, (London: Cresset Press, 1939).

27. Wilson, "Morality," 53-70.

Chapter IV

1. The conflict between conscious self-interest and other-consciousness is certainly not the only process producing internal conflicts with distress or anxiety, etc. Surely Oedipal and other complexes produced by other social relations produce anxiety and distress, and some of these are likely intertwined with that produced by what I have collectively called other-consciousness. Psychiatrist and psychologists will not be put out of business even if the morality of equality is an entirely accurate description of morality.

2. Will Durant, *Caesar and Christ*, vol. 3 of *The Story of Civilization*, (New York: Simon & Schuster 1944), 566.

3. Will Durant, *The Age of Faith* vol. 4 of *The Story of Civilization* (New York: Simon & Schuster 1950), 554.

4. Paul Allard, transcribed by Michael C. Tinkler, *The Catholic Encyclopedia*, vol. XIV, 1912 by Robert Appleton Company, Online Edition Copyright 1999 by Kevin Knight, *Nihil Obstat, July 1, 1912*. Remy Lafort, S.T.D., Censor, *Imprimatur*. John Cardinal Farley, Archbishop of New York, http://www.newadvent.org/cathen/14036a.htm.

5. Will Durant, *The Reformation*, vol. 6 of *The Story of Civilization*, (New York: Simon & Schuster 1957), 449.

6. Henry Cleveland, *Alexander H. Stevens, in Public and Private with Letters and Speeches, Before, During and since the War,* (Philadelphia: National Publishing Co. 1866), 126-29.

7. Florida's law, as an example, provides:

§ 828.12. Cruelty to animals

(1) A person who unnecessarily overloads, overdrives, torments, deprives of necessary sustenance or shelter, or unnecessarily mutilates, or kills any animal, or causes the same to be done, or carries in or upon any vehicle, or otherwise, any animal in a cruel or inhumane manner, is guilty of a misdemeanor of the first degree, punishable as provided in s. 775.082 or by a fine of not more than $5,000, or both.

8. Durant, *Caesar and Christ,* 398; Duruy, *History of Rome,* 5:295-296, 640.

9. Will Durant and Ariel Durant, *The Age of Napoleon,* vol. 11 of *The Story of Civilization* (New York: Simon & Schuster 1975), 368.

10. William Blackstone, *Commentaries on the Laws of England,* (1765; reprint, Buffalo, New York: William S. Hein & Co., 1992), 1:430.

11. Durant, *The Reformation,* 416.

12. Carl N. Degler, *In Search of Human Nature* (New York: Oxford Univ. Press, 1991).

13. Lawyers who remember studying proximate cause in torts class in law school will recognize this as adopting the views of Judge Andrews in the famous case of *Palsgraff v. Long Island Railway Company,* 248 N.Y. 339, 162 N.E. 99 (N.Y.Ct. of App.1928)(Andrews, J., dissenting).

14. This, of course, assumes that the person is of the age of majority and competent. It does not mean that all people have equal ability to judge the consequences given equal knowledge of the alternatives and the information available to understand the consequences of each alternative.

15. Durant, *Caesar and Christ,* 400.

16. Section 384.24, Florida Statutes. For a case applying this principle and citing other authorities supporting its application, *See Hogan v. Tavzel,* 660 So.2d 350 (Fla. 5th DCA 1995).

17. This does not include the relationship between a parent and a minor child, i.e., a child who has not yet chosen whether to sign the Social Contract.

18. 2 Sam. 11:15

19. The government could by law establish a presumption that absent agreement to the contrary, spouses promise fidelity. Numerous laws currently establish the default terms of relationships between individuals when they do not specifically agree to the contrary. For instance, when a merchant sells a product to a consumer, he warrants that it is of merchantable quality unless the warranty is specifically disclaimed. When two or more people form a partnership they are presumed to have equal interests in the profits and losses of the partnership unless they specifically agree to a different division.

20. Actual consciousness may not always be necessary as with a presumptive promise of fidelity upon marriage absent a specific agreement to the contrary, and the woman does not affirmatively state that she has not promised fidelity to her husband.

21. The definition of an "individual" must not be forgotten here: a self and other-conscious human able and trying to make choices in creating and achieving his or her volitional will based on the equal value of all similarly conscious and motivated humans.

22. Victor-Marie Hugo, *Les Miserables,* trans. Charles E. Wilbour (New York: Modern Library, n.d.).

23. A citizen may use destructive power in self-defense against another citizen. Society, no matter how vigilant, will never be able to prevent all destructive power. When it cannot, self-defense is allowed.

Chapter V

1. Carl N. Degler, *In Search of Human Nature: The Decline and Revival of Darwinism in American Social Thought,* (New York, Oxford: Oxford Univ. Press, 1991), 81.
2. Ibid., 216.
3. Ibid., 59.
4. Quoted in Degler, *Human Nature,* 60, quoting Loren Eiseley, *Darwin's Century: Evolution and the Men Who Discovered it* (Garden City: Doubleday; Anchor Books, 1961), 303, 312-313.
5. Degler, *Human Nature,* 15. Deggler noted, however, "... no American social scientists, despite their acceptance of Darwinian beliefs in regard to other matters, drew upon that explanation for racial differences."
6. Ibid., 34-35.
7. Ibid., 36.
8. Ibid., 37-40.
9. *Buck v. Bell,* 274 U.S. 200 (1927).
10. Id., at 205.
11. Id., at 208.
12. Degler, *Human Nature,* 48.
13. Ibid., 52. Degler argues that the intelligence testing played a minor if not insignificant role in the Immigration Act of 1923, but he cites several others who take an opposite view.
14. James M. Cattell, quoted in Degler, *Human Nature,* 30.
15. Rousseau makes the same argument in his *Second Discourse* that all of the ills of mankind were due to society. Jean-Jacques Rousseau, *The First and Second Discourses,* ed. R. D. Masters, trans. R. D. Masters and Judith R. Masters, (New York: St. Martin's, 1964), 101-181.
16. Degler, *Human Nature,* 139-140.
17. Ibid., 140.
18. Jacob, "Evolution and Tinkering," 27.
19. Abraham Maslow, *Motivation and Personality,* 2d ed. (New York, Eavanston, London: Harper & Row, 1970), 35-58.
20. Aristotle *Rhetoric* 2:1378b33-35-1379a1-5.

Chapter VI

1. Locke, *Two Treatises of Government*, ed. Thomas I. Cook, (New York: Hafner Press, 1973)(hereinafter, Locke, *Second Treatise*, followed by the paragraph number).
2. Locke, *Second Treatise*, ¶ 11.
3. Locke, *Second Treatise*, ¶ 190.
4. Locke, *Second Treatise*, ¶ 19.
5. Locke, *Second Treatise*, ¶ 27.
6. Locke, *Second Treatise*, ¶ 10, 11.
7. Locke, *Second Treatise*, ¶192.
8. Locke, *Second Treatise*, ¶ 85.
9. Locke, *Second Treatise*, ¶ 95.
10. Locke, *Second Treatise*, ¶3.
11. *Miami Herald*, March 19, 2001.
12. *Webster's Encyclopedic Unabridged Dictionary*, Barnes & Noble Books ed. 1992, s.v. "artificial," "artifice."
13. Deut. 5:18, 19, 21.
14. Locke, *Second Treatise*, ¶ 7.
15. Locke, *Second Treatise*, ¶ 125.
16. *The Western Tradition, from the Ancient World to Louis XIV*, ed. Eugene Weber, 2d ed. (D.C.: Heath & Co., 1966).
17. The enforcing authority's methods and their efficacy is a separate issue deserving complete attention, but is beyond the scope of this work.
18. Punishing a violator is not unique to humans. In many primate species, when a dominant male witnesses a subordinate male mate with one of the dominant male's females, although the act is done, the dominant male will invariable attack the younger male. From all appearances, the attack is intended to discourage a repeat of the disapproved act and to reinforce dominance.
19. Richard Thomson, *An Essay on the Magna Charta of King John*, (1829; reprint, Birmingham, Ala.: Legal Classics Library Edition, 1982),
20. Some 400 years later, Charles I would also face military defeat and Parliament's demands for restrictions on royal powers. Unlike John, Charles refused, and lost his head.
21. Thomson, *Magna Charta*, 31-32.
22. There are no natural duties to correspond to the natural right to try to do anything. There is no other will to direct how the person must act. I do not deny those people who would assert that God is such a will, but for me, until God speaks for himself, and not through the mouths of humans, and especially with so many different voices and religions, I cannot accept such human expressions of God's will as anything more than a human efforts to cloak an individual's own will with greater authority.
23. Locke, *Second Treatise*, ¶ 96.

Chapter VII

1. For a discussion of the many political theories and legal history that influenced the Constitution of the United States, see Edward S. Corwin, *The "Higher Law" Background of American Constitutional Law*, (Ithaca, N.Y.: Cornell Univ. Press, 5th reprint, 1963).

2. Herbert W. Schneider, introduction to *Leviathan*, by Thomas Hobbes, (1651; Indianapolis, New York: Bobbs-Merrill Co., 12th reprint, Library of Liberal Arts Press, 1958)

3. Thomas Hobbes, *Leviathan*, (1651; Indianapolis-New York: Bobbs-Merrill Co., 12th reprint, Library of Liberal Arts Press, 1958), 86.

4. Ibid.

5. Ibid., 107.

6. The law of nature and its corollary, natural justice, were born of the idea of right reason almost from the beginning of western philosophy. And reason as the ultimate test of the common law of England had its origins perhaps as early as the creation of a system of circuit courts by Henry II in the twelfth century, but it was firmly established by the time of Coke. In 1610, Coke in *dictum* in *Dr. Bonham's Case* claimed the right of the common law to declare void an act of Parliament as "against common right and reason." He later retreated from this position, but judicial review would not die with the retreat. Corwin, *"Higher Law."*

7. Ibid., 109.

8. Ibid., 110. Hobbes also quotes Matthew 7:12 and Luke 6:31 for the biblical statement of the golden rule.

9. For a fuller, but still brief summary of the events of Locke's life, and his political philosophy, see Thomas I. Cook, Introduction to *Two Treatises of Government*, by John Locke (New York: Hafner Press, 1973).

10. Locke's law of nature is complicated by his views of God's will as the ultimate source of authority for that law. Reason is the best means available for determining how men should live in the temporal world, so reason is the basis of the temporal law of nature. For a fuller explanation of Locke's law of nature, see Leo Strauss, *Natural Right and History*, (Chicago, London: Univ. of Chicago Press, paperback edition, 1965), 202-215.

11. This point of Locke's philosophy was inconsistent with the English common law of Locke's own day. One of the grounds Coke states for the common law to declare a statute of Parliament void is if it "should ordain that the same person should be party and judge, ..." And, this view emanated from the common law embodiment of reason. Corwin, *"Higher Law,"* 51-53. Perhaps it was merely a straw man to be knocked down by the social contract and the law of nature.

12. Locke, *Second Treatises*, ¶ 99.

13. Roger Masters, Introduction to *Jean-Jacques Rousseau, The First and Second Discourses*, ed. by Roger Masters, trans. Roger D. Masters and Judith R. Masters (New York: St. Martin's Press 1964) 230-232, n. 6, 7.

14. Rousseau, *Social Contract*, xxx.

15. Ibid.

16. Rousseau, *Discourses*.

17. Rousseau, *Social Contract*, 38.
18. Rousseau, *Social Contract*, xxx.
19. Lenore Ealy suggested this relationship between the goal of morality and polity.
20. Compare Locke, *Second Treatise*, ¶ 241.

Chapter VIII

1. Howard, "Rights in Passage," 3-15.
2. Ibid., 4.; Corwin, *"Higher Law,"* 54-55.
3. The Mayflower Compact provides, in part:

> In the name of God, Amen. We, whose names are underwritten, the Loyal Subjects of our dread Sovereign Lord, King James, by the Grace of God, of England, France and Ireland, King, Defender of the Faith, e&.
>
> Having undertaken for the Glory of God, and Advancement of the Christian Faith, and the Honour of our King and Country, a voyage to plant the first colony in the northern parts of Virginia; do by these presents, solemnly and mutually in the Presence of God and one of another, covenant and combine ourselves together into a civil Body Politick, for our better Ordering and Preservation, and Furtherance of the Ends aforesaid; And by Virtue hereof to enact, constitute, and frame, such just and equal Laws, Ordinances, Acts, Constitutions and Offices, from time to time, as shall be thought most meet and convenient for the General good of the Colony; unto which we promise all due submission and obedience.
>
> In Witness whereof we have hereunto subscribed our names at Cape Cod the eleventh of November, in the Reign of our Sovereign Lord, King James of England, France and Ireland, the eighteenth, and of Scotland the fifty-fourth. Anno Domini, 1620.

There followed the signatures of 41 of the 102 passengers, 37 of whom were members of the "Separatists" who were fleeing religious persecution in Europe. This compact established the first basis in the new world for written laws.

The preamble of the Fundamental Orders of Connecticut provides:

> January 14, 1639
> For as much as it hath pleased Almighty God by the wise disposition of his divine providence so to order and dispose of things that we the Inhabitants and Residents of Windsor, Hartford and Wethersfield are now cohabiting and dwelling in and upon the River of Connectecotte and the lands thereunto adjoining; and well knowing where a people are gathered together the word of God requires that to maintain the peace and union of such a people there should be an orderly and decent

Government established according to God, to order and dispose of the affairs of the people at all seasons as occasion shall require; do therefore associate and conjoin ourselves to be as one Public State or Commonwealth; and do for ourselves and our successors and such as shall be adjoined to us at any time hereafter, enter into Combination and Confederation together, to maintain and preserve the liberty and purity of the Gospel of our Lord Jesus which we now profess, as also, the discipline of the Churches, which according to the truth of the said Gospel is now practiced amongst us; as also in our civil affairs to be guided and governed according to such Laws, Rules, Orders and Decrees as shall be made, ordered, and decreed as followeth:

Prepared by Gerald Murphy (The Cleveland Free-Net - aa300) Distributed by permission of the Cybercasting Services Division of the National Public Telecomputing Network (NPTN).

4. Howard,"Rights in Passage," 11.
5. Quoted in ibid., 11-12.
6. Ibid., 17.
7. John P. Kaminski, "The Constitution without a Bill of Rights," in *The Bill of Rights and the States*, ed. Patrick T. Conley and John P. Kaminski (Madison, Wis.: Madison House, 1992), 16.
8. Ibid., 21.
9. Ibid., 24.
10. Ibid. This view of state constitutions also seems inconsistent with the Lockean theory that by the social contract the people give up only those rights and powers to government necessary to interpret, protect and enforce their natural rights.
11. Hamilton and other proponents of a strong central government also opposed a federal bill of rights. See *The Federalist,* No. 84 (New York: Cooperative Publication Society, 1902); see generally, Clinton L. Rossiter, *1787: The Grand Convention* (New York: Macmillan, 1966), 284, 302-303.
12. Kenneth R. Bowling, "'A Tub to the Whale'" The Adoption of the Bill of Rights," in *The Bill of Rights and the States*, ed. Patrick T. Conley and John P. Kaminski (Madison, Wis.: Madison House, 1992), 46-54.
13. Ibid., 54.
14. Helen E. Veit, Kenneth R. Bowling, Charlene Bangs Bickford, ed., *Congress, Creating the Bill of Rights, The Documentary Record from the First Federal* (Baltimore: Johns Hopkins Univ. Press, 1991).
15. *The Federalist,* No. 51.
16. Alexander Hamilton and other advocates of a strong central government opposed a bill of rights as unnecessary because the Federal Government was not granted the power to intrude upon fundamental personal rights. He also argued:

I go further, and affirm that bills of rights, in the sense and in the extent in which they are contended for, are not only unnecessary in the proposed constitution, but would even be dangerous. They would contain various exceptions to powers which are not granted; and on this very account, would afford a colourable pretext to claim more than were granted. For why declare that things shall not be done which there is no power to do? Why for instance, should it be said, that the liberty of the press shall not be restrained, when no power is given by which restrictions may be imposed? I will not contend that such a provision would confer a regulating power; but it is evident that it would furnish, to men disposed to usurp, a plausible pretence for claiming that power.

The Federalist, No. 84.
    17.   3 U.S. (3 Dall.) 386 (1798).
    18.   *Baldwin v. Fish and Game Commission of Montana,* 436 U.S. 371, 394- (1977)(Brennan, J., dissenting), quoting Professor Tribe:

Behind the 1825 *Corfield* opinion lay the nineteenth century controversy over the status of 'natural rights' in constitutional litigation. Some judges had supposed an inherent limitation on state and federal legislation that compelled courts to strike down any law 'contrary to the first great principles of the social compact.' They were the proponents of the natural rights doctrine which, without specific constitutional moorings, posited 'certain vital principles in our free republican governments, which will determine and overrule an apparent abuse of legislative powers.'

Corfield can be understood as an attempt to import the natural rights doctrine into the Constitution by way of the privileges and immunities clause of article IV. By attaching the fundamental rights of state citizenship to the privileges and immunities clause, Justice Washington would have created federal judicial protection against state encroachment upon the 'natural rights' of citizens. (footnotes omitted).

Laurence H. Tribe, *American Constitutional Law* (Mineola, N.Y.: Foundation Press, 1978), 405-406. *See also,* Keven C. Newsom, "Setting Incorporationism Straight: A Reinterpretation of the Slaughter-House Cases," Yale L. Rev. (2000).
    19.   Id., at 395, n. 1.
    20.   5 U.S. (1 Cranch) 137 (1803).
    21.   60 U.S. (19 How.) 397 (1857).
    22.   *Barron v. The Mayor and City of Baltimore,* 32 U.S. (7 Pet.) 243 (1833).
    23.   Intellectually honest means are available. See e.g., *Adamson v. People of State of California,* 332 U.S. 46, 68 (1947)(Black, J., dissenting); Newsom, "Setting Incorporationism Straight," and authorities cited therein.
    24.   Article I §§ 2, 9, cl. 1, 4; Article V.
    25.   *In re Slaughter-House Cases,* 83 U.S. 36 (1873). Compare with the revisionist interpretation of this case in Newsom, "Setting Incorporationism Straight."
    26.   94 U.S. 113 (1877).
    27.   Id., at 133-134.
    28.   113 U. S. 27 (1884)

29. 123 U.S. 623 (1887).
30. 165 U.S. 578 (1897).
31. 169 U.S. 366 (1898).
32. 198 U.S. 45 (1905).
33. 208 U.S. 412 (1908).
34. 291 U.S. 502 (1934).
35. Some of these cases are as follows:

Panama Refining Co. v. Ryan, 293 U.S. 388 (1935). The National Industrial Recovery Act (NIRA) allowed the president to establish "codes of fair competition" to increase prices and improve labor conditions, with the approval of industrial organizations or trade associations. It was struck down as an excessive delegation of legislative power to the executive branch.

Railroad Retirement Board v. Alton R.R. Co., 295 U.S. 330 (1935). The Railroad Retirement Act of 1934 required and regulated a pension system for railroad employees. It was struck down as exceeding the federal government's power under the commerce clause.

Schecter Poultry Corp. v. United States, 295 U.S. 495 (1935). The national economic crisis was simply insufficient for the federal government's power to deal with the "internal" matters of the states whose job it was to deal with economic conditions within their borders. The Court again struck down the NIRA code of competition for poultry dealers which regulated the conditions and price of labor.

United States v. Butler, 297 U.S. 1 (1936). The Adjustment Act of 1933 allowing payments to farmers not to grow certain crops from a tax imposed on processors of the products not grown, was found to violate the 10th Amendment. Setting the quantity and quality of agricultural production was a matter reserved to the states. And, the federal government could not pay people not to grow because that would be purchasing submission to federal regulation outside its power.

Carter v. Carter Coal Co., 298 U.S. 238 (1936). The Bitumous Coal Conservation Act (1935) required coal producers to follow maximum hours negotiated by miners and producers of more than two-thirds of the annual national tonnage production for the previous year, set a minimum wage in the same way, and imposed a tax on those who did not comply. The act also regulated coal prices. Setting requirements for private producers was an unconstitutional delegation to private persons of legislative power. 10th Am analysis of scope of fed power.

Moorehead v. New York, ex rel. Tipaldo, 298 U.S. 587 (1936). The court struck down as violative of the liberty of contract a minimum wage law for women.

36. *Norman v. Baltimore & O. Ry. Co.*, 294 U.S. 240 (1935)(abrogation of gold clauses in contracts upheld as regulation of national currency for which 10th amendment gave states no role); *Tennessee Electric Power Co. v. Tennessee Valley Authority*, 306 U.S. 118 (1939), federal government competition in establishing dams and generating electricity upheld.

37. *West Coast Hotel Co. v. Parrish*, 300 U.S. 379 (1937); *NLRB v. Jones and Laughlin Steel Corp.*, 301 U.S. 1 (1937).

38. 335 U.S. 525 (1945).
39. 348 U.S. 483 (1955).
40. In *Railway Express Agency v. New York,* 336 U.S. 106 (1949), a statute prohibiting advertising on delivery vehicles except for the owner's business, supposedly to reduce distractions for other drivers and pedestrians, was upheld as long as its scheme "has relation to the purpose for which it is made and does not contain the kind of discrimination against which the equal protection clause affords protection."

City of New Orleans v. Dukes, 427 U.S. 297 (1976) involved an equal protection challenge to a prohibition of pushcart vendors in the French Quarter, except for grandfathered vendors of which there were only two. The Court held "the judiciary may not sit as a super-legislature to judge the wisdom or desirability of legislative policy determinations made in areas that neither affect fundamental rights nor proceed along suspect lines." In the process, the Court overruled the only post 1937 case suggesting otherwise. *Morey v. Doud,* 354 U.S. 457 (1957).

41. *Goldfarb v. Virginia State Bar,* 421 U.S. 773 (1975).
42. *Bates v. State Bar of Arizona,* 433 U.S. 350 (1977), and other professional advertising cases later reversed this trend on fundamental rights grounds, i.e., the right to free speech.
43. *Virginia State Bd. of Pharmacy v. Virginia Citizens Consumer Council, Inc.,* 425 U.S. 748 (1976): "[T]he free flow of commercial information is indispensable . . . to the proper allocation of resources in a free enterprise system . . . [and] to the formation of intelligent opinions as to how that system ought to be regulated or altered." Id., at 765. See also *City of Cincinnati v. Discovery Network, Inc.* 507 U.S. 410 (1995)(summarizing factors applicable to permissible government regulation of commercial speech); *Florida Bar v. Went for It, Inc.* 515 U.S. 618 (1995)(summarizing the history of and the Court's change of course on First Amendment protection of commercial speech).
44. 211 U.S. 78 (1908).
45. The Court also summarized prior formulations used as follows:

Third. But, consistently with the requirements of due process, no change in ancient procedure can be made which disregards those fundamental principles, to be ascertained from time to time by judicial action, which have relation to process of law, and protect the citizen in his private right, and guard him against the arbitrary action of government. This idea has been many times expressed in differing words by this court, and it seems well to cite some expressions of it. The words 'due process of law' 'were intended to secure the individual from the arbitrary exercise of the powers of government, unrestrained by the established principles of private rights and distributive justice.' [citations omitted] 'This court has never attempted to define with precision the words 'due process of law.' . . . It is sufficient to say that there are certain immutable principles of justice which inhere in the very idea of free government which no member of the Union may disregard.' [citation omitted] 'The same words refer to that law of the land in each state, which derives its authority from the inherent and reserved powers of the state, exerted within the limits of those fundamental principles of liberty and justice which lie at the base of all our civil and political institutions.' [citation omitted] 'The limit of the full control which the state has in the proceedings of its courts, both in civil and criminal cases, is subject only to the qualification that such procedure must not work a denial of fundamental rights or conflict with specific and applicable provisions of the Federal Constitution.' [citation omitted].

Twining, at 101-102.

46. *Buchanan v. Warley,* 245 U.S. 60 (1917). This decision has been argued to be a judicial effort to restrict racially discriminatory legislation. Schmidt, *Principle and Prejudice: The Supreme Court and Race in the Progressive Era,* Part 1: The Heyday of Jim Crow, 82 Colum. Law Rev. 444 (1982).

47. *Meyers v. Nebraska,* 262 U.S. 390 (1923).

48. *Gitlow v. New York,* 268 U.S. 652 (1925). See also *Powell v. Alabama,* 287 U.S. 45 (1935); *Brown v. Mississippi,* 297 U.S. 278 (1936).

49. *Powell v. Alabama,* 287 U.S. 45 (1935); *Brown v. Mississippi,* 297 U.S. 278 (1936).

50. *Rochin v. California,* 342 U.S. 165 (1952).

51. *Malinski v. People of State of New York,* 324 U.S. 401, 413-420 (1945)

52. In *Hurtado v. California,* 110 U.S. 516, 527 (1884), the Court held that the Due Process Clause did not require the States to prosecute all infamous crimes by the indictment of a grand jury as the Fifth Amendment required in Federal Court. In the more than 100 years since *Hurtado,* a number of the protections in the Bill of Rights were applied to the States through the Fourteenth Amendment:

Fourth Amendment's exclusionary rule: *Mapp v. Ohio,* 367 U.S. 643 (1961), overruling *Wolf v. Colorado,* 338 U.S. 25 (1949);
Fifth Amendment's privilege against self-incrimination : *Malloy v. Hogan,* 378 U.S. 1 (1964), overruling *Twining v. New Jersey,* 211 U.S. 78 (1908);
Double Jeopardy Clause of the Fifth Amendment: *Benton v. Maryland,* 395 U.S. 784 (1969), overruling *Palko v. Connecticut,* 302 U.S. 319 (1937);
Sixth Amendment's right to counsel : *Gideon v. Wainwright,* 372 U. S. 335, (1963), overruling *Betts v. Brady,* 316 U.S. 455 (1942);
Sixth Amendment right to speedy trial: *Klopfer v. North Carolina,* 386 U.S. 213 (1967);
Sixth Amendment right to compulsory process : *Washington v. Texas,* 388 U.S. 14, (1967);
Sixth Amendment right to jury trial: *Duncan v. Louisiana,* 391 U.S. 145, (1968).

See also, John E. Nowak, Roland D. Rotunda, and J. Nelson Young, *Constitutional Law,* Hornbook Series 3d ed. (St. Paul, Minn.: West Publishing Co., 1983), 315-318.

53. *Poe v. Ullman,* 367 U.S. 497, 541-43, 550-54 (1961)(Harlan, J., dissenting).

54. 381 U.S. 479 (1965).
55. 410 U.S. 113 (1973).
56. 505 U.S. 833 (1992).
57. See *Ohio v. Akron Center for Reproductive Health*, 497 U.S. 502 (1990); *Hodgson v. Minnesota*, 497 U.S. 417 (1990); *Webster v. Reproductive Health Services*, 492 U.S. 490 (1989)
58. *Loving v. Virginia*, 388 U.S. 1 (1967) (marriage); *Skinner v. Oklahoma*, 316 U.S. 535 (1942)(procreation); *Prince v. Massachusetts*, 321 U.S. 158 (1944) (family relationships); *Pierce v. Society of Sisters*, 268 U.S. 510 (1925)(child rearing and education); *Griswold v. Connecticut*, 381 U.S. 479 (1965) (contraception). *Eisenstadt v. Baird*, 405 U.S. 438 (1972)(bearing or begetting a child).
59. *Akron v. Akron Center for Reproductive Health*, 462 U.S. 416 (1983) (Akron I); *Thornburgh v. American College of Obstetricians and Gynecologists*, 476 U.S. 747 (1986); *Webster v. Reproductive Health Services*, 492 U.S. 490 (1989).
60. He also pointed out that in the nineteen years after *Roe*, of the fifteen Justices who have passed on the basic issue in *Roe*, eleven have voted with the majority, Chief Justice Burger, Justices Douglas, Brennan, Stewart, Marshall, Powell, Blackmun, O'Connor, Kennedy, Souter, and Stevens. Only the four then on the Court, Chief Justice Rehnquist, Justices Scalia, White and Thomas, have disagreed.
61. *Roe* analogized the right to abort a fetus to those in *Pierce v. Society of Sisters*, 268 U.S. 510 (1925); *Meyer v. Nebraska*, 262 U.S. 390 (1923); *Loving v. Virginia*, 388 U.S. 1 (1967); and *Griswold v. Connecticut*, 381 U.S. 479 (1965).
62. Nowak, *Constitutional Law*, 367.
63. There are still cases that use the language of prohibiting public expenditures for private benefit; however, every new multimillion dollar sports stadium paid for with public money proves that fundamental law is "in vain."
64. Corwin, *"Higher Law," 73.*
65. *Knowlton v. Moore*, 178 U.S. 41, 109-110 (1900).
66. Compare *Olcott v. Fond du Lac County*, 83 U.S. 678 (1872), in which the Supreme Court held that a tax used to pay for a private railroad expansion was a "public use" of the tax. In so doing, the Court overruled the Wisconsin Supreme Court's holding that the use was unconstitutional under the State Constitution as a private use. This result almost certainly would not be repeated after *Erie R.R. v. Tompkins,* 304 U.S. 64 (1938), in which the Supreme Court held that henceforth it would defer to a state supreme court on the determination of questions of state law.
67. Social Security was deemed to be for the "general welfare" because of the crushing unemployment of the Great Depression.

> ... During the years 1929 to 1936, when the country was passing through a cyclical depression, the number of the unemployed mounted to unprecedented heights. Often the average was more than 10 million; at times

a peak was attained of 16 million or more. Disaster to the breadwinner meant disaster to dependents. Accordingly the roll of the unemployed, itself formidable enough, was only a partial roll of the destitute or needy. The fact developed quickly that the states were unable to give the requisite relief. The problem had become national in area and dimensions. There was need of help from the nation if the people were not to starve. It is too late today for the argument to be heard with tolerance that in a crisis so extreme the use of the moneys of the nation to relieve the unemployed and their dependents is a use for any purpose narrower than the promotion of the general welfare.

Steward Machine Co. v. Davis, 301 U.S. 548, 586-587 (1937); Compare *United States v. Butler*, 297 U.S. 1, 65, 66 (1937); *Helvering v. Davis*, 301 U.S. 619, 672 (1937).

68. While there has never been a billionare's tax, as early as 1921, a tax of 73% of all income over $1,000,000 was imposed, 8% normal, and 65% surtax. *Statutes at Large* 42 (1921): 233. In 1934, the tax was 63%, 4% normal and 59% surtax. *Statutes at Large* 48 (1934): 684-686. In 1935, the tax was 77%, 78%, and 79% respectively on income of $1,000,000 to $2,000,000, $2,000,000 to $5,000,000, and over $5,000,000. *Statutes at Large* 49 (1935): 1014-1015. For the even higher rates on lower incomes, see note 69.

69. The first personal income tax rate after ratification of the Sixteenth Amendment was a one percent "normal Tax" on all incomes, and an "additional tax" as follows:

Income	Additional Tax
$20,000 to $50,000	1%
$50,000 to $75,000	2%
$75,000 to $100,000	3%
$100,000 to $250,000	4%
$250,000 to $500,000	5%
over $500,000	6%.

Statutes at Large 38 (1913): 166.

By 1954 there was a "normal tax" on all incomes of 3%, and a "surtax" as follows:

Income	Surtax Tax	
over $16,000	$4,336	plus 50% of the excess
over $26,000	$8,696	plus 63% of the excess
over $50,000	$23,096	plus 72% of the excess
over $80,000	$42,516	plus 80% of the excess
over $200,000	$154,716	plus 89% of the excess.

Statutes at Large 65 (1951): 459. The above table has only representative rates. Compare *Fulman v. U. S.*, 434 U.S. 528 (1978); *Quaker City Cab Co. v. Commonwealth of Pennsylvania*, 48 S.Ct. 553, 407 n. 5 (1928)(Brandeis, J., dissenting).

Chapter IX

1. *Pullum v. Cincinati Inc.,* 476 So.2d 657 (Fla. 1985)(Fla. Supreme Court reversing its prior holding that a product liability statute of repose was unconstitutional, reinstating the statute, and ultimately applying its decision retroactively); *Gore v. Harris,* 772 So.2d 1243 (Fla. 2000)(rewriting the Florida Election Code after the election).
2. See Chapter VIII.
3. *United States v. Villato,* 2 U.S. (2 Dall.) 370 (1797); *Inglis v. Trustees of Sailor's Snug Harbour in City of New York,* 28 U.S. (3 Pet.) 99 (1830); *Shanks v. Dupont,* 28 U.S. (3 Pet.) 242 (1830); *Ex Parte Milligan,* 71 U.S. (4 Wall.) 2 (1866).
4. Charles Frankel, Introduction to *The Social Contract* by Jean-Jacques Rousseau, Hafner Library of Classics (New York: Hafner Publishing Co. 1947), xxi. For a discussion of the classic view of the role of society, justice and virtue, see Strauss, *Natural Right,* 120-164.
5. *The Federalist*, No. 78.
6. Compare Hamilton's view that, "To avoid an arbitrary discretion in the courts, it is indispensable that they should be bound down by strict rules and precedents, which serve to define and point out their duty in every particular case that comes before them." Id., at 529; *See also,* 1 J. Story, *Commentaries on Equity Jurisprudence* ,§§ 18-20, 9th ed. (I. Redfield, 1866), 15-17.
7. 71 U.S. (4 Wall.) 2 (1866).
8. The riot acts of the past imposed direct liability on government entities for failing to protect private citizens from a riot. *See e.g., City of Chicago v. Sturges,* 222 U.S. 313 (1911).

Chapter X

1. John Rawls, *A Theory of Justice,* (Cambridge: Harvard Univ. Press, Belknap Press,1971).
2. Ibid., 13. Space prohibits a full comparison of the New Social Contract with Rawls' *Theory of Justice.* The quoted terms are defined and used by Rawls to explain his social contract theory. An interested reader would do well to read Rawls in the original.
3. Ibid., 14.
4. Ibid., 39. "The only way therefore to dispute intuitionism is to set forth the recognizably ethical criteria that account for the weights which, in our considered judgments, we think appropriate to give to the plurality of principles. A refutation of intuitionism consists in presenting the sort of constructive criteria that are said not to exist." I did not arrive at the term "constructive power" as a response to this remark by Rawls. Rather, I chose it probably ten years or more before I ever read the first page of Rawls. It does, however, seem a ingenuous

coincidence.

5. Paul H. Mussen, John J. Conger and Jerome Kagan. ed. *Child Development and Personality,* 5th ed. (New York: Harper & Row, 1979), 506.

6. Ibid.

7. An example of a fiduciary duty involving a real estate broker is the case of *Silverman v. Pitterman,* 574 S.2d 275 (Fla. 3d DCA 1991). When Mrs. Silverman divorced her husband, their home was ordered sold and the proceeds to be divided equally with her husband. On her husband's recommendation, they hired Pitterman, a real estate broker, to sell the house. Before entering into the listing agreement, Mrs. Silverman knew that Pitterman had acted as her former husband's expert witness in the couple's divorce. Mrs. Silverman, however, did not know that Pitterman was romantically involved with her ex-husband's divorce attorney. Mrs. Silverman claimed that had she known of that romantic involvement, she would not have consented to hiring Pitterman as the broker or the sale to the buyer he produced. She claimed that Pitterman was required to disclose all material facts, and that his relationship with her ex-husband's divorce attorney was material to her decision to enter into the listing agreement. The court held that the facts were sufficient to require a jury to decide whether Pitterman had breached his fiduciary duty to disclose all material facts within his knowledge.

8. Section 678.10, Fla. Stat.

9. *Grimshaw v. Ford Motor Co.*, 119 Cal.App.3d 757, 174 Cal.Rptr. 348 (1981) (pinto gas tank fire resulting in jury verdict for $125 million in punitive damages).

10. This too is not a substantial departure from current law. A manufacturer of an inherently dangerous product has an affirmative obligation to provide purchasers with an adequate warning of any inherent risk associated with its use. An adequate warning must "warn with a degree of intensity that would cause a reasonable man to exercise for his own safety the caution commensurate with the potential damages." *Lollie v. General Motors Corporation,* 407 So.2d 613, 615 (Fla. 1st DCA 1982). *Square D Company v. Hayson,* 621 So.2d 1373 (Fla. 1st DCA 1993). Compare *Upjohn Company, v. MacMurdo,* 562 So.2d 680 (Fla. 1990.)(adequacy of warning for prescription drugs directed to physician not patient).

11. Blackstone, *Commentaries,* 1:435-439.

12. Georgia Probate Form GPCSF 41.

13. Compare *Wisconsin v. Yoder,* 406 U.S. 205 (1972). The Court upheld the constitutional right of the Amish to withdraw their children from public school before reaching the age at which mandatory public school attendance was no longer required. The Social Contract would permit the same result if the child received the education necessary to attain moral capacity and choose whether to sign the Social Contract.

14. See Damasio, *Descartes' Error,* for a description of a person who after removal of a benign brain tumor was incapable of making choices that conformed to socially acceptable norms. He seemed normal in every other way, and tested normal on all the usual standardized tests for intelligence and neuropsychological functioning.

15. It is interesting to note that the early common law of England, and the United States until recently, a child was considered an economic asset of the father. Parents are still entitled to their children's earnings during minority. Only upon reaching the age of majority does a child becomes fully entitled to all of his earnings. Blackstone, *Commentaries*, 1:441.

16. 662 So.2d 1328 (Fla. 3d DCA 1995).

17. For a discussion of the history of self-incrimination as a fundamental right, see *Twining v. State of New Jersey*, 211 U.S. 78 (1908).

18. In *Giglio v. United States*, 405 U.S. 150, 153 (1972), the Supreme Court held:

> As long ago as *Mooney v. Holohan*, ... (1935), this Court made clear that deliberate deception of a court and jurors by the presentation of known false evidence is incompatible with 'rudimentary demands of justice.' This was reaffirmed in *Pyle v. Kansas*, ... (1942). In *Napue v. Illinois*, ... (1959), we said, '(t)he same result obtains when the State, although not soliciting false evidence, allows it to go uncorrected when it appears.' ... Thereafter *Brady v. Maryland*, ... held that suppression of material evidence justifies a new trial 'irrespective of the good faith or bad faith of the prosecution.' ... When the 'reliability of a given witness may well be determinative of guilt or innocence,' nondisclosure of evidence affecting credibility falls within this general rule. ... We do not, however, automatically require a new trial whenever 'a combing of the prosecutors' files after the trial has disclosed evidence possibly useful to the defense but not likely to have changed the verdict ...' *United States v. Keogh*, ... (1968). A finding of materiality of the evidence is required under *Brady*, ... A new trial is required if 'the false testimony could ... in any reasonable likelihood have affected the judgment of the jury ...' Napue ...

19. *Metropolitan Dade County v. Martinsen*, 736 So.2d 794 (Fla. 3d DCA 1999).

20. Rules Regulating the Florida Bar, 4-3.3:

(a) False Evidence; Duty to Disclose. A lawyer shall not knowingly:
   (1) make a false statement of material fact or law to a tribunal;
   (2) fail to disclose a material fact to a tribunal when disclosure is necessary to avoid assisting a criminal or fraudulent act by the client;
   (3) fail to disclose to the tribunal legal authority in the controlling jurisdiction known to the lawyer to be directly adverse to the position of the client and not disclosed by opposing counsel; or
   (4) permit any witness, including a criminal defendant, to offer testimony or other evidence that the lawyer knows to be false. A lawyer may not offer testimony that the lawyer knows to be false in the form of a narrative unless so ordered by the tribunal. If a lawyer has offered material evidence and thereafter comes to know of its falsity, the lawyer shall take reasonable remedial measures.

(b) Extent of Lawyer's Duties. The duties stated in subdivision (a) continue beyond the conclusion of the proceeding and apply even if compliance requires disclosure of information otherwise protected by rule 4-1.6.

(c) Evidence Believed to be False. A lawyer may refuse to offer evidence that the lawyer reasonably believes is false.

(d) Ex Parte Proceedings. In an ex parte proceeding a lawyer shall inform the tribunal of all material facts known to the lawyer that will enable the tribunal to make an informed decision, whether or not the facts are adverse.

21. For a summary of the history of the case see *Spaziano v. State*, 692 So. 2d 174 (Fla. 1997).

22. *Lafferty v. Allstate Ins. Co.*, 425 So.2d 1147 (Fla. 4th DCA 1982).

23. Allstate ultimately paid the entire judgment in the quadriplegic case, partly because it did not appeal the original judgment. *Aaron v. Allstate Inc. Co.*, 559 So. 2d 275 (Fla. 4th DCA 1998).

24. This is a much broader statement of the natural law doctrine that the fundamental law prohibits the government to take from A to give to B. See, John V. Orth,"Taking from A and giving to B: substantive due process and the case of the shifting paradigm." Constitutional Commentary, Summer (1997), 337-345.

25. These functions likely will never be completely met, so community well-being by prohibiting and preventing destructive uses of power will always be a concern, but the government's use of destructive power must always be kept in this context and not be allowed to pour over into the realm of government using destructive power for any other reasons.

26. Note that this presupposes that there has been a determination that the person has actually used destructive power. If the identity of a person who has used destructive power is not known, then the use of destructive power to determine who has used destructive power must be the least destructive power necessary to achieve the government's objective.

27. If the Social Contract succeeds in its objective of eliminating destructive power from human interaction, the need for punishment will become unnecessary. I do not believe that this will require a fundamental change in human nature, but a modification of behavior for which man is peculiarly capable. The Social Contract is premised on human nature being unchangeable, but the particulars of human behavior being exceedingly malleable. If all parties to the Social Contract understand destructive power, it can be eliminated through conditioning and education and the use of the Society's power against those who insist upon using destructive power. Anyone who use destructive power will, if the use is severe or persistent enough, be removed as a party to the Social Contract and a citizen of Society, thus removing them as a source of destructive power. They will, once expelled, become, as Locke said, the same as a wild animal, a man-eating tiger in India, or a rogue elephant in Kenya or a polar bear in Alaska.

28. 686 So.2d 653 (Fla. 2d DCA 1997).

29. Id. at 657, quoting *North Miami v. Seaway Corp.*, 151 Fla. 301, 9 So.2d 705, 707 (Fla.1942).

Index

ability to choose 15, 161, 162, 180, 208
abortion xv, xvi, 144-147, 230
abstract reasoning 6, 14, 39, 177
act 8-11, 19, of free will 18, 41
Adams, John 131
adaptability 12, 25, 228
adversary system 210-213, (*See* judiciary)
Aelius Priscus 41
Aeschines 30
affective role-taking 36, 62 (*See also* empathy)
affirmative action xiii, xv, xvi, 169
affirmative obligation, of government 171, 172, 201, 202, 214, 216 227 (*see also* government)
age of majority 74, 159, 160, 235, 241
age of maturity 52, 192, 235, 241
agriculture 24, 109, 121
Allgeyer v. Louisiana 136, 141
Allstate Ins. Co. 212
alternative 14-16, 18, 22, 30, 31, 35, 41-44, 53-59, 68-75, 80, 81, 168, 177, 205; future states 15; means 22, 69
altruism 23, 24, 49, 238
American avocet 33, 80
American Revolution xi, xii, 86, 105, 106, 113, 125, 149; post war period: abolition of all debts 126
animals xix, 5, 6, 9-14, 19-25, 27, 29-33, 37, 39, 44, 46, 48, 50, rights activists 60, societies xix, 23, 25, 26, 152; individualistic 66, 81, 89, 90, 119, 152, 153, 186, 187, 192, 194
Anne Frank 80
anti-federalists 128
anti-trust laws 141, 216, 228
Antoninus Pius 61
anxiety 37, 43, 45, 56, 59, 62, 89 (*See also* other-consciousness)

ape 14, 25, 33, 34, 100, 101, 194
apprehension 56, 178
Aristotle 57, 58, 90; final cause 49
artificial duty 96, 97, 99, 101, 107, 108
artificial right 96-111, 122, 136, 154, 155, 158, 162, 169, 195-198, 202, 204-206, 209, 212, 213, 220-225, 230, 240, 241; to life 95; can be denied 94, 95; human inventions 22, 95; separation of might and right 97
Augustus Caesar 26
autonomic, learning 12, 15; motivations 90; will 9-12, 14, 16, 18, 19, 21, 30, 49, 65, 81, 82, 90; self-interest 43 (*See also* will)

Bacon, Francis 114
bacteria 7, 12, 47
bar exam 159, 205
Barbier v. Connelly 134, 136
basic desires 18, 89, 90 (*See also* autonomic)
Bastogne, Battle of 72
Bathsheba 78
behavior xviii, 4-6, 11-15, 17-19, 23-25, 29, 31, 33, 35, 38, 40, 49, 50, 55, 62, 85-90, 100, 109, 143, 153, 154, 177, 180, 200, 237
Beziers, Bishop of 57
Bill of Rights xi, xiii, xvi, 103, 109, 125-129, 133, 136, 142, 144, 145, 157, 207; apply to states 133, 142; apply to federal 132; ignored 132; penumbras of 144; federal superfluous 126 (*See also* rights)
biochemical 9, 11, 39
biological, function as mother 61; purpose 62; society xix, xx, 23-27, 29, 51, 53, 60, 63, 81, 83, 91, 95, 106, 152-154, 164, 169-171, 199, 228; inferior 86

95, 106, 152-154, 164, 169-171, 199, 228; inferior 86
biology 4-8, 23, 88
birds 15, 44, 47, 65
Black, Justice Hugo 143
Blackmun, Justice Harry 145
black-necked stilt 33, 80 (*See also* birds)
body coloring 10, 33, 34
body politic 95, 121, 122
Brigham, Carl 87
British Constitution (*See* constitution)
bronze cuckoo 29 (*See also* birds)
Buck v. Bell 87
Bundy, Ted 30

Calder v. Bull 130, 147, 148
Callicles 53
camp, necessities (*See* necessities)
Cannae, Battle of 72
cannibals 44, 45, 47, 51, 56, 80, 109
categorical imperative (See morality)
Catholic church (*See* church)
Cattell, James 88
cause 7-9, 11, 13, 14, 16, 17, 19, 20, 36, 37, 48, 49, 54, 63, 67, 70, 88, 100, 107, 118, 148, 171, 186, 188, 189, 200, 201, 208, 217, 231, 232
caveat emptor 76, 183
caveat venditor 76
central nervous system 9-11
chaffinch 15 (*See also* birds)
charity 39, 57, 74, 75, 177
Charles I 103, 113
Charles II 103, 113, 114
Chase, Justice 130, 131, 144, 145, 147, 148, 164
cheetah 29, 30, 65 (*See also* animals)
chemistry 4, 7, 8, 17, 20
chimpanzees 13, 14, 23, 26, 32, 33, 194 (*See also* animals)
choice (this is not indexed because it appears throughout the text; for selected references *See* moral)
Christian xiii, 40, 45, 57, 58, 107, 110, 124, 158, 175, 177; kingdoms 26
church 21, 103, 158, 202; Catholic 57, 58,

citizen 52, 81, 82, 95, 105, 119, 122, 131, 133, 135-137, 139, 142, 147, 148, 150, 151, 159, 160-162, 165, 166, 169-172, 174- 176, 178-182, 185, 187, 192- 206, 209, 212-218, 220-235, 237, 240, 241
civil disobedience 221
civil law 69, 76, 166, 226, 239, 240
civil liberties cases 141-147
civil necessities (See necessities)
Civil War xvii, 58, 61, 103, 111, 113, 131-132, 136
Civil War Amendments 132, 136
civilization 19, 25, 86, 87, 97, 140
civilized society 3, 63, 76, 151
claims xvi, 4, 33, 37, 49, 55, 66, 80, 97, 121, 123, 145, 163, 174, 177, 188, 203, 205, 210, 212, 214
Clarke, Dr. Edward 87
Claudius, Emperor 62
Clinton, President William J. 128, 210
code (*See* ethics, Hammurabi, Uniform Commercial)
coercive force xii-xviii, xx, 129, 148, 149, 157, 158, 164, 176
Coke, Lord Edward 115, 118, 125, 126
collective experience 167, 187
colonies 23, 104, 125, 126, 162
common law 30, 70, 115, 125-127, 146, 156, 171, 224 30, 71, 114, 124-126, 155, 170, 194, 224; English 61, 62, 117, 145
communication 14 (*See also* language)
competition 43, 49, 113, 121, 125, 141, 169, 216; for religious supremacy 112
complex xix, xx, 4-6, 8-11, 13, 15, 19, 20, 24-26, 29, 34, 37-39, 41, 48, 52, 69, 89, 90, 101, 153, 154, 229; motivations 90; symbolic cues 37
complexity xix, xx, 3-11, 13, 16, 17, 23-27, 32, 34, 37-39, 48, 50-52, 81, 89, 96, 109, 150, 153-156, 176, 177, 199, 213, 214, 225, 228, 239; learned behavior 11-13; history as nurture 89
concepts 4, 6, 13, 14, 37, 40, 50, 70, 147, 186
conditioned behavior 12, 15, 33, 50, 118
confession 56, 142, 143, 158, 238

Index

conflicts xi, xv, 43, 46, 49, 50, 53, 56, 65, 66, 90, 91, 109, 166, 176, 225, 239
conform 38, 40, 42, 160
conscience 39, 43, 47, 56, 143, 144, 146
conscious xix, xx, 6, 10-19, 21, 22, 25, 30-34, 36, 38-44, 46-58, 63, 68, 69, 71, 72, 78-81, 90, 96, 98, 106, 109, 110, 123, 154, 155, 160, 165, 166, 175, 176, 178, 181, 182, 185, 187, 188, 190, 205, 214, 216, 220, 222-224, 226; conviction xix, 39, 63; desire 95; learning 12-14; manipulation 33, 34; self-interest 32, 43, 44, 53, 54, 57, 80, 90, 154, 176; use of destructive power 68, 69, 78, 175, 188, 190, 222, 223, 224, 226; will 10, 11, 16, 48, 96, 106, 154; deception 33
consciously, equate 43, 45; organized 25; valuing 62
consciousness 5, 10-18, 22, 30-33, 35, 36, 38-40, 42-47, 49-63, 65, 66, 68, 69, 72, 75, 80, 90, 105, 109, 110, 123, 154, 155, 161, 167, 176, 177, 194, 196, 231, 241; of relationships 13, 14; of consequences 16, 32
consent 123, 136, 180; informed 191; to formation of political state 116, 118, 119, 157, 158; tacit 119, 158,
consequences xix, 16-18, 22, 30-32, 40-46, 50, 54-56, 59, 68-75, 80, 107, 116, 149, 166, 167, 176, 186, 187, 190, 191, 201, 202, 208, 217, 219, 223, 224
consideration 55, 70, 186
constitution xi-xiv, xvi, xvii, 103, 105, 109-111, 113, 117, 125-136, 138-142, 144, 146-151, 155, 157, 163, 164, 171, 178, 198, 207, 227, 240; British 117, 126; limitations 119; delegated powers, federal xiv, 128, 129, 141; privileges and immunities clause 131; procedural due process 135; super-majorities 148
constitution, amendments xiv, 128, 129, 131, 145, 197, 240; Eighth 207; Eighteenth xv, 111, 148; Fifth 142-144, 207; First 110, 140, 141, 146, 207, 208; Fourteenth 132-141, 144-147, 207; Ninth 144, 157; Second 207; Sixth 142, 207; Sixteenth xiv, xv 148-149; Third 207; Thirteenth xiv, 111, 132, 147, 149; Twenty-first 111, super-majority xiv, 148 (*See also* law, constitutional)
constitutional convention xvii, 126, 127
constitutional monarchy 103, 113, 120
constraints 5, 6, 16, 17, 24, 27, 29, 63-65, 89, 90, 103 177
constructive power xix, 67, 69, 70, 75, 78, 81, 82, 84, 90, 91, 109, 149, 154, 155, 158-161, 164-171, 174, 176, 177, 179, 181, 182, 185, 195, 202, 203, 206, 209, 214-217, 219-221, 223, 225-237, 239, 241
Continental Congress 106, 125-127
contraceptives 143, 145 (*See* necessities)
conventional, moral thinking 180; rights theory 97
cooperate 20, 21
cooperation 5, 14, 21, advantages of social 23-25, 50, 51, 54, 63, 120
corporation 21, 168, 181, 189, 215
crime 24, 31, 40-42, 45, 52, 57, 78, 139, 159, 161, 170, 181, 192-194, 206, 209, 211, 222, 223, 226
criminal justice xviii, 40, 53, 133, 142, 160
criminal law (*See* law)
criminal procedure 207
criminal responsibility 41
crocodile 10, 11, 19, 20, 29, 30 (*See also* animals)
Cromwell, Oliver 102, 112, 113
cruel 29, 61, 126, 207, 230
Crusoe, Robinson 44-47
cuckoo, bronze 29, 30
cultural determinism (*See* determinism)
cunning 50, 113, 210
curriculum 62, 160, 193
Curtis, Justice 146, 156

Darwin, Charles 31, 51, 63, 85-87
David, King 41, 79
death xv, 22, 24, 25, 45, 50-52, 62, 63, 65, 66, 83, 94, 95, 97, 100, 101, 110, 113-116, 119, 148, 160, 175, 188-190, 211, 217, 222-224
deceit 29, 210, 33-36, 81, 120; false alarm call 35; intentional 35, 36, 218
Declaration of Independence xi, xvii, 26 63, 102, 106, 123-125, 148, 154, 161
defence 45, 116
DeFoe, Daniel 46
Degler, Carl 62, 86-88
delinquency 88
depression 43
depression, economic 124, 126
determinism 5, 17, 89; cultural 18, 88-89; environmental xviii; mechanistic 3
Dred Scott xvii, 62, 131, 143, 146
drugs xiv, xvii, 77, 167, 189,
due process (*See* law, constitutional)
duty 27, 39, 40, 95, 96, 98, 100, 103, 106, 107, 127, 134, 142, 154, 162, 180, 182, 184, 185, 192, 199, 210, 217; fiduciary 185

economic, growth 179, 232; power 21, 67, 69, 216; production 24
economy 140, 185
education (*See* moral education)
Edward I 31
Edward the Confessor 100
effect 7, 8, 11, 14, 20, 36, 39, 42, 45, 86, 103, 134, 143, 167, 174, 181, 214, 216, 227, 236
egoism 51, 56-58, 60, 114; psychological 56-58, 60 175, 176; self-interest xix, 44, 50, 53, 63, 81, 114; long-term self-interest 56, 60; short-term consequences 56
Eighteenth Amendment (*See* constitution, *see also* law, constitutional)
eighteenth century 26, 85, 105

Einstein, Albert 6, 17
elephants 6, 23, 26, 50
Emancipation Proclamation 148
emerge xix, xx, 6, 13, 26, 29, 38, 39, 43, 54, 82, 91, 108, 109, 122, 149, 151-153, 155, 160, 177, 199, 214, 228, 239
emergent properties xix, 5, 6, 8-12, 17, 25, 26, 27, 29, 31, 39, 40, 43, 47, 48, 51-53, 63, 95, 152, 153
emotion 36, 39; capacity 38; biochemical correlates 39
empathy 30, 32, 33, 36-38, 44; role-taking 36; homeless 24, 37; refugees, famine 37
endocrine 11, 19
enemies 33, 45, 107, 113
enforcing authority (*See* government)
England 31, 41, 61, 62, 86, 100-102, 113-115, 118, 119, 124, 192, 194
English xi, xvi, 14, 30, 41, 46, 62, 100-102, 104, 106, 112, 116, 117, 124, 125, 141, 142, 145; Barons 101, 102, 104; Civil War 102, 112; common law (*See* common law); ecclesiastics 101; history 104; laws 100; liberties xi, xvi, 124, 125; lords 100; throne 102, 116
enlightenment 26, 85, 105, 119, 231
entropy 48
environment 17, 23, 32, 88, 89, 166, 167, 187
epigenetic 50, 63
equal xi, xii, xvi-xix, 38, 39, 44, 47-49, 51, 52, 54, 55, 57, 59, 62, 64, 66, 67, 74, 75, 77, 79, 81, 84, 88, 90, 91, 103, 114, 116, 117, 119, 120, 124, 130, 132-135, 137, 140, 143, 147, 150, 154, 168, 177, 178, 189, 194, 214, 217-219, 229; education and treatment of women 62; opportunity 168, 214; protection (*See* constitutional law); right to gravity 66; value xix, 51, 52, 54, 55, 57, 64, 66, 67, 81, 91, 154, 177, 178; weight 44
equality iii, xii, xv, xvii-xx, 38-40, 43, 50-54, 59, 62-64, 66, 67, 74, 75, 81, 84, 92, 96, 108, 109, 112, 116, 120-124, 126, 131, 133, 135, 147,

148, 150, 152-154, 157, 160, 162, 164, 166, 167, 169, 177, 214, 236, 237, 239; false 109; of individuals 81, 122; of man xii, 40, 52, 62
equilibrium 5, 7, 8, 48, 49 (*See also* thermodynamics)
ethics xix, 46, 158, 177, 180
eugenics 85, 87, 233
evolution 6, 9, 12, 14, 15, 24, 27, 31, 50, 63, 86, 90, 109, 236, 239
evolutionary biology (*See* biology)
Ex Parte Milligan 157, 163
exchange 21, 68, 71, 72, 74-77, 79, 166, 176, 182-185, 190, 191, 206, 209, 212, 213, 215, 220, 226, 231
exclusive listing agreement 80
existing state 7, 16, 17, 20, 48, 52, 64-66, 68, 99, 106, 108, 109, 152, 161
extinct 24, 25

fear xix, 22, 45, 89, 97, 105, 110, 114, 115, 119, 166, 191, 198, 200, 232, 236, 237; of violent death 97
federal government (*See* government)
federal troops 98, 99
feebleminded 86, 87, 157
fetus 144, 145
fidelity, marital 46, 79, 80
fiduciary duty (*See* duty)
Fifth Amendment (*See* constitution, see also law, constitutional)
Final Solution 148
fire 19, 68, 108, 133, 166, 188-190
firefly 33 (*See also* animals)
Filmer, Sir Robert 116
First Amendment (*See* constitution, see also law, constitutional)
fish 23, 48, 130, 194 (*See also* animals)
Florida Statutes 167, 186, 201, 212
flycatcher 29, 30 (*See also* birds, animals)
Food and Drug Administration 187
Ford Motor Company 188-190, 206
foresight 16, 42, 43, 69, 70, 71, 119, 165, 185-187, 224

Foster, Jodie 42, 79
founding fathers xi-xiii, 59, 123, 128, 131 (*See also* constitution)
Frankfurter, Justice Felix 141, 142
fraud 77, 182, 183, 222
free speech xv, 96, 140
free will xvii, 17-19, 41, 72
freedom xiii, 19, 26, 55, 56, 61, 65, 94, 132, 141, 159, 162, 169, 177, 207, 215, 221, 229, 230, 236
Fundamental Orders of Connecticut 124

Galileo 113
General Motors 178, 189, 206
general will 120, 121, 150, 157, 162, 169 (*See also* Rousseau)
genetics 5, 6, 23-25, 27, 49, 50, 55, 63, 64, 89, 169 (*See also* population genetics)
George Washington 127
Ginger 12, 13, 18
global empathy 36 (*See also* empathy)
Glorious Revolution 102
goal of life 25, 114, 179; economic growth 179
God 3, 6, 9, 19, 45, 49, 52, 59, 62, 102-105, 107, 115, 121, 124, 236
Goddard, Herbert 86, 88
Goldberg, Justice Arthur 143
Golden Rule 45, 58-60, 114, 116, 122, 177, 236
good faith and honesty in fact 173, 182, 183, 185, 208, 218 (*See also* Social Contract)
Goodall, Jane 33
Gorgias 54
government xi-xviii, xx, 26, 39, 79, 80, 85, 94, 96, 97, 103, 104, 107-110,115-118, 120-122, 124-132, 134, 135, 140, 141, 146-148, 150, 151, 154-157, 162-170, 173-176, 178, 179, 181, 182, 186, 187, 189, 190, 192-209, 213-228, 232-241; as recipient of natural right 117; federal xiii, 127, 128, 131, 132, 140, 170, 198, 240; form of xi, 103, 109, 110, 121, 125, 197, 198, 200, 204; limited xi, 26, 116, 128, 129, 157, 162

government, under Social Contract affirmative obligation 170, 189, 201, 202, 216; defining possessions 80; enforcing authority 98, 99, 104, 108, 109, 156; spending 196; discrimination 220
gravity 8, 14, 49, 66
Great Charter of King John (*See* Magna Charta)
Great Depression 140, 141, 149, 202, 230
greatest good (See utilitarianism) 59, 60, 110, 176, 177, 214
Greece 40
Greek 19, 27, 30, 120, 232; democracies and oligarchies 105
greenhouse gases 167, 187
Gregory I, Pope 58
Griswold v. Connecticut 143-145
guarantee 22, 82, 84, 150, 171, 176, 177, 185, 207, 208, 225, 228, 236
guardian 39, 159, 165, 192, 194, 203, 204

habeas corpus 126, 163
half-truth 182, 183, 189 (*See also* power, constructive)
Hall v. Humana Hospital Daytona Beach 225, 226
Hameroff, Stuart 10
Hamilton, Alexander 128, 162 127, 128, 162
Hammurabi's Code 100, 101 105
Hannibal 73
happiness xi, xv, xix, 60, 63, 83, 84, 97, 103, 125, 130, 133, 169, 170, 174, 179-182, 203, 209, 214-217, 231, 238, 241
Harlan, Jr., Justice John, 143
health, safety, welfare and morals (*See* police power)
hedonistic principle 57
Henry VIII 31
hereditary 86, 197, 233; monarchy 198
heredity advocates 88
hierarchy, of concepts 6; dominance 54, 99; of government obligations 219; of laws 178; of people 86; social 99, 107, 231
Hinckley, John xvii, 41-43, 79
historical xix, 5, 89, 99, 116, 124, 145, 150
history xi, 5, 84, 99, 104, 110, 125, 160, 198, 220
Hitler, Adolph 30, 107
HIV 77
Hobbes, Thomas xviii, 46, 50, 58, 94, 96, 97, 112-117, 119-122, 124, 138, 155, 162, 175
Holden v. Hardy 136
Holmes, Oliver Wendell, Jr. 30, 31, 87, 138
homeless 24, 37
homeostasis 89
honesty in fact (*See* Social Contract)
Hooker, Robert 39, 40, 52
horizon of foresight 69, 70
hospital 37, 141, 225, 226
house xi, 13, 16, 21, 49, 55-57, 60, 65, 67, 68, 70, 80, 81, 96, 99, 100, 124, 125, 127, 130-132, 147, 157, 169, 183, 184, 193, 195, 201, 206, 217, 218, 229, 231, 237
human brain xix, 6, 17, 193
human nature iii, 4, 62, 85-89, 97, 116, 122, 222, 228
human rights (*See* artificial rights)
human society xix, 5, 6, 11, 21, 24-27, 51, 61, 63, 82, 95, 96, 108,122, 150, 153, 166, 171, 241
hunger 11, 19, 68, 170
hunger strike 19
hunt 12, 21, 23, 29
hyena 23, 29, 30 (*See also* animals)

idea 40, 56, 89, 114, 119, 122, 124, 128, 141, 150, 155, 238; of equality 62
identification 38, 160
Illinois Constitution 132
imagine 36, 38, 65, 105, 106, 195, 211, 225
imagined states of reality 105
immigrants 192, 195
immigration 87
inanimate xix, 4, 7, 9, 30-32, 49
income tax (*See* tax)

Index

independence (*See* judiciary)
individual
   morally capable (See moral, capacity); consent to government 118; freedom 26
individualism iii, xi, 26, 52, 57, 60, 64, 82, 90, 179, 231
individualistic society iii, iv, xv, xviii-xx, 5, 53, 64, 67, 82-84, 89-92, 96, 108-110, 112, 123, 149, 150, 152, 154-156, 159-161, 163-165, 168-171, 177, 179-181, 198, 199, 214, 221, 225, 227-229, 237, 239, 240; not inevitable 109; greatest opportunities for happiness 83, 181
incrementalism 128
infanticide 25, 62, 193
infants 25, 32, 36, 85
inferior 25, 59, 62, 87, 147, 185, 198
informed consent 191
inheritance tax (*See* tax)
inhibited behaviors 50, 51, 153
innocence 31, 41, 209
insanity defense 41-43
instinct theory 86
instrumental association 35
integration xix, 5, 6, 25, 26, 52, 82
intellect 86, 113, 121, 205 (*See also* moral capacity)
intelligence 25, 66, 86-88, 169, 193, 211
intentional interference with contract 80
internal conflict 43-47, 54-57, 60, 64, 67, 81, 90, 91, 108, 153, 154, 176, 194
internet v, 10, 239, 240
interpretation, child's 36, of Golden Rule 58-60; of uses of destructive power 71, 190; of natural rights 118; of constitution 127, 132, 140, 143, 146, of common law rules 149, 155, of Social Contract 198
involuntary persuasion 73, 75, 76, 78-80, 166, 182, 191, 209, 217, 222, 223
Ipswich 147
Iredell, Justice James 129, 140, 142, 154

Islamic heresy 110
Israel 94

Jacob, Francois 4-7, 89
jaguar 23 (*See also* animals)
James, William 86,
James Cattell 88
James I 112
Jay, John 125
Jean Valjean 83
Jefferson, Thomas 11, 52, 63, 90, 127
Jehovah's Witness 191
Jesus 58, 124
Jews xv, 30, 81
John, King 101, 102, 107, 116, 124,
Jones, Paula case 210
judge xi, xii, xvi, xvii, 41, 67, 71, 74, 103, 117, 129, 128, 130, 134, 137, 138, 139, 140, 142, 181, 204, 205, 207, 209, 211, 212, 221 (*See also* judiciary)
judicial review 114, 131
judiciary, Social Contract: above suspicion 204; adequately and completely remedy 206; allegiance to Social Contract 197; decisions explained 205; future ambitions 204; independence 162, 174, 199, 203-205, 209; mercy 58, 150; paranoia by judges 205; selection 205; timeliness of decisions 174, 203, 205, 206, 219
justice xiv-xvi, xviii, 4, 16, 27, 39-41, 44, 53, 87, 95, 104, 107, 114, 115, 120, 122, 123, 129, 130, 133-147, 150, 154, 156, 160, 162, 163, 175, 177, 209, 210

Kagan, Jerome 36, 37, 180
Kallikak 86, 87
Kant, Immanuel 39, 58, 175, 177
Kennedy, Justice Anthony 144, 145
Kholberg, Lawrence 180
kill 11, 12, 20, 22, 29-31, 42, 44, 45, 47, 56, 63, 81, 95, 96, 100, 104, 113, 117, 153, 200
kindness 46, 58, 86
komodo dragon 50

labor 55, 65, 66, 78, 94, 110, 136, 137, 139, 140, 232
language 4-6, 14, 33, 34, 37, 39, 54, 66, 120, 121, 127, 130, 141,147,159; communication 14; computer lexigrams 33; gorilla 34; word domain 34
last resort (*See* necessities) 83, 164, 165, 174, 196, 208, 217, 229, 232
law
　constitutional: equal protection xii, xvi, 132-135, 140, 143, 150; *ex post facto* and attainder 126; due process: fair procedures xii, xvi, 126, 132-137, 140-145, 150, 207, 214; as under common law 126; fundamental rights 130, 140, 141, 143, 208; obligation of contracts, impairment 126; social substantive due process 134, 136, 140, 144, 214; welfare legislation xvi, 140
　criminal law (*See* law) 40, 42, 69, 89, 158, 164
　English 102
　of nature xiii, 17, 97, 109, 114, 116-118, 121-123, 125, 131, 147, 150, 156, 162, 163, 175; as reason 114, 117; about truth-telling 77
　Social Contract, hierarchy under 178; knowledge of 225
　in state of nature 115
law school 71, 158, 205
lawyer xi, xii, xvii, 41, 71, 84, 89, 128, 142, 149, 158, 203, 205-207, 209-213; parsing 210;
learned behavior 11-13 (*See also* complexity)
Lee, Richard Henry 125, 127, 156
legal preferences 168
legal rights (*See* rights)
legal, segregation 168; standards 40; system 37, 67, 107, 211, 225; test 183; theories 30, 212
Leviathan 113
lex petronia 62
liberal democracy 1, xi, xiv, xv, 61, 109, 110, 152-154, 179, 198, 227
liberty xi, xiii, xix, 47, 55, 63, 65, 103, 104, 114, 117, 118, 122, 124-126, 128, 129, 132-135, 137-146,150, 157, 176
license 158, 162, 169, 214, 215, 223, 240
limited government (*See* government)
Lincoln Fed. Labor Union v. NW Iron & Metal Co. 140
linnet 15 (*See also* birds)
lions 23, 29, 153, 196 (*See also* animals)
Livermore, Samuel 128, 156
Lochner v. New York 137, 139, 140, 145
Locke, John xi, xiii, xvi, xviii, 112, 115-118, 124; agreement with Hobbes and Rousseau 122; children's capacity 39; differs from Hobbes 121, 155; law of nature 97, 150; limited government xii, xiii, 128, 129, 147, 162; majority rule 118, 162; natural rights 46, 94, 96, 97, 109, 116, 125; New Social Contract 175, 176; on divine right 116; consent 118, 157; on equality 40, 52; political power defined 116; purpose of political philosophy 116, 122; religious belief 52, 115; Second Treatise xi, 94, 97, 109, 116, 118, 122; social contract 116-118, 128, 156, 157,162; state of nature 117
logic 38, 50, 121, 148
long-term self-interest 56, 60
Louisiana 135, 143
love xv, 19, 37, 39, 40, 65, 66, 77, 79, 89, 208, 231
Luther, Martin 59, 62

M'Naghten's case 41
Madison, James 127,
Magna Charta xi, 101, 102, 104, 106, 108, 124, 135
majority rule xiv, xv, 118, 124, 156, 161
Marbury v. Madison 130, 163
Marcus Aurelius 41
marriage 78-80, 144, 231, 237
Marshall, Chief Justice John xiv, 130, 134, 156 xiv, 130, 131, 134, 145,

156
Marx, Karl 85, 106
Maslow, Abraham 89, 90 (*See* autonomic will)
Massachusetts 126, 138, 144, 147
material information 77, 183, 182-185, 222
Maxwell's theory 4
Mayflower Compact 124
mayhem 22, 69, 223
McAuliffe, Gen. 73
medical care 24, 82, 170, 223, 226, 228 (*See also* necessities)
medical school 87, 158, 216
medicare xiii, 149, 170, 227
member, of Society 19, 20, 39, 61, 82, 83, 97, 104, 108, 156-161, 165, 166, 168, 176, 178, 180-182, 185, 187, 190, 192, 196, 199, 201, 203, 204, 208, 218, 220, 221, 232, 241 of social group 23, 26, 32, 50, 51, 61, 153, of family 61, 233
Menendez xvii
Mengele, Dr. Joseph 30
mentally deficient 42, 43, 230
microtubules 10
Middle Ages 58, 109
might makes right 27, 50, 51, 54-57, 59, 61, 66, 67, 70, 74, 83, 107, 109, 116, 153, 154, 161, 162, 169, 197, 240
Miles, L. H. 33, 34, 183, 188
military 25, 101, 163, 199, 218
Milligan, Ex Parte 157, 163, 197
Missouri Compromise 131
modification, (*See* Social Contract)
Monroe, James 127
moral
   basis of Society 82, 150, 157, 163, 176
   blame 30, 37, 41, 42
   capacity xvii-xx, 6, 37, 39, 40, 42, 52, 53, 55, 63, 67, 74, 89, 90, 158-161, 164, 165, 178, 179, 181, 192-195, 202, 203, 208, 220, 223, 224, 240, 241; demonstration of 158-159, 181, 224; denial of 89; education 38, 158-161; foundation of Society 84, 165, 202, 228; full 37, 52, 160; loss of 223; standard of competency 194
   choice 45, 46, 50, 69, 81-83, 89, 153
   dilemma 45, 56, 81
   philosophers 180
   philosophy 54, 57, 108, 114, 150, 237, 238
   principle 52, 54, 69, 78, 81, 82, 114, 181, 227, 231, 236, 241
   reasoning, stages 180
   sense of blame 30
   standard 120, 121
   tones of political debate 121
morality iii, xviii-xx, i, 3, 4, 6, 21, 23, 25, 29, 30, 42-44, 47, 50, 52, 54-56, 58, 60, 64-67, 70, 75, 81, 84, 90, 92, 96, 105, 108, 109, 114, 122, 135, 150, 152, 154, 157, 160, 162, 164, 166, 177, 194, 214, 231, 236, 237, 239; categorical imperative 57, 124, 177; cost-benefit analysis 114; of equality iii, xviii-xx, 54, 64, 67, 84, 92, 96, 108, 109, 122, 135, 150, 152, 154, 157, 160, 162, 164, 166, 177, 214, 236, 237, 239; limitations 237; rational 6, 108; rational self-interest as xix, 63, 114; utilitarianism 109
morally capable 64, 69, 74-76, 78, 80-82, 91, 155, 156, 159-161, 166, 167, 171, 176, 189, 222, 227 (*See also* moral, capacity)
mother 30-32, 41, 62, 87, 180
motive 68
Mugler v. Kansas 134
Muller v. Oregon 139
Munn v. Illinois 132, 168
murder 22, 50, 69, 223
murderer 30, 44, 69, 95, 96, 160
mutual mistake 77

NAMBLA xv, 208
Narbonne, Archbishop of 57
national defense 164, 168
natural, justice 135, 137, 138, 142, 150, 154; reason 40, 117; right 22, 26, 66, 81, 82, 95, 107, 117, 118, 146, 160, 176, 178, 195, 204, 235; rejected by Supreme Court

131; selection 31, 50, 51, 56, 86, 88, 108
Nature iii, xiii, xviii, xix, 3-5, 8, 9, 16, 17, 22, 36, 37, 39-41, 47, 49, 53, 62, 74, 78, 85-90, 94, 96, 97, 103, 109, 113-123, 125, 129, 131, 142, 147, 150, 156, 162, 163, 175, 179, 197, 201, 205, 206, 222, 228
Nazi xv, 81, 87, 109, 157
Nebbia v. New York 139, 140
necessities xx, 5, 39, 82-84, 139, 149, 164, 165, 168, 171, 174, 176, 177, 181, 192, 193, 195, 199, 201-203, 206, 220, 227-230, 232-235; civil necessities 83, 84, 168, 174, 192, 199, 201-203, 206, 228, 232; demanding 229; entitlement to 202; camp 229, 230, 233-235; credit for work 229; last resort, government as 83, 164, 165, 174, 196, 208, 217, 229, 232; parents responsibility 193; physical necessities xx, 82, 83, 206, 228, 229
need 59, 79; for government xx, 164, for logical consistency 38, for knowledge of the law 225, 226; for morality 47, 55, 56 63, 64, 83, 90; synonym for want 79; to use destructive power 83, 90, 162
negligent acts 37, 224
nest 15,18, 29, 33, 66 (*See also* birds)
New Deal 139, 140
New Hampshire 125, 126, 128, 139
New Social Contract (*See* Social Contract)
New York xi, 5, 6, 14, 33, 36, 39, 41, 44, 58, 59, 62, 83, 86, 88, 89, 94, 97, 113, 116, 119, 125, 127, 128, 137-141, 157, 180, 193, 223
Newton, Sir Issac xx, 6, 8, 17
Newton's laws 4
Ninth Amendment (*See* constitution, *see also* law, constitutional)
noncitizen 161, 165, 165, 192, 227
nonmoral animals 81
non-members, of Society 178, 195, 196, 218, 240
Norman Conquest 101, 104

Nowak, John 146

O'Connor, Justice Sandra Day 144, 145
obey xvii, 4, 8, 105, 115, 120, 134, 175, 181, 221, 241
objective 7-11, 13-17, 20-22, 27, 42, 52, 61, 64, 66, 82, 83, 90, 95, 105, 108, 109, 115, 117, 122, 123, 154, 155, 170, 174, 182, 185, 193, 199, 214, 216, 217, 219, 222, 227, 231
opportunity xiii, 16, 19, 64, 83, 84, 88, 90, 108, 160, 168-170, 174, 182, 189, 203, 214-217, 220, 227, 228, 232, 236, 238, 241; for individual happiness 83, 169, 170, 214, 215, 217; freedom to try 169; judgment 182
orangutans 32, 33, 194
order of complexity 5, 8, 9, 11, 24, 52, 82, 152, 153, 155
other-consciousness 33, 36, 38-40, 43-47, 50-64, 66, 67, 81, 90, 108, 109, 122, 153, 154, 160, 166, 176, 177, 194, 196, 231, 241
ought xii, xx, 3, 27, 55, 56, 85, 88, 90, 95, 96, 98, 100, 103-107, 110, 117, 122, 130, 138, 140, 146, 150, 153-155, 157, 162, 163, 237, 238

pagan 40, 47, 62
paramecium 9, 11, 12, 15
parent xvii, 24, 37-39, 65, 66, 74, 79, 88, 98, 159, 160, 165, 180, 181, 192-194, 202, 203, 230, 232, 234; abuse or neglect 192, 234; responsibility for necessities 193
Parliament 102, 112-114, 117, 119, 124, 147
parliamentary supremacy 112, 125
partnership 21, 79, 215, 237
Pavlov's dog 12, 15
pedophilia xv, 161
Peel, Robert 41
Pennsylvania 127, 144, 149
perceptual role-taking 36 (*See also* empathy)
person identity 37 (*See also* psychology)
person permanence 36, 37 (*See also*

psychology)
personal income tax xiv, 147-149 (*See also* tax)
personal responsibility xvii, xviii, 180, 189
personality 25, 66, 89, 180 (*See also* psychology)
perspective-taking 36, 63 affective 36; cognitive 36, perceptual (*See also* empathy)
persuasion 21, 67, 69, 71-80, 166, 167, 175, 176, 182, 185, 189-191, 209, 212, 213, 217, 222, 223, 226, 237, 238; conscious 72, 73; unconscious 72
PETA xix, 46
philosophers 50, 52, 58, 59, 85, 112, 180
philosophy v, xi-xiii, xvi, xviii, xx, 6, 7, 22, 40, 46, 54, 57, 85, 108, 110, 113, 114, 116, 117, 119-123, 128, 131, 144, 150, 154, 155, 177, 179, 231, 236-238
physical destructive power (*See* power)
physical necessities (*See* necessities)
physical power (*See* power)
physics student 48, 49
physiological 19, 38, 89
Planned Parenthood of Southeastern Pennsylvania v. Casey 144
Plato 59, 62
plea, of ignorance 77; of insanity 161
pleasure 57, 83
Plessy v. Ferguson xvii
Plutarch 30, 119
polar bear 23, 24, 222 (*See also* animals)
police 24, 98-100, 132-139, 141, 142, 157, 164-167, 170, 186, 196, 200, 201, 209, 211, 217-219, 223, 226
police power (*See* power)
political majority xiii, xvi, 134-137, 147, 149, 150, 162, 163, 168, 170, 216, 224, 227
political philosophy xi-xiii, xvi, xviii, xx, 6, 7, 40, 46, 85, 110, 116, 119, 123, 128, 154, 155

political society xi, xiii, xv, xviii, 4, 21, 94, 116-118, 122, 128, 153-155, 163, 164
pool 8, 9, 89, 187, 233
poor xiii, 24, 59, 114, 169
Pope 58, 101
population genetics 23-25, 27, 49, 50, 55, 63, 64, 89, 169
possession xix, 45, 59, 64-82, 84, 96, 98, 99, 106, 108-110, 116, 134, 141, 154, 156, 165-169, 170, 173, 176, 177, 179, 184, 185, 186, 191, 208, 209, 212, 213, 220, 228, 231, 232, 237; basic 66; distribution of 74; ephemeral 65; experiences as 65; government defined 80; inconstant 66; in relationships with people 79; in life 65; non-human 66; objective of will 66; taking 69; sufficiency of power 96; transfer of 71; value changes 68
possible future states 7, 9, 15-17, 48, 49, 152
power xiii-xvii, xix, xx, 7, 8, 10, 17, 20-22, 26, 27, 44, 47, 50-52, 54, 55, 57, 60-84, 88, 90, 91, 95- 110, 113-119, 121, 122, 125- 129, 131-140, 142, 144, 146- 150, 152-171, 173- 193, 195- 206, 208, 209, 212- 237, 239- 241; of alliance 20, 21, 54, 67, 83, 99, 104, 108, 109, 122, 148, 153-156, 161, 162, 169, 178, 195, 200, 201, 204, 223, 240; control of energy 8, 20, 48; of life and death 62; of persuasion 21, 67, 69, 71, 75-77, 209, 213; physical 20, 21, 67-69, 98-100, 175, 209, 213, 222, 223, 240; destructive, physical 71, 78, 182, 201, 217, 218, 222, 223; police 132-139, 165-167, 170, 186; to avoid claims of involuntary persuasion 191; to try 65, 96, 153, 159, 163
Praetorian Guard 147
predators 12, 21, 23, 29, 33
president, Adams 130; Clinton 210; Reagan xvii, 42; Roosevelt 140
prevarication 182
pre-moral behaviors 51 (*See also*

moral, morality)
pre-social condition 113 (*See also* state of nature)
Prigogine, Ilya 5, 17
primitive people 31, 86
privacy 143-145, 218
privileges and immunities clause 130 (*See also* constitution)
probability 5, 23, 48, 51, 186-188
procedural due process (*See* law, constitutional)
progress 60, 61, 109, 114, 120
progressive taxes (*See* tax)
Prohibition xiv, 82, 83, 127, 130, 135, 139, 141, 143, 178, 227, 236
property xiii, xiv, xix, 6, 8-12, 17, 25, 27, 29, 31, 32, 39-41, 43, 47, 51, 52, 60-62, 64, 65, 68, 69, 76, 95, 96, 98, 99, 101, 102, 115, 117-119, 121, 122, 126, 127, 130, 132-136, 138, 140, 142, 144, 147, 148, 150, 154, 158, 176, 182, 188, 190, 192, 194, 207, 216, 218, 221, 231-233, 236
prostitution 168, 217
psychological egoism (*See* egoism)
psychology xviii, 5, 6, 35, 85, 86, 117
punish xv, xviii, 18, 40, 41, 61, 68, 82, 88, 97, 98, 118, 161, 165, 166, 181, 195, 200, 218, 224, 229
punishment 41, 42, 56, 98, 100, 101, 106, 111, 116, 118, 134, 161, 166, 167, 178, 194, 207, 214, 221-223, 234; proportional 117
purpose xiii, 7-9, 11, 13, 14, 62, 69, 95, 116, 117, 128, 129, 131, 137, 140, 141, 146, 147, 149, 150, 157, 158, 161, 163, 165, 168, 169, 193, 201, 208, 214, 215, 219, 236; of political society and government 119
purposeful movement 7-10
Pythagoras 58

quadriplegic 185, 186, 212

race hypothesis 87, 90
rate xiv, 10, 11, 23, 88, 148, 150, 218
rational xix, 6, 38, 42, 44, 50, 52, 53, 59, 62, 80, 98, 109, 115, 139, 140, 146, 151, 175, 188
rational morality (*See* morality)
rational self-interest xix, 44, 50, 51, 52, 59, 80, 115 (*See also* egoism, morality)
rationalization 58-60,157
Reagan, President Ronald xvii, 42
reason xii, xiii, xvi, 6, 12-16, 38-41, 46, 50, 59, 83, 108, 115, 118, 122, 123, 125, 130, 139, 143, 147, 157, 176-178, 183, 184, 193, 200, 204, 206, 219, 220, 225, 228; tool to reach objectives 122
reasoned behavior 13
reed bunting 15 (*See also* birds)
Reformation 26, 57, 58, 61, 114
regressive taxes (*See* tax)
reinforce 37, 52, 100
relativism xix, xx, 150
religion xiii, xv, xx, 3, 4, 52, 58, 105, 106, 108, 109, 113, 115-117, 120, 123, 125, 127, 151, 159, 169, 177, 179, 191, 207, 220, 231, 233, 236-238; intolerance 113; liberty 127; toleration 117
remote consequences 22
representative government 127, 149
reproduction 5, 23, 24, 49, 51, 153, 233
republic 26, 105, 124
republicanism 126, 198
residents 59, 125, 142, 171, 201, 229
responsible xvii, 41, 70, 75, 88, 159, 160, 164, 166, 170, 180, 190, 192, 194, 199, 203, 208, 213, 231; for one's acts 89
restraint 123, 136, 160
revenge 30, 31
reversion to might makes right 69, 163
Rey v. Perez-Gurri 200
Rhode Island 126, 127, 140
richest one percent xiv
right xi-xiii, xv, xvi, xviii, 7, 9, 21, 22, 26, 27, 37-39, 41-44, 46, 47, 50-56, 58-62, 65, 66, 69, 73, 80-82, 85, 88, 89, 95-102, 104, 107, 108, 110, 111, 114-120, 122,

Index

123, 125,126, 128, 131, 132, 136- 142, 144-147, 149, 150, 154-158, 161-164, 170, 176, 178, 180, 181, 193, 195-197,201-203, 207-210, 221, 230, 231, 235, 236, 238, 240; of nature 95-112; of privacy 144-146; of revolution 119, 126, 158, 163; of self-preservation 95, 97; of majority 95, 163; to make laws 95, 119

rights xi, xiii, xvi, 22, 27, 46, 60, 62, 64, 83, 95-111, 117-119, 121-129, 131-136, 140-145, 147, 148, 151, 154, 155, 157, 158, 162-164, 169, 174-176, 178-181, 192, 195-198, 203-209, 212, 213, 220-226, 240, 241

Bill of Rights (*See* Bill of Rights); states bills of 126, 127; unalienable xi, 62, 104, 107, 127; Virginia Declaration 126; legal xvi, 83, 98, 136, 147, 157, 158, 178, 181, 221

Roberts, Justice xvi, 140, 141
Rochin v. California 142, 147, 151
Roe v. Wade 144-146, 150
Rome 25, 26, 40, 41, 61, 72, 76, 105, 148; empire 26, 61; law 41, 61, 76; republic 26, 105; Romans 26, 30, 72, 232
romantic view 121
Roosevelt, President Franklin xvi,141
Rousseau, Jean-Jacques xviii, 14, 88, 113, 119, 120, 122, 161, 163; First and Second Discourses 120; moral, collective body 121; abandoning to a foundling home 120; Emile 120; Calvinist Geneva 120; will of all 122, 158, 232 (*See also* general will)
rule xii, xiv, xv, 18, 23, 25, 41, 42, 45, 51-55, 57-59, 63, 66, 74, 80, 82, 90, 91, 110, 115, 117, 119, 123, 125, 129, 130, 135, 144, 145, 157, 162, 167, 168, 177, 209-212, 230, 236, 237
Runnymede 102, 108
Russia 178

satin bower bird 49
Saxon laws 102
Scalia, Justice Antonin 145, 146
schools 23, 153
science xvii-xx, 3-5, 7, 10, 52, 85, 87, 88, 108, 113-115, 143, 187, 231
scientific racism 86
searches and seizures 207, 208 (*See also* constitutional law)
Second Treatise xi, 95, 98, 110, 117, 119, 123 (*See also* Locke, John)
segregation 99, 169
self-consciousness 31, 32, 35, 36, 38, 40, 43, 47, 51, 62, 65, 154
self-defense 82, 115, 142, 173, 182, 219, 226
self-evident xi, 38, 90, 104, 220, 241
self-incrimination 142, 143, 208
self-interest xix, 31, 32, 43, 44, 46, 50, 52-60, 62, 63, 66, 73, 74, 80, 90, 115, 116, 121, 154, 175, 176, 188, 231, 237, 238
self-organization 5, 7, 48, 49
self-preservation 45, 46, 80, 95, 96, 98, 115, 120, 121, 175
seventeenth century 103, 116, 119
sex 18, 19, 27, 64, 76-78, 86, 87, 167, 168, 220, 238
sexual odometer law 168
sexual preferences xv
sexually transmitted diseases xv, 78
shareholders 188
Sharon, Ariel 95
situational cues 36
Sixteenth Amendment (*See* constitution, *see also* constitutional law)
sixteenth century 26, 31
Skinner,B.F. 86, 145
slavery xii, xiv, xvii, 57, 58, 61, 111, 127, 132, 147, 149, 151, 158; abolishing slave trade 132; abolishing slavery 61; abused slave 61; Archbishop of Narbonne 57; banned slavery 127; British Empire outlawed the slave trade 61; Constitution enshrined slavery 132; enslaving 54, 56, 59; fugitive slave clause 132; freedom 55; importa-

tion of slaves 61; laws forbidding slaves 57; maltreated slaves 61; Negro slaves xii, 58; importation outlawed 61; Saracen slaves 57; sick slave 61; natural condition 58; decline in Medieval Europe 58; useless slaves 61
slaves xii, 54, 55, 57, 58, 61, 62, 76, 95, 102, 111, 123, 132, 136, 149
social behaviors 23-25, 100, 154
social compact 121, 128, 130, 131
Social Contract xviii, xx, 14, 18, 78, 113, 116, 118-125, 128, 151-153, 155-159, 161-167, 169, 171-182, 184-188, 190, 192-210, 212-217, 220-225, 227-230, 232, 234-241; amendment 224, 225; good faith and honesty in fact 173, 182-185, 185, 208, 218; immigrants 192, 195; modification 173, 175, 222, 224, 225; New xviii, xx, 18, 155, 157, 173, 177; preamble 125, 179; repudiation of 223, 224; signing 162, 180, 181, 184; termination for uses of involuntary persuasion 223
Social Darwinists 50
social organization 14, 24, 25, 156, 232
Social Security xiii, 149, 150, 159, 171, 196, 227, 240
society, guarantees 83, 176, 203, 232; prohibition of destructive power 82; legal rights and remedies 221; consciously organized 25; mon-key and ape 99, 100
sociologists 5, 86
sociology xviii, 4, 5, 85
sociobiology 23
Socrates 50, 82
soldiers xii, 24, 101, 129, 201
Solon 30
sophists 27, 50
Souter, Justice 144, 145
Sparta 25
spatial reasoning 13, 14
Spaziano case 211

SPCA xix, 46
special case 6, 8, 11, 16, 48
species xi, 5, 12, 13, 15, 16, 18, 20, 23-26, 32, 33, 50, 60, 62, 65, 86, 101, 110, 154, 235
Stalin's logic 149
state legislatures 127, 140, 147
state of nature xviii, xix, 98, 114-118, 120, 121, 123, 157
state of war 113, 114, 117
statement of will (*See* will)
statutes 76, 77, 119, 137, 139, 146, 150, 156, 212, 225
Stephens, Alexander 58
sterilization 87
Stevens, Justice John Paul 146
stimuli 9, 11, 12, 19
substantive due process 135, 137, 141, 145, 214 (*See also* constitutional law)
sufficient power 50, 59, 63, 64, 97-100, 105, 123
suicide 72, 200, 201
suppressing cues 35
Supreme Court xvi, xvii, 61, 87, 99, 129, 131-133, 136, 141, 142, 148-151, 155, 156, 164, 165, 197, 206, 209, 211, 212
sympathetic reaction 38
symphony xviii, 64
systems xviii-xx, 5-8, 10, 11, 15, 17, 19, 23-27, 29, 33, 37-39, 43, 48, 49, 51, 52, 64, 89, 90, 97, 99, 100, 105, 108, 143, 153, 154, 161, 175, 199, 228, 239; of artificial rights and duties (*See* artificial duty, artificial rights)

tacit acquiescence 119, 156
Tarquin kings 26
tax 232, 233; Billionaire's 150; income xiv, 60, 148-150, 214, 218; breaks 169; inheritance 147, 232; rate xiv, 150
television intoxication xvii, 89
temporary visitors or immigrants (*See* ward)
temporary ward (*See* ward)
teutonic 30
thermodynamics 5, 8, 48, 49

Thirteenth Amendment (*See* constitution, *see also* constitutional law)
three-fifths compromise 131 (*See* constitution)
tiger 23, 24, 118, 222 (*See also* animals)
timely (*See* judiciary)
Tindal, Lord Chief Justice 41
Tojo 107
tools 13, 20, 21, 109
torts 69, 70, 186
tree pipit 15 (*See also* birds)
trial by jury 127, 164, 207
tribal chieftains 105
Twenty-first (*See* constitution, *see also* constitutional law)
Twining v. State of New Jersey 141, 208

umbrella 40-42
unalienable rights (*See* rights)
unconscious, destructive power 78; persuasion 71; use of destructive power 68, 166
unconstitutional xvi, 131, 132, 137, 139, 141, 146, 149, 156, 164
understand xvii, xviii, 15, 16, 18, 25, 38-41, 46, 48, 56, 62, 68, 71- 73, 97, 109, 122, 151, 160, 162, 163, 177, 179, 180, 189, 222
understanding xvi, xviii, 6, 8, 9, 11-19, 22, 31, 34, 37, 41, 48, 52, 58, 62, 63, 72, 106, 107, 117, 122, 152, 156, 161, 162, 177, 181, 226
Underwriter's Laboratories 188
Uniform Commercial Code 79, 212, 215
Union Army 163
universal equality xii, xvii, xviii, 51-53, 58, 63, 65, 66, 73, 74, 109, 110, 113, 123-125, 127, 132, 134, 136, 149, 151, 154, 155, 168, 170
unreasonable risk of injury 167, 173, 185-187, 190, 215
Uriah 79
Utah 136

utilitarianism 59, 60, 88, 110, 148, 150, 151, 170, 175, 176, 214, 216; greatest good 59, 60, 110, 176, 177, 214
utility 51, 59, 140

vacuum 48, 49
value xi, 26, 38, 40, 47-56, 59, 62, 63, 65-67, 69, 71-77, 80, 91, 107, 108, 155, 168, 176-179, 181, 182, 184, 185, 189-191, 215, 231, 233, 238
Verne, Jules 105
victimless crimes 228
violence xii, 127, 130, 176, 200, 201, 208, 223
Virginia 87, 124, 125, 127, 140, 144, 145; Declaration of Rights 125
virus 4, 9, 78, 88
visitors 192, 195
volitional will (*See* will)
Voltaire 105
voluntary persuasion 71-79, 168, 175, 176, 182, 185, 189-191, 212, 226, 237, 238
Von Bulow, Klaus 211

Wallace, George 99
Wallace, Alfred Russel 86
ward 40, 126, 150, 161, 162, 165, 166, 169, 171-175, 176, 181, 182, 185, 191-195, 197-199, 201-203, 206, 221-224, 226-230, 233-235, 240
Ward, Samuel 125
Washington, George 127,
Washington, Justice 130
wasp 29, 30
Watson, John B. 85
weaver bird 15 (*See also* birds)
welfare xv, xvi, 105, 129, 130, 133, 136-138, 140, 141, 146, 149, 150, 170, 196
Thomas, Justice Clarence 145
will xii-xvii, xx, 3-12, 14-27, 29, 30, 37-39, 41-45, 47-76, 78-84, 90, 95-101, 104-110, 112, 115, 117, 120-122, 124, 125, 128-130, 134, 136, 141, 143-145, 148, 150, 152-157, 159-171, 173-183, 185-

193, 195-201, 203-207, 209, 210, 213-222, 224, 226-229, 231-241; autonomic 9-12, 14, 16, 18, 19, 21, 30, 49, 66, 82, 83, 90; statement of 100, 105, 108, 110, 122, 154-156, 220; of God 3, 9, 105, 108; volitional 18, 19, 63, 80, 90, 109, 154, 168-170, 179, 180, 215, 221, 231, 232, 236-238

William the Conqueror 101 103, 112, 116, 119, 192
William and Mary 113, 120
William III 117
William James 86
William McDougall 86
Williamson v. Lee Optical Co. 141
Wilson, Edward O. 23-24, 50
Wilson, James 128
wolves 21, 23, 26, 29, 31, 154, 196
women 61, 62, 87, 88, 90, 102, 111, 123, 140, 141, 145, 169, 234
World War II 73, 107

Zamora, Ronny xvii
zero sum game 185